American Universities and Colleges:

A Dictionary of Name Changes

by

ALICE H. SONGE

The Scarecrow Press, Inc.
Metuchen, N.J. & London
1978

Library of Congress Cataloging in Publication Data

Songe, Alice H
     American universities and colleges.

     1.   Universities and colleges--United States--Directories.
I.   Title.
L901.S57   378.73   78-5497
ISBN 0-8108-1137-5

CONTENTS

CATJun4'79

3-21-79 8.0 9.35

iii

PREFACE

"What's in a name?" The familiar Shakespearean quotation seems to have assumed greater significance in the changing social and economic climates of American university and college campuses. Such names as Female Seminary, Colored People's University or State Normal College have long been outmoded. In recent years the reorganization of state university systems has given new and often impersonal names to older, long-established institutions. Even numerous church-related schools have discarded their former, more religious titles for names more secular in nature.

Name changes for institutions of higher education have also occurred because of economic factors that forced them to merge with others as a means of survival. Most, however, changed names as they progressed from simple beginnings, often as a grammar or secondary school, to college and university status. Unfortunately, in many instances, the names of some formerly well known alma maters have been lost as these institutions were forced to close altogether.

In all of its aspects, this study of name changes of American universities and colleges has proven to be most revealing, and as far as can be determined, this is the first listing of its kind in dictionary form. The aim is to present, as far as it is possible to do so, an alphabetical list of the names of all the four-year, degree-granting universities and colleges in the continental United States and outlying territories that have undergone name changes since they were founded, accompanied by the former names of these institutions and the years in which these names were adopted. Included in this alphabetical list are the names of those institutions that have closed since the 1964/65 school year and the date of closing. An appendix gives further information as to the location of the academic records for these defunct institutions.

The approach to this work is informative and factual, yet wide enough in scope to include related historical data, such as changes in geographic location and the names of the founders for many of the non-public institutions.

It is hoped that this book will serve as a contribution to American educational history, and will serve the academic community as well as other sectors of the public. Employers and others in personnel administration should find it most useful in seeking academic records for job applicants, a task often made difficult by name changes or closings of institutions.

Library staff members in reference and cataloging should find this volume a great time-saver in searching pertinent information concerning our colleges and universities and in determining the official names for institutions for correct corporate entries.

The author acknowledges the assistance of many persons in the compilation of this dictionary. Particular appreciation is expressed to the librarians who furnished information on the name changes of their institutions, to the personnel of the state boards of higher education for providing factual data on school closings, and to Mrs. Jo Anne Cassell of the National Institute of Education Library for her assistance in making certain resources of that library available.

For invaluable assistance for manuscript production the author wishes to thank Mrs. Robert Evans, Sister Ethel Lunsford, R.C.E. and Mrs. Dorothy Cadmun of the Kelly Girl Services--all of Asheville, N.C. where most of the work for this book was done.

INTRODUCTION

This reference work does not claim to be definitive by any means. Research procedures for gathering data were limited mainly to reference to printed sources, supplemented by written requests for information to university and college librarians and to state boards of higher education in selected states. Frequently, the facts needed were not available in printed sources nor forthcoming from those to whom letters were sent asking for information.

According to the Education Directory: Colleges and Universities 1976-77, published by the U.S. National Center for Educational Statistics (Washington, D.C.: U.S. Govt. Print. Off., 1977), there are 1,928 four-year institutions in the "Aggregate U.S.," meaning the 50 states, the District of Columbia and outlying areas or territories. From the resources mentioned above, it was possible to find information on 1,618 institutions and to discover that 1,120 had undergone name changes since founded.

There are 3,745 entries in this dictionary: 1,120 entries for the names of institutions that have name changes (to be referred to as main entries), 2,512 entries for the names formerly held by these schools (to be referred to as "see" references) and 114 entries for the names of four-year institutions that have closed since the 1964/65 school year (through the 1976/77 academic session).

The published sources used for this research were 1) American Universities and Colleges, edited by W. Todd Furniss. 11th ed. (Washington, D.C.: American Council on Education, 1973); 2) The College Blue Book, Vol. I: U.S. Colleges, Narrative Description. 14th ed. (New York: CCM Information Corporation, 1973); 3) Education Directory: College and Universities 1968/69-1976/77, by Arthur Podolsky and Carolyn R. Smith, National Center for Educational Statistics (Washington, D.C.: U.S. Govt. Print. Off., 1975-); 4) U.S. Office of Education. Education Directory: Higher Education 1965/66-1967/68 (Washington, D.C.: U.S. Govt. Print. Off., 1965-).

The main entry for each institution lists the following information: Present name; city and state where located, with Zip Code number; type of institution (i.e., state or non-public); present owners or administrators, if non-public; original name used when founded; date and name of founders, if non-public; name changes, indicated by the word "Became," and the year of change; date when present name was adopted; any mergers with other institutions; changes in geographic location; change in administrative control, if any, from private to state control, state to private control, municipal to state control, etc.

Since this reference work is concerned only with name changes and related data, the main entries do not include information as to when the institutions were chartered, incorporated or accredited; when first instruction was offered or first degrees awarded; changes in status from secondary school or junior college to four-year institution, except where a name change is involved. Former names of institutions that have closed are also not given.

The "see" references in the main text list the names previously used by the institutions, the year this name was adopted, and a reference to the present name used.

Entries for the names of institutions that have closed include the location of the school, and the month and year of closing where such information was available. Where the exact date of closing was not available, the school year is given. It must be noted that some of the sources used presented conflicting statements in regard to the institutions that have closed. Many of the institutions listed as four-year schools had in reality become two-year colleges at the time operations ceased. In such cases information supplied by the state boards of higher education is used as the final authority.

Following the main text, an Appendix in chart form contains an alphabetical listing by state of the institutions listed as closed in the main text; the present location of the academic records for these defunct institutions, where available; and the state sources from which the information was obtained or not obtained.

Selection of colleges and universities to be searched was confined to all four-year, degree-granting institutions, including those in law, medicine, chiropractic, etc., where the four-year limit is not required. Unless regionally accredited, institutions such as Bible colleges, seminaries and theological institutions that train students exclusively for some form of the ministry were not included. However, those that offer some secular programs were searched or contacted for possible name changes. All Bible colleges, seminaries and theological institutions that have closed within the time period 1964/65 to 1976/77 are listed regardless of accreditation status or programs.

THE DICTIONARY

Abilene Baptist College 1891. See Hardin-Simmons University, Abilene, Tex.

Abilene Christian College 1971. See Abilene Christian University, Abilene, Tex.

ABILENE CHRISTIAN UNIVERSITY. Abilene, Tex. 79601. Nonpublic institution. Affiliated with the Church of Christ. Established as Childers Classical Institute 1906. Merged with Fort Worth Christian College 1971 and Christian College of the Southwest, Dallas, 1971. Became: Abilene Christian College 1971. Adopted present name 1976.

The Academy at Due West 1835. See Erskine College, Due West, S.C.

Academy at Red Wing, Minn. 1862. See Gustavus Adolphus College, St. Peter, Minn.

The Academy of Idaho 1901. See Idaho State University, Pocatello, Ida.

Academy of Mount St. Joseph 1906. See College of Mount St. Joseph on the Ohio, Mt. St. Joseph, Ohio.

Academy of Mount Saint Vincent 1847. See College of Mount Saint Vincent, Riverdale, N.Y.

Academy of Our Lady of the Elms 1897, Pittsfield, Mass. See College of Our Lady of the Elms, Chicopee, Mass.

Academy of Philadelphia 1753. See University of Pennsylvania, Philadelphia, Pa.

Academy of the Holy Angels College Department 1941. See Our Lady of Holy Cross College, New Orleans, La.

Academy of the Holy Angels Normal School 1916. See Our Lady of Holy Cross College, New Orleans, La.

Academy of the Holy Infancy 1853. See Manhattan College, Riverdale, Bronx, N.Y.

1

ADAMS STATE COLLEGE. Alamosa, Colo. 81101. State institution. Established as State Normal School at Alamosa 1921. Became: Adams State Normal School 1923; Adams State Teachers College of Southern Colorado 1929. Adopted present name 1945.

Adams State Normal School 1923. See Adams State College, Alamosa, Colo.

Adams State Teachers College of Southern Colorado 1929. See Adams State College, Alamosa, Colo.

AddRan Christian College 1889. See Texas Christian University, Fort Worth, Tex.

AddRan Male and Female College 1873. See Texas Christian University, Fort Worth, Tex.

Adelphi Academy 1863. See Adelphi University, Garden City, N.Y.

Adelphi College 1896. See Adelphi University, Garden City, N.Y.

Adelphi Suffolk College of Adelphi University 1959. See Dowling College, Oakdale, N.Y.

ADELPHI UNIVERSITY. Garden City, N.Y. 11530. Non-public institution. Established as Adelphi Academy 1863. Became: Adelphi College 1896. Adopted present name 1963.

ADRIAN COLLEGE. Adrian, Mich. 49221. Non-public institution. Affiliated with The United Methodist Church. Established under present name 1859. Merged with Methodist Protestant College at West Lafayette, Ohio 1916.

AGNES SCOTT COLLEGE. Decatur, Ga. 30030. Non-public institution. Established as Decatur Female Seminary 1889. Became: Agnes Scott Institute 1890. Adopted present name 1906.

Agnes Scott Institute 1890. See Agnes Scott College, Decatur, Ga.

Agricultural and Industrial State College 1927. See Tennessee State University, Nashville, Tenn.

Agricultural and Industrial State Normal College 1924. See Tennessee State University, Nashville, Tenn.

Agricultural and Industrial State Normal School 1912. See Tennessee State University, Nashville, Tenn.

Agricultural and Mechanical College, Fourth District 1923. See University of Arkansas at Monticello, Monticello, Ark.

Agricultural and Mechanical College of Alabama 1872. See Auburn University, Auburn, Ala.

Agricultural and Mechanical College of Kentucky 1878. See University of Kentucky, Lexington, Ky.

Agricultural and Mechanical College of Kentucky University 1865. See University of Kentucky, Lexington, Ky.

Agricultural and Mechanical College of Louisiana 1877. See Louisiana State University and Agricultural and Mechanical College, Baton Rouge, La.

Agricultural and Mechanical College of Texas 1871. See Texas Agricultural and Mechanical University, College Station, Tex.

Agricultural and Technical College for the Colored Race 1891. See North Carolina Agricultural and Technical State University, Greensboro, N.C.

Agricultural and Technical College of North Carolina 1915. See North Carolina Agricultural and Technical State University, Greensboro, N.C.

Agricultural College, Experiment Station and School of Science of the State of Washington 1891. See Washington State University, Pullman, Wash.

Agricultural College of Colorado 1870. See Colorado State University, Fort Collins, Colo.

Agricultural College of South Dakota 1881. See South Dakota State University, Brookings, S.D.

Agricultural College of State of Michigan 1855. See Michigan State University, East Lansing, Mich.

Agricultural College of the State of Montana at Bozeman 1893. See Montana State University, Bozeman, Mont.

Agricultural College of Utah 1888. See Utah State University, Logan, Ut.

Agricultural College of West Virginia 1867. See West Virginia University, Morgantown, W.Va.

Agriculture College of Pennsylvania 1862. See The Pennsylvania State University, University Park, Pa.

Air Corps Engineering School 1926. See Air Force Institute of Technology, Dayton, Ohio.

AIR FORCE INSTITUTE OF TECHNOLOGY. Dayton, Oh. 45433. Federal institution. Operated by the U.S. Department of the Air Force. Established as Air School of Engineering 1919. Became: Air Service Engineering School 1920; Air Corps Engineering School

1926; Army-Air Force Institute of Technology 1946. Adopted present name 1947.

Air School of Engineering 1919. See Air Force Institute of Technology, Dayton, Oh.

Air Service Engineering School 1920. See Air Force Institute of Technology, Dayton, Oh.

Alabama Agricultural and Mechanical College 1948. See Alabama Agricultural and Mechanical University, Normal, Ala.

ALABAMA AGRICULTURAL AND MECHANICAL UNIVERSITY. Normal, Ala. 35762. State institution. Established as Huntsville Normal School 1875. Became: State Normal and Industrial School at Huntsville 1878; State Agricultural and Mechanical College for Negroes 1890; State Agricultural and Mechanical Institute for Negroes 1919; Alabama Agricultural and Mechanical College 1948. Adopted present name 1969.

Alabama College 1892. See University of Montevallo, Montevallo, Ala.

Alabama Colored Peoples University 1887. See Alabama State University, Montgomery, Ala.

Alabama Conference Female College 1872. See Huntingdon College, Montgomery, Ala.

Alabama Normal College 1882. See Livingston University, Livingston, Ala.

Alabama Polytechnic Institute 1899. See Auburn University, Auburn, Ala.

Alabama State College 1954. See Alabama State University, Montgomery, Ala.

Alabama State College for Negroes 1946. See Alabama State University, Montgomery, Ala.

ALABAMA STATE UNIVERSITY. Montgomery, Ala. 36101. State institution. Established as State Normal School and University for Colored Students and Teachers 1873. Became: Alabama Colored Peoples University 1887; State Normal School for Colored Students 1889; State Teachers College 1929; Alabama State College for Negroes 1946; Alabama State College 1954. Adopted present name 1969.

The Alaska Agricultural College and School of Mines 1917. See University of Alaska, College, Alas.

Alaska Methodist University, Anchorage, Alas. Closed 1976/77 School Year.

Albany Bible and Manual Training Institute 1903. See Albany State
College, Albany, Ga.

Albany College 1867. See Lewis and Clark College, Portland, Ore.

ALBANY STATE COLLEGE. Albany, Ga. 31705. State institution.
Established as Albany Bible and Manual Training Institute 1903. Became: Georgia Normal and Agricultural College 1917. Adopted present name 1943.

ALBION COLLEGE. Albion, Mich. 49224. Non-public institution.
Related to The United Methodist Church. Established as Spring Arbor Seminary 1835. Became: Wesleyan Seminary at Albion 1839;
added Albion Female Collegiate Institute 1850; Wesleyan Seminary
and Female College at Albion 1857. Adopted present name 1861.

Albion Female Collegiate Institute 1850. See Albion College, Albion, Mich.

ALBRIGHT COLLEGE. Reading, Pa. 19604. Non-public institution.
Affiliated with the United Methodist Church. Established as Union
Seminary 1856. Became: Central Pennsylvania College 1887.
Adopted present name after merging with Albright Collegiate Institute 1902. Merged with Schuylkill Seminary 1928 and became Albright College of the Evangelical Church 1928. Readopted present
name 1972.

Albright College of the Evangelical Church 1928. See Albright College, Reading, Pa.

Albright Collegiate Institute 1902. See Albright College, Reading,
Pa.

Alcorn Agricultural and Mechanical College 1878. See Alcorn State
University, Alcorn Rural Station, Lorman, Miss.

ALCORN STATE UNIVERSITY. Alcorn Rural Station, Lorman,
Miss. 39096. State institution. Established as Alcorn University
1871. Became: Alcorn Agricultural and Mechanical College 1878.
Adopted present name 1974.

Alcorn University 1871. See Alcorn Agricultural and Mechanical
College, Alcorn Rural Station, Lorman, Miss.

ALDERSON-BROADDUS COLLEGE. Philippi, W. Va. 26416. Non-
public institution. Affiliated with the American Baptist Convention.
Established as Broaddus Academy 1871. Became: Broaddus College
and Academy 1917. Merged with Alderson Junior College 1932.
Adopted present name 1932.

Alderson Junior College 1932. See Alderson-Broaddus College,
Philippi, W. Va.

Alfred Academy 1843. See Alfred University, Alfred, N. Y.

Alfred Select School 1836. See Alfred University, Alfred, N. Y.

ALFRED UNIVERSITY. Alfred, N. Y. 14902. Non-public institution.
Established as Alfred Select School 1836, by Seventh Day Baptists.
Became: Alfred Academy 1843. Adopted present name 1857.

Allentown Bible Institute 1934. See United Wesleyan College, Allentown, Pa.

Allentown College for Women 1893. See Cedar Crest College,
Allentown, Pa.

Allentown Collegiate Institute and Military Academy 1864. See
Muhlenberg College, Allentown, Pa.

Allentown Female College 1867. See Cedar Crest College, Allentown, Pa.

Allentown Seminary 1848. See Muhlenberg College, Allentown, Pa.

ALLIANCE COLLEGE. Cambridge Springs, Pa. 16403. Non-public
institution. Sponsored by the Polish National Alliance of the U. S. A.
Established as Polish National Alliance College 1912. Adopted present name 1928.

Alma College, Los Gatos, California 1934. See The Jesuit School
of Theology at Berkeley, Calif.

Almira College 1855. See Greenville College, Greenville, Ill.

Alta Vista Agricultural College 1876. See Prairie View Agricultural and Mechanical University, Prairie View, Tex.

ALVERNO COLLEGE. Milwaukee, Wisc. 53215. Non-public insti-
tution. Owned by the Sisters of St. Francis, Roman Catholic Church.
Established as St. Joseph Normal School 1887. Became: Alverno
Teachers College 1936. Adopted present name 1946.

Alverno Teachers College 1936. See Alverno College, Milwaukee,
Wisc.

American College of Neuro-ophthalmology and Ocular Myology 1909.
See West Coast University, Los Angeles, Calif.

AMERICAN GRADUATE SCHOOL. Glendale, Ariz. 85301. Non-
public institution. Established as American Institute for Foreign
Trade 1946. Became: Thunderbird Graduate School of International
Management 1968. Adopted present name 1976.

American Institute for Foreign Trade 1946. See American Graduate
School, Glendale, Ariz.

AMERICAN INTERNATIONAL COLLEGE. Springfield, Mass. 01109.
Non-public institution. Established as French-Protestant College,
Lowell, Mass. 1885. Became: French-American College 1894,
after moving to present location 1888. Adopted present name 1905.

American Literary, Scientific and Military Academy 1819. See Norwich University, Northfield, Vt.

American School of Osteopathy 1892. See Kirksville College of
Osteopathic Medicine, Kirksville, Mo.

Anderson Bible School and Seminary 1925. See Anderson College,
Anderson, Ind.

Anderson Bible Training School 1917. See Anderson College, Anderson, Ind.

ANDERSON COLLEGE. Anderson, Ind. 46011. Non-public institu-
tion. Affiliated with the Church of God. Established as Anderson
Bible Training School 1917. Became: Anderson Bible School and
Seminary 1925; Anderson College and Technological Seminary 1929.
Adopted present name 1964.

Anderson College and Technological Seminary 1929. See Anderson
College, Anderson, Ind.

Andrew Still College of Osteopathy and Surgery 1926. See Kirksville College of Osteopathic Medicine, Kirksville, Mo.

ANDREWS UNIVERSITY. Berrien Springs, Mich. 49104. Non-public
institution. Controlled by the General Conference of Seventh-Day
Adventists. Established as Battle Creek College 1874. Became:
Emanuel Missionery College 1901; merged with Seventh-Day Adventist
Theological Seminary and adopted present name 1934.

Angelo State College 1965. See Angelo State University, San Angelo,
Tex.

ANGELO STATE UNIVERSITY. San Angelo, Tex. 76901. State institution. Established as San Angelo Junior College 1928. Became:
Angelo State College 1965. Adopted present name 1969.

Anna S. C. Blake Manual Training School 1891. See University
of California, Santa Barbara, Santa Barbara, Calif.

ANNHURST COLLEGE. Woodstock, Conn. 06281. Non-public institution. Conducted by the Daughters of the Holy Spirit, Roman Catholic. Established as Ker-Anna Junior College 1941. Adopted present name 1943.

Appalachian State Normal School 1925. See University of North
Carolina at Boone, Boone, N.C.

Appalachian State Teachers College 1929. <u>See</u> University of North Carolina at Boone, Boone, N.C.

Appalachian State University 1967. <u>See</u> University of North Carolina at Boone, Boone, N.C.

Appalachian Training School 1903. <u>See</u> University of North Carolina at Boone, Boone, N.C.

AQUINAS COLLEGE. Grand Rapids, Mich. 49506. Non-public institution. Owned by the Dominican Sisters of Grand Rapids, Roman Catholic Church. Established as Novitiate Normal School 1886. Became: Sacred Heart College 1923; Catholic Junior College 1931. Adopted present name 1940.

Aquinas Institute of Philosophy and Theology 1961. <u>See</u> Aquinas Institute of Theology, Dubuque, Ia.

AQUINAS INSTITUTE OF THEOLOGY. Dubuque, Ia. 52001. Non-public institution. Owned by the Dominican Fathers of the Province of St. Albert the Great, Roman Catholic Church. Established as College of St. Thomas Aquinas in River Forest, Ill. 1939. Separated from School of Philosophy and moved to present location 1951. Became: The Dominican College of St. Rose of Lima 1950. Branches reorganized as Aquinas Institute of Philosophy and Theology 1961. Adopted present name 1970 with merger of branches.

Aquinas Institute of Theology, River Forest, Ill. Closed May 1972.

Arizona Bible College of Biola College, Phoenix, Ariz. Closed June 1971.

Arizona State College at Flagstaff 1945. <u>See</u> Northern Arizona University, Flagstaff, Ariz.

Arizona State College at Tempe 1945. <u>See</u> Arizona State University, Tempe, Ariz.

Arizona State Teachers College 1929. <u>See</u> Arizona State University, Tempe, Ariz.

Arizona State Teachers College at Flagstaff 1929. <u>See</u> Northern Arizona University, Flagstaff, Ariz.

ARIZONA STATE UNIVERSITY. Tempe, Ariz. 85281. State institution. Established as Territorial Normal School 1885. Became: Arizona Territorial Normal School 1889; Normal School of Arizona 1896; Tempe Normal School of Arizona 1903; Tempe State Teachers College 1925; Arizona State Teachers College 1929; Arizona State College at Tempe 1945. Adopted present name 1958.

Arizona Territorial Normal School 1889. <u>See</u> Arizona State University, Tempe, Ariz.

Arkadelphia Methodist College 1890. See Henderson State University, Arkadelphia, Ark.

Arkansas Agricultural and Mechanical College 1939. See University of Arkansas at Monticello, Monticello, Ark.

Arkansas Agricultural, Mechanical and Normal College 1928. See University of Arkansas at Pine Bluff, Pine Bluff, Ark.

Arkansas Christian College, Morrilton, Ark. 1919. See Harding College, Searcy, Ark.

Arkansas Cumberland College 1891. See The College of the Ozarks, Clarksville, Ark. 72830.

Arkansas Industrial University 1871. See University of Arkansas, Fayetteville, Ark.

Arkansas Polytechnic College 1925. See Arkansas Tech University, Russellville, Ark.

Arkansas State College 1933. See Arkansas State University, State University, Ark.

Arkansas State Normal School 1907. See State College of Arkansas, Conway, Ark.

Arkansas State Teachers College 1925. See State College of Arkansas, Conway, Ark.

ARKANSAS STATE UNIVERSITY. State University, Ark. 72467.
State institution. Established as First District Agricultural School
1909. Became: State Agricultural and Mechanical College 1925;
Arkansas State College 1933. Adopted present name 1967.

ARKANSAS TECH UNIVERSITY. Russellville, Ark. 72801. State
institution. Established as Second District Agricultural School 1909.
Became: Arkansas Polytechnic College 1925. Adopted present name
1976.

Arlington College 1895. See University of Texas at Arlington, Arlington, Tex.

Arlington State College 1949. See University of Texas at Arlington, Arlington, Tex.

Arlington Training School 1913. See University of Texas at Arlington, Arlington, Tex.

Armour Institute of Technology. See Illinois Institute of Technology, Chicago, Ill.

ARMSTRONG COLLEGE. Berkeley, Calif. 94704. Non-public institution. Established as California School for Private Secretaries 1918. Adopted present official name Armstrong Schools of Business 1923.

Armstrong College of Savannah 1935. See Armstrong State College, Savannah, Ga.

Armstrong Schools of Business 1923. See Armstrong College, Berkeley, Calif.

ARMSTRONG STATE COLLEGE. Savannah, Ga. 31406. State institution. Established as Armstrong College of Savannah 1935. Adopted present name 1964.

Army-Air Force Institute of Technology 1946. See Air Force Institute of Technology, Dayton, Ohio.

Arnold and Marie Schwartz College of Pharmacy and Health Sciences. See Long Island University Arnold and Marie Schwartz College of Pharmacy and Health Sciences.

Aroostook State College 1965. See University of Maine at Presque Isle, Presque Isle, Me.

Aroostook State College of the University of Maine 1968. See University of Maine at Presque Isle, Presque Isle, Me.

Aroostook State Normal School 1903. See University of Maine at Presque Isle, Presque Isle, Me.

Aroostook State Teachers College 1952. See University of Maine at Presque Isle, Me.

ART CENTER COLLEGE OF DESIGN. Los Angeles, Calif. 90020. Non-public institution. Established as Art Center School 1930. Adopted present name 1966.

Art Center School 1930. See Art Center College of Design, Los Angeles, Calif.

ART INSTITUTE OF CHICAGO. Chicago, Ill. 60603. Non-public institution. Established as Chicago Academy of Design 1866. Became: Chicago Academy of Fine Arts 1879. Adopted present official name Schools of the Art Institute of Chicago 1882.

Arts and Technological College 1947. See Texas Agricultural and Industrial University at Corpus Christi, Corpus Christi, Tex.

Asheville-Biltmore College 1936. See University of North Carolina at Asheville, Asheville, N.C.

Asheville Farm School 1894. See Warren Wilson College, Swannanoa, N.C.

11   Ashland

ASHLAND COLLEGE. Ashland, Oh. 44805. Non-public institution.
Affiliated with the Brethren Church. Established as Ashland University 1878. Adopted present name 1888.

Ashland University 1878. See Ashland College, Ashland, Oh.

Ashmun Institute 1854. See Lincoln University, Lincoln University,
Pa.

Assisi Junior College 1925. See College of Saint Francis, Joliet,
Ill.

Assumption College, Richardton, N.D. Closed June 1972.

ASSUMPTION COLLEGE. Worcester, Mass. 10609. Non-public institution. Sponsored by the Augustinians of the Assumption, Roman
Catholic Church. Established as Trustees of Assumption College
1904. Adopted present name 1968.

The Athenaeum 1831. See Xavier University, Cincinnati, Oh.

THE ATHENAEUM OF OHIO. Norwood, Cincinnati, Oh. 45212.
Non-public institution. Owned by the Roman Catholic Archdiocese
of Cincinnati. Established as Seminary of Saint Francis Xavier 1829
in Cincinnati. Established college section The Athenaeum 1831.
Moved to St. Martins, Ohio 1839 after separating from The Athenaeum. Became: Mount St. Mary's of the West 1851, after moving
back to Cincinnati. Adopted present name 1928.

Athens College 1907. See Athens State College, Athens, Ala.

Athens College for Young Women 1889. See Athens State College,
Athens, Ala.

Athens Female Academy 1822. See Athens State College, Athens,
Ala.

Athens Female College 1857. See Tennessee Wesleyan College,
Athens, Tenn.

Athens Female Institute 1872. See Athens State College, Athens,
Ala.

Athens School of the University of Chattanooga 1906. See Tennessee Wesleyan College, Athens, Tenn.

ATHENS STATE COLLEGE. Athens, Ala. 35611. Non-public insti-
tution. Owned by the North Alabama Conference, United Methodist
Church. Established as Athens Female Academy 1822. Became:
Female Institute of the Tennessee Annual Conference 1843; Athens
Female Institute 1872; Athens College for Young Women 1889; Athens
College 1907. Adopted present name 1976.

Atlanta Baptist College 1897.   See   Morehouse College, Atlanta, Ga.

Atlanta Baptist College 1973.   See   Mercer University, Macon, Ga.

Atlanta Baptist Female Seminary 1881.   See   Spelman College, Atlanta, Ga.

ATLANTA COLLEGE OF ART.   Atlanta, Ga. 30309.   Non-public institution.   Established as High Museum School of Art 1928.   Became: Atlanta School of Art 1962.   Adopted present name 1914.

Atlanta Division, University of Georgia 1947.   See   Georgia State University, Atlanta, Ga.

Atlanta School of Art 1962.   See   Atlanta College of Art, Atlanta, Ga.

ATLANTIC CHRISTIAN COLLEGE.   Wilson, N.C. 27893.   Non-public institution.   Affiliated with the Christian Church (Disciples of Christ).   Established as Atlantic Christian College Company 1902.   Adopted present name 1964.

Atlantic Christian College Company 1902.   See   Atlantic Christian College, Wilson, N.C.

Atlantic States Chiropractic Institute of Brooklyn, N.Y.   See   Columbia Institute of Chiropractic, Glen Head, N.Y.

ATLANTIC UNION COLLEGE.   South Lancaster, Mass. 05161.   Non-public institution.   Affiliated with the Atlantic Union Conference of the Seventh-day Adventists.   Established as That New England School 1882.   Became: South Lancaster Academy 1883; Lancaster Junior College 1918.   Adopted present name 1922.

AUBURN UNIVERSITY.   Auburn, Ala. 36830.   State institution.   Established as East Alabama Male College 1856, by Methodist Episcopal Church, South.   Control transferred to state and became Agricultural and Mechanical College of Alabama 1872; Alabama Polytechnic Institute 1899.   Adopted present name 1960.

AUGSBURG COLLEGE.   Minneapolis, Minn. 55404.   Non-public institution.   Owned by The American Lutheran Church.   Established as Augsburg Seminary in Wisconsin 1869; moved to Minneapolis 1872.   Adopted present name 1963.

Augsburg Seminary and Marshall Academy 1869.   See   Augustana College, Sioux Falls, S.D.

Augsburg Seminary in Wisconsin 1869.   See   Augsburg College, Minneapolis, Minn.

Augusta Academy 1749.   See   Washington and Lee University, Lexington, Va.

Augusta Baptist Seminary 1879. See Morehouse College, Atlanta, Ga.

AUGUSTA COLLEGE. Augusta, Ga. 30904. State institution. Established as Junior College of Augusta 1925. Adopted present name 1958.

Augusta Female Academy 1842. See Mary Baldwin College, Staunton, Va.

Augusta Institute 1867. See Morehouse College, Atlanta, Ga.

Augustana College 1884. See Augustana College, Sioux Falls, S.D.

AUGUSTANA COLLEGE. Rock Island, Ill. 61201. Non-public institution. Affiliated with the Lutheran Church in America. Established as Augustana Seminary 1860. Became: Augustana College and Theological Seminary 1865. Adopted present name 1948.

AUGUSTANA COLLEGE. Sioux Falls, S.D. 57102. Non-public institution. Affiliated with the American Lutheran Church. Established as Augustana College and Seminary 1860, Chicago, Ill. Moved to Paxton, Ill. 1863. Became: Augsburg Seminary and Marshall Academy 1869 after moving to Marshall, Wis; Augustana Seminary and Academy 1881, after moving to Beloit, Ia; Augustana College 1884 after moving to Canton, S.D.; Augustana College and Normal School 1918, after moving to Sioux Falls. Merged with Lutheran Normal School 1918. Adopted present name 1926.

Augustana College and Normal School 1918. See Augustana College, Sioux Falls, S.D.

Augustana College and Seminary 1860, Chicago, Ill. See Augustana College, Sioux Falls, S.D.

Augustana College and Theological Seminary 1865. See Augustana College, Rock Island, Ill.

Augustana Seminary 1860. See Augustana College, Rock Island, Ill.

Augustana Seminary and Academy 1881. See Augustana College, Sioux Falls, S.D.

Augustinian College of the Merrimack Valley 1947. See Merrimack College, North Andover, Mass.

AURORA COLLEGE. Aurora, Ill. 60507. Non-public institution. Affiliated with the Advent Christian Church. Established as Mendota College 1893. Adopted present name 1912.

Austin Peay Normal School 1927. See Austin Peay State University, Clarksville, Tenn.

Austin Peay State College 1943. See Austin Peay State University, Clarksville, Tenn.

AUSTIN PEAY STATE UNIVERSITY. Clarksville, Tenn. 37040. State institution. Established as Austin Peay Normal School 1927. Became: Austin Peay State College 1943. Adopted present name 1967.

AVERETT COLLEGE. Danville, Va. 24541. Non-public institution. Affiliated with the Virginia Baptist Association. Established as Danville Female Institute 1854. Became: Baptist Female Seminary 1858; Union Female College 1859; Trustees of Roanoke Female College 1863; Roanoke Female College, 1893; Roanoke College 1904; Roanoke Institute 1910; Averett Junior College 1919. Adopted present name 1968.

Averett Junior College 1919. See Averett College, Danville, Va.

AVILA COLLEGE. Kansas City, Mo. 64145. Non-public institution. Affiliated with the Sisters of St. Joseph of Carondelet, Roman Catholic Church. Established as College of St. Teresa 1916. Adopted present name 1963.

Azusa College 1899. See Azusa Pacific College, Azusa, Calif.

AZUSA PACIFIC COLLEGE. Azusa, Calif. 91702. Non-public institution. Established as Azusa College 1899. Merged with Los Angeles Pacific College 1965 and adopted present name 1965.

- B -

BABSON COLLEGE. Wellesley, Mass. 02157. Non-public institution. Established as Babson Institute 1919. Adopted present name 1969.

Babson Institute 1919. See Babson College, Wellesley, Mass.

Baker Theological Institute 1870. See Clafin College, Orangeburg, S. D.

Balboa University 1952. See United States International University, San Diego, Calif.

Baldwin Institute 1845. See Baldwin-Wallace College, Berea, Ohio.

Baldwin School 1853. See Macalester College, St. Paul, Minn.

Baldwin University 1855. See Baldwin-Wallace College, Berea, Ohio.

Baldwin University 1864. See Macalester College, St. Paul, Minn.

BALDWIN-WALLACE COLLEGE.   Berea, Oh. 44017.   Non-public
institution.   Affiliated with the East Ohio Conference of The United
Methodist Church.   Established as Baldwin Institute 1845.   Became:
Baldwin University 1855.   Created German Wallace College 1863,
as German department.   Adopted present name 1913, after merger
of the two colleges.

Ball State Teachers College 1920.   See   Ball State University, Muncie, Ind.

BALL STATE UNIVERSITY.   Muncie, Ind. 47306.   State institution.
Established as Eastern Indiana Normal University 1898.   Became:
Palmer University 1902; Indiana Normal School 1905; Muncie Normal
Institute 1912; Indiana State Normal School, Eastern Division 1918;
Ball State Teachers College 1920.   Adopted present name 1965.

Baltimore College of Commerce, Baltimore, Md.   Closed Feb. 1973.

Bangor Maine School of Commerce 1926.   See   Husson College,
Bangor, Me.

BANK STREET COLLEGE OF EDUCATION.   New York, N.Y. 10025.
Non-public institution.   Established as Bureau of Education Experiments 1916.   Adopted present name 1950.

Baptist Bible Institute 1917.   See   New Orleans Baptist Theological
Seminary, New Orleans, La.

Baptist College at McMinnville 1854.   See   Linfield College, Mc-
Minnville, Ore.

Baptist Female College 1857.   See   Stephens College, Columbia, Mo.

Baptist Female Seminary 1858.   See   Averett College, Danville, Va.

Baptist Female University 1891.   See   Meredith College, Raleigh,
N.C.

Baptist University for Women 1905.   See   Meredith College, Raleigh,
N.C.

BARAT COLLEGE.   Lake Forest, Ill. 60045.   Non-public institution.
Owned by the Religious of the Sacred Heart, Roman Catholic Church.
Established as Barat College of the Sacred Heart 1857.   Adopted
present name 1969.

Barat College of the Sacred Heart 1857.   See   Barat College, Lake
Forest, Ill.

Barber Memorial College 1930.   See   Barber-Scotia College, Concord, N.C.

BARBER-SCOTIA COLLEGE.   Concord, N.C. 28025.   Non-public

institution. Owned and controlled by the Board of National Missions of the United Presbyterian Church in the U.S. Established as Scotia Seminary 1867. Became: Scotia Women's College 1916. Merged with Barber Memorial College 1930 and adopted present name.

Barboursville College 1889. See Morris Harvey College, Charleston, W. Va.

Barboursville Seminary 1888. See Morris Harvey College, Charleston, W. Va.

BARD COLLEGE. Annandale-on-Hudson, N.Y. 12504. Non-public institution. Established as St. Stephens College 1860. Became: Undergraduate College of Columbia University 1928. Adopted present name 1934. Became independent 1944.

Barre Normal School 1838. See Westfield State College, Westfield, Mass.

BARRINGTON COLLEGE. Barrington, R.I. 02806. Non-public institution. Established as Bethel Bible Institute 1900. Became: Providence Bible Institute 1929. Adopted present name 1959.

BARTLESVILLE WESLEYAN COLLEGE. Bartlesville, Okla. 74003. Non-public institution. Affiliated with the Wesleyan Church. Established as Central Pilgrim College 1959 by the Pilgrim Holiness Church of America. Adopted present name 1970.

Battle Creek College 1874. See Andrews University, Berrien Springs, Mich.

Baylor College for Women 1924. See Mary Hardin-Baylor College, Belton, Tex.

BAYLOR COLLEGE OF MEDICINE. Houston, Tex. 77025. Non-public institution. Established as Baylor University College of Medicine 1903. Adopted present name 1969.

Baylor Female College 1866. See Mary Hardin-Baylor College, Belton, Tex.

Baylor Theological Seminary, Waco, Tex. See Southwestern Baptist Theological Seminary, Fort Worth, Tex.

Baylor University College of Medicine 1903. See Baylor College of Medicine, Houston, Tex.

BEAVER COLLEGE. Glenside, Pa. 19038. Non-public institution. Affiliated with The United Presbyterian Church in the U.S.A. Established as Beaver Female Seminary 1853. Became: Beaver College and Musical Institute 1872. Adopted present name 1907.

Beaver College and Musical Institute 1872. See Beaver College, Glenside, Pa.

Beaver Female Seminary 1853. See Beaver College, Glenside, Pa.

BELHAVEN COLLEGE. Jackson, Miss. 39202. Non-public institution. Owned by the Synod of Mississippi, Presbyterian Church in the U.S. Established under present name 1894. Merged with McComb Female Institute 1910, with Mississippi Synodical College of Holly Springs 1939.

Belknap College, Center Harbor, N.H. Closed June 1974.

BELMONT ABBEY. Belmont, N.C. 28012. Non-public institution. Sponsored by the Southern Benedictine Society of N.C., Inc. Established as St. Mary's College 1876. Adopted present name 1913.

BELMONT COLLEGE. Nashville, Tenn. 37203. Non-public institution. Affiliated with the Tennessee Baptist Convention. Established as Ward-Belmont, Inc. 1951. Adopted present name 1962.

Bemidji State College 1957. See Bemidji State University, Bemidji, Minn.

Bemidji State Normal School 1913. See Bemidji State University, Bemidji, Minn.

Bemidji State Teachers College 1921. See Bemidji State University, Bemidji, Minn.

BEMIDJI STATE UNIVERSITY. Bemidji, Minn. 56601. State institution. Established as Bemidji State Normal School 1913. Became: Bemidji State Teachers College 1921; Bemidji State College 1957. Adopted present name 1976.

BENEDICT COLLEGE. Columbia, S.C. 29204. Non-public institution. Affiliated with the Baptist Church. Established as Benedict Institute 1870, by Mrs. Bathsheba A. Benedict. Adopted present name 1890.

Benedict Institute 1870. See Benedict College, Columbia, S.C.

BENEDICTINE COLLEGE. Atchison, Kan. 66002. Non-public institution. Owned by the Benedictine Abbey of Atchison and the Benedictine Sisters of Pontifical Jurisdiction, Roman Catholic Church. Established as St. Benedict's College 1859. Established St. Scholastica's Academy 1863. Became: Mount St. Scholastica College 1924. Adopted present name 1971 with merger of the two colleges.

Benedictine Society of Alabama 1893. See Southern Benedictine College, St. Bernard, Ala.

BENTLEY COLLEGE. Waltham, Mass. 02154. Non-public institution. Established as Bentley School of Accounting and Finance 1917. Became: Bentley College of Accounting and Finance 1961. Adopted present name 1971.

Bentley College of Accounting and Finance 1961. See Bentley College, Waltham, Mass.

Bentley School of Accounting and Finance 1917. See Bentley College, Waltham, Mass.

Berkeley Bible Seminary 1896. See Chapman College, Orange, Calif.

BERKLEE COLLEGE OF MUSIC. Boston, Mass. 02215. Non-public institution. Established as Berklee School of Music 1945. Adopted present name 1970.

Berklee School of Music 1945. See Berklee College of Music, Boston, Mass.

BERNARD M. BARUCH COLLEGE. New York, N. Y. 10010. Municipal institution. Established as School of Business and Civic Administration of The City College 1919. Became: Bernard M. Baruch School of Business and Public Administration of the City College 1954. Adopted present official name Bernard M. Baruch College of The City University of New York 1968, after becoming independent college in CUNY system.

Bernard M. Baruch College of the City University of New York 1968. See Bernard M. Baruch College, New York, N. Y.

Bernard M. Baruch School of Business and Public Administration of the City College 1954. See Bernard M. Baruch College, New York, N. Y.

BERRY COLLEGE. Mount Berry, Ga. 30149. Non-public institution. Established as Boys' Industrial School 1902. Became: Berry School 1908. Adopted present official name The Berry Schools 1917.

Berry School 1908. See Berry College, Mount Berry, Ga.

The Berry Schools 1917. See Berry College, Mount Berry, Ga.

Bessie Tift College 1907. See Tift College, Forsyth, Ga.

BETHANY BIBLE COLLEGE. Santa Cruz, Calif. 95060. Non-public institution. Affiliated with The Assemblies of God. Established as Glad Tidings Bible Training School of San Francisco 1919; Glad Tidings Bible Institute 1924; moved to present location 1950. Adopted present name 1954.

BETHANY COLLEGE. Lindsborg, Kan. 67456. Non-public institution. Owned by the Central State Synod of The Lutheran Church in America. Established as Bethany College 1881. Adopted present name 1886.

Bethany Bible Seminary 1931. See Bethany Theological Seminary, Oak Brook, Ill.

Bethany Bible Training School 1905. <u>See</u> Bethany Theological Seminary, Oak Brook, Ill.

Bethany College 1881. <u>See</u> Bethany College, Lindsborg, Kan.

BETHANY NAZARENE COLLEGE. Bethany, Okla. 73008. Non-public institution. Owned by the South Central Educational Zone of the Church of the Nazarene. Established as Oklahoma Holiness College 1909. Became: Bethany-Peniel College 1920 after merger with Peniel University 1920. Adopted present name 1955.

Bethany-Peniel College 1920. <u>See</u> Bethany Nazarene College, Bethany, Okla.

BETHANY THEOLOGICAL SEMINARY. Oak Brook, Ill. 60521. Non-public institution. Owned by the Church of the Brethren. Established as Bethany Bible Training School 1905. Became: Bethany Bible Seminary 1931. Adopted present name 1963.

Bethel Academy and Seminary 1914. <u>See</u> Bethel College, St. Paul, Minn.

Bethel Bible Institute 1900. <u>See</u> Barrington College, Barrington, R.I.

BETHEL COLLEGE. McKenzie, Tenn. 38201. Non-public institution. Affiliated with the Cumberland Presbyterian Church. Established as Bethel Seminary 1842. Adopted present name 1850.

BETHEL COLLEGE. North Newton, Kan. 67117. Non-public institution. Affiliated with the Mennonite Church. Established as The Bethel College of the Mennonite Church of North America 1887. Adopted present name 1961.

BETHEL COLLEGE. St. Paul, Minn. 55108. Non-public institution. Owned by the Baptist General Conference. Established as Scandinavian Department of Baptist Union Theological Seminary of the University of Chicago 1871. Became: Bethel Academy and Seminary 1914 after gaining independence; Bethel Institute 1920; Bethel College and Seminary 1945. Adopted present name 1974.

Bethel College and Seminary 1945. <u>See</u> Bethel College, St. Paul, Minn.

The Bethel College of the Mennonite Church of North America 1887. <u>See</u> Bethel College, North Newton, Kan.

Bethel Institute 1920. <u>See</u> Bethel College, St. Paul, Minn.

Bethel Seminary 1842. <u>See</u> Bethel College, McKenzie, Tenn.

BETHUNE-COOKMAN COLLEGE. Daytona Beach, Fla. 32015. Non-public institution. Affiliated with the Florida Conference of the United

Methodist Church.   Established as Daytona Cookman Collegiate Institute 1923.   Adopted present name 1925.

Beulah Park Bible School 1921.   See   United Wesleyan College, Allentown, Pa.

Bible Institute of Chicago 1946.   See   Trinity College, Deerfield, Ill.

Bible Institute of Los Angeles 1907.   See   Biola College, La Mirada, Calif.

Bible Institute of Pennsylvania 1913.   See   Philadelphia College of Bible, Philadelphia, Pa.

Bible Missionary Institute 1937.   See   Westmont College, Santa Barbara, Calif.

Bible Training School 1918.   See   Lee College, Cleveland, Tenn.

Biddle Memorial Institute 1867.   See   Johnson C. Smith University, Charlotte, N. C.

Biddle University 1876.   See   Johnson C. Smith University, Charlotte, N. C.

Big Rapids Industrial School 1884.   See   Ferris State College, Big Rapids, Mich.

Billings Polytechnic Institute 1946.   See   Rocky Mountain College, Billings, Mont.

Biltmore College 1934.   See   University of North Carolina at Asheville, Asheville, N. C.

Biola Bible College 1947.   See   Biola College, La Mirada, Calif.

BIOLA COLLEGE.   La Mirada, Calif. 90638.   Non-public institution. Established as Bible Institute of Los Angeles 1907.   Became: Biola Bible College 1947; Biola Schools and Colleges 1956.   Adopted present name 1971.

Biola Schools and Colleges 1956.   See   Biola College, La Mirada, Calif.

Birmingham College 1918.   See   Birmingham-Southern College, Birmingham, Ala.

BIRMINGHAM-SOUTHERN COLLEGE.   Birmingham, Ala. 35204. Non-public institution.   Owned by The United Methodist Church.   Established as Southern University 1856.   Merged with Birmingham College 1918.   Adopted present name 1918.

BLACK HILLS STATE COLLEGE.   Spearfish, S. D. 57783.   State

institution. Established as Dakota Territorial Normal School 1883.
Became: Spearfish Normal School 1898; Black Hills Teachers College 1941. Adopted present name 1964.

Black Hills Teachers College 1941. See Black Hills State College,
Spearfish, S. D.

Bliss College, Lewiston, Me. Closed June 1972.

BLOOMFIELD COLLEGE. Bloomfield, N. J. 07003. Non-public
institution. Affiliated with the United Presbyterian Church in the
U.S. Established as German Theological School 1868. Became:
Bloomfield Theological Seminary 1913; Bloomfield College and Seminary 1926. Adopted present name 1960.

Bloomfield College and Seminary 1926. See Bloomfield College,
Bloomfield, N. J.

Bloomfield Theological Seminary 1913. See Bloomfield College,
Bloomfield, N. J.

Bloomsburg Academy 1839. See Bloomsburg State College, Bloomsburg, Pa.

Bloomsburg Literary Institute 1856. See Bloomsburg State College,
Bloomsburg, Pa.

Bloomsburg Literary Institute and State Normal School 1869. See
Bloomsburg State College, Bloomsburg, Pa.

BLOOMSBURG STATE COLLEGE. Bloomsburg, Pa. 17815. State
institution. Established as Bloomsburg Academy 1839. Became:
Bloomsburg Literary Institute 1856; Bloomsburg Literary Institute
and State Normal School 1869; Bloomsburg State Normal School 1916;
Bloomsburg State Teachers College 1927. Adopted present name 1960.

Bloomsburg State Normal School 1916. See Bloomsburg State College, Bloomsburg, Pa.

Bloomsburg State Teachers College 1927. See Bloomsburg State
College, Bloomsburg, Pa.

Blount College 1794. See The University of Tennessee, Knoxville,
Knoxville, Tenn.

BLUE MOUNTAIN COLLEGE, Blue Mountain, Miss. 38610. Nonpublic institution. Owned by the Mississippi Baptist Convention
(Southern Baptist). Established as Blue Mountain Female Institute
1873. Became: Blue Mountain Female College 1877. Adopted present name 1909.

Blue Mountain Female College 1877. See Blue Mountain College,
Blue Mountain, Miss.

Blue Mountain Female Institute 1873. See Blue Mountain College,
Blue Mountain, Miss.

Bluefield Colored Institute 1895. See Bluefield State College, Bluefield, W. Va.

BLUEFIELD STATE COLLEGE. Bluefield, W. Va. 24701. State
institution. Established as Bluefield Colored Institute 1895. Became: Bluefield State Teachers College 1931. Adopted present name
1943.

Bluefield State Teachers College 1931. See Bluefield State College,
Bluefield, W. Va.

BLUFFTON COLLEGE. Bluffton, Oh. 45817. Non-public institution.
Affiliated with The General Conference Mennonite Church. Established as Central Mennonite College 1899. Adopted present name
1914.

Boiling Springs High School 1905. See Gardner-Webb College,
Boiling Springs, N. C.

Boise Junior College 1932. See Boise State University, Boise, Ida.

Boise State College 1969. See Boise State University, Boise, Ida.

BOISE STATE UNIVERSITY. Boise, Ida. 83707. State institution.
Established as Boise Junior College 1932 by private group, control
assumed by state 1939. Became: Boise State College 1969.
Adopted present name 1974.

BORROMEO COLLEGE OF OHIO. Wickliffe, Oh. 44092. Non-public institution. Owned by the Roman Catholic Diocese of Cleveland.
Established as Borromeo Seminary 1954. Became: Borromeo Seminary of Ohio 1957. Adopted present name 1974.

Borromeo Seminary 1954. See Borromeo College of Ohio, Wickliffe, Ohio.

Borromeo Seminary of Ohio 1957. See Borromeo College of Ohio,
Wickliffe, Oh. 44092.

Boston-Bouvé College 1964. See Northeastern University, Boston,
Mass.

BOSTON COLLEGE. Chestnut Hill, Mass. 02167. Non-public institution. Affiliated with the Society of Jesus, Roman Catholic Church.
Established under present name 1863. Merged with Newton College
of the Sacred Heart 1974.

Boston Conservatory of Oratory 1880. See Emerson College, Boston, Mass.

Boston Ecclesiastical Seminary 1883. See St. John's Seminary,
Brighton, Mass.

Boston Normal School 1852. See Boston State College, Boston,
Mass.

BOSTON STATE COLLEGE. Boston, Mass. 02115. State institution.
Established as Boston Normal School 1852. Became: Girls High
and Normal School 1854; Teachers College of the City of Boston 1924;
State Teachers College at Boston 1952; State College at Boston 1960.
Adopted present name 1968.

Boston Theological Seminary 1867. See Boston University, Boston,
Mass.

BOSTON UNIVERSITY. Boston, Mass. 02215. Non-public institution. Established as Methodist General Biblical Institute 1839 in
Newbury, Vermont. Became: Boston Theological Seminary, after
moving to Boston 1867. Adopted present name 1869.

Bowie Normal and Industrial School for the Training of Colored
Youth 1925. See Bowie State College, Bowie, Md.

BOWIE STATE COLLEGE. Bowie, Md. 20715. State institution.
Established as Industrial School for Colored Youth 1867. Became:
Bowie Normal and Industrial School for the Training of Colored
Youth 1925; Maryland State Teachers College at Bowie 1938. Adopted
present name 1963.

Bowling Green State College 1929. See Bowling Green State University, Bowling Green, Ohio.

Bowling Green State Normal College 1910. See Bowling Green
State University, Bowling Green, Ohio.

BOWLING GREEN STATE UNIVERSITY. Bowling Green, Oh. 43403.
State institution. Established as Bowling Green State Normal College
1910. Became: Bowling Green State College 1929. Adopted present
name 1935.

Boys' Industrial School 1902. See Berry College, Mount Berry, Ga.

Bradford Durfee College of Technology. See Southeastern Massachusetts University, North Dartmouth, Mass.

Bradley Polytechnic Institute 1896. See Bradley University, Peoria,
Ill.

BRADLEY UNIVERSITY. Peoria, Ill. 61606. Non-public institution.
Established as Bradley Polytechnic Institute 1896. Adopted present
name 1946.

Branch Agricultural College 1913. See Southern Utah State College,
Cedar City, Ut.

Branch Normal College 1873. See University of Arkansas at Pine Bluff, Pine Bluff, Ark.

Branch Normal School 1897. See Southern Utah State College, Cedar City, Ut.

BRENAU COLLEGE. Gainesville, Ga. 30501. Non-public institution. Established as Georgia Baptist Female Seminary 1878. Adopted present name 1900.

Brentwood College, Brentwood, N. Y. Closed June 1971.

BRESCIA COLLEGE. Owensboro, Ky. 42301. Non-public institution. Affiliated with the Roman Catholic Church. Established as Mount Saint Joseph Academy 1878. Became: Mount Saint Joseph Junior College 1925. Adopted present name 1950.

Brethren's Normal College 1876. See Juniata College, Huntingdon, Pa.

Brevard Engineering College 1958. See Florida Institute of Technology, Melbourne, Fla.

Briarcliff College. Briarcliff Manor, N. Y. Closed July 1977.

BRIDGEWATER COLLEGE. Bridgewater, Va. 22812. Non-public institution. Affiliated with the Church of the Brethren. Established as Spring Creek Normal School 1880. Became: Virginia Normal School 1882. Adopted present name 1890.

Bridgewater Normal School 1840. See Bridgewater State College, Bridgewater, Mass.

BRIDGEWATER STATE COLLEGE. Bridgewater, Mass. 02324. State institution. Established as Bridgewater Normal School 1840. Became: Bridgewater State Teachers College 1932. State College at Bridgewater 1960. Adopted present name 1968.

Bridgewater State Teachers College 1932. See Bridgewater State College, Bridgewater, Mass.

Brigham Young Academy 1875. See Brigham Young University Main Campus, Provo, Ut.

Brigham Young University 1903. See Brigham Young University Main Campus, Provo, Ut.

BRIGHAM YOUNG UNIVERSITY MAIN CAMPUS. Provo, Ut. 84601. Non-public institution. Controlled and owned by the Church of Jesus Christ of the Latter Day Saints. Established as Brigham Young Academy 1875. Became: Brigham Young University 1903. Adopted present name 1974.

Broaddus Academy 1871. See Alderson-Broaddus College, Philippi, W. Va.

Broaddus College and Academy 1917. See Alderson-Broaddus College, Philippi, W. Va.

Brockport Collegiate Institute 1836. See State University of New York College at Brockport, Brockport, N. Y.

Brockport State Normal School 1866. See State University of New York College at Brockport, Brockport, N. Y.

Brockway College 1851. See Ripon College, Ripon, Wisc.

BROOKLYN COLLEGE. Brooklyn, N. Y. 11210. Municipal institution. Established under present name 1930. Adopted present official name Brooklyn College of The City University of New York 1961.

Brooklyn College of Pharmacy 1929. See Long Island University Arnold and Marie Schwartz College of Pharmacy and Health Sciences, Brooklyn, N. Y.

Brooklyn College of The City University of New York 1961. See Brooklyn College, Brooklyn, N. Y.

Brooklyn Collegiate and Polytechnic Institute 1854. See Polytechnic Institute of New York, Brooklyn, N. Y.

BROOKS INSTITUTE. Santa Barbara, Calif. 93108. Non-public institution. Established as Brooks Institute of Photography 1945. Adopted present name 1968.

Brooks Institute of Photography 1945. See Brooks Institute, Santa Barbara, Calif.

BROWN UNIVERSITY. Providence, R. I. 02912. Non-public institution. Established as Rhode Island College 1764. Adopted present name 1804.

Brown's Schoolhouse 1838. See Duke University, Durham, N. C.

BRYAN COLLEGE. Dayton, Tenn. 37321. Non-public institution. Established under present official name William Jennings Bryan College 1930.

Bryant and Stratton Business College 1863. See Bryant College, Smithfield, R. I.

BRYANT COLLEGE. Smithfield, R. I. 02917. Non-public institution. Established as Bryant and Stratton Business College 1863. Adopted present official name Bryant College of Business Administration 1934.

Bryant College of Business Administration 1934. See Bryant College, Smithfield, R. I.

Bryant, Lusk and Stratton Business College 1853. See Dyke College, Cleveland, Oh.

Buchel College 1870. See University of Akron, Akron, Oh.

BUCKNELL UNIVERSITY. Lewisburg, Pa. 17837. Non-public institution. Established as University at Lewisburg 1846, by the Baptist Church. Adopted present name 1886.

Bucknell University Junior College 1933. See Wilkes College, Wilkes-Barre, Pa.

Buffalo Male and Female Institute 1866. See Milligan College, Milligan College, Tenn.

Buffalo State Normal School 1867. See State University of New York College at Buffalo, Buffalo, N. Y.

Buie's Creek Academy 1887. See Campbell College, Buie's Creek, N. C.

Bullock School 1821. See Widener College, Chester, Pa.

Bureau of Education Experiments 1916. See Bank Street College of Education, New York, N. Y.

BUTLER UNIVERSITY. Indianapolis, Ind. 46208. Non-public institution. Established as North Western Christian University 1850. Adopted present name 1877.

- C -

C. W. POST CENTER. Greenvale, N. Y. 11548. Non-public institution. Established as Merriweather Campus of Long Island University 1954. Adopted present name 1969.

CALDWELL COLLEGE. Caldwell, N. J. 07006. Non-public institution. Affiliated with the Sisters of St. Dominic, Roman Catholic Church. Established as Caldwell College for Women 1939. Adopted present name 1969.

Caldwell College for Women 1939. See Caldwell College, Caldwell, N. J.

California Academy 1852. See California State College, California, Pa.

California Christian College 1923. See Chapman College, Orange, Calif.

CALIFORNIA COLLEGE OF ARTS AND CRAFTS. Oakland, Calif.
94618. Non-public institution. Established as School of the California Guild of Arts and Crafts in Berkeley 1907. Became: California School of Arts and Crafts 1908. Adopted present name 1936.

California College of Chiropody 1914. See California College of
Podiatric Medicine, San Francisco, Calif.

CALIFORNIA COLLEGE OF PODIATRIC MEDICINE. San Francisco,
Calif. 94115. Non-public institution. Established as California Col-
lege of Chiropody 1914. Became: California Podiatry College (and
Hospital) 1960. Adopted present name 1964.

California Concordia College, Oakland, Calif. Closed June 1973.

CALIFORNIA INSTITUTE OF TECHNOLOGY. Pasadena, Calif.
91109. Non-public institution. Established as Throop Polytechnic
Institute 1891. Became: Throop College of Technology 1913.
Adopted present name 1920.

CALIFORNIA MARITIME ACADEMY. Vallejo, Calif. 94590. State
institution. Established as California Nautical School 1929. Adopted
present name 1940.

California Nautical School 1929. See California Maritime Academy,
Vallejo, Calif.

California Podiatry College and Hospital 1960. See California College of Podiatric Medicine, San Francisco, Calif.

California Polytechnic School 1901. See California Polytechnic State
University, San Luis Obispo, San Luis Obispo, Calif.

CALIFORNIA POLYTECHNIC STATE UNIVERSITY, SAN LUIS OBISPO.
San Luis Obispo, Calif. 93401. State institution. Established as
California Polytechnic school 1901. Became: California State Poly-
technic College, San Luis Obispo 1947. Adopted present name 1972.

California School for Private Secretaries 1918. See Armstrong
College, Berkeley, Calif.

California School of Arts and Crafts 1908. See California College
of Arts and Crafts, Oakland, Calif.

California School of Christianity 1921. See Chapman College,
Orange, Calif.

California School of Fine Arts 1916. See San Francisco Art Institute, San Francisco, Calif.

CALIFORNIA STATE COLLEGE. California, Pa. 15419. State institution. Established as California Academy 1852. Became: Southwestern State Normal School 1874; California State Normal School

1914; California State Teachers College 1928.   Adopted present name
1959.

California State College at Fullerton 1964.   See   California State
University, Fullerton, Fullerton, Calif.

California State College at Hayward 1963.   See   Hayward State University, Hayward, Calif.

California State College at Los Angeles 1964.   See   California State
University, Los Angeles, Los Angeles, Calif.

CALIFORNIA STATE COLLEGE, BAKERSFIELD.   Bakersfield,
Calif. 93309.   State institution.   Established as California State
College, Kern County 1965.   Adopted present name 1967.

California State College, Fullerton 1969.   See   California State University, Fullerton, Fullerton, Calif.

California State College, Hayward 1968.   See   Hayward State University, Hayward, Calif.

California State College, Kern County 1965.   See   California State
College, Bakersfield, Bakersfield, Calif.

California State College, Long Beach 1968.   See   California State
University, Long Beach, Long Beach, Calif.

California State College, Los Angeles 1968.   See   California State
University, Los Angeles, Calif.

CALIFORNIA STATE COLLEGE, SONOMA.   Rohnert Park, Calif.
94928.   State institution.   Established as Sonoma State College 1960.
Adopted present name 1972.

CALIFORNIA STATE COLLEGE, STANISLAUS.   Turlock, Calif.
95380.   State institution.   Established as Stanislaus State College
1957.   Adopted present name 1972.

California State Normal School 1862.   See   San Jose State University,
San Jose, Calif.

California State Normal School 1914.   See   California State College,
California, Pa.

California State Polytechnic College, Kellogg-Voorhis 1956.   See
California State Polytechnic University, Pomona, Calif.

California State Polytechnic College, Kellogg-Voorhis, Pomona 1966.
See   California State Polytechnic University, Pomona, Calif.

California State Polytechnic College, San Luis Obispo 1947.   See
California Polytechnic State University, San Luis Obispo, San Luis
Obispo, Calif.

California State Polytechnic College--Voorhis Campus 1938. See
California State Polytechnic University, Pomona, Calif.

CALIFORNIA STATE POLYTECHNIC UNIVERSITY. Pomona, Calif.
91768. State institution. Established as California State Polytechnic
College--Voorhis Campus 1938. Became: California State Polytechnic College, Kellogg--Voorhis 1956; California State Polytechnic College, Kellogg-Voorhis, Pomona 1966. Adopted present name 1972.

California State Teachers College 1928. See California State College, California, Pa.

CALIFORNIA STATE UNIVERSITY, CHICO. Chico, Calif. 95926.
State institution. Established as Chico State Normal School 1887.
Became: Chico State Teachers College 1921; Chico State College
1935. Adopted present name 1972.

CALIFORNIA STATE UNIVERSITY, FRESNO. Fresno, Calif. 93710.
State institution. Established as Fresno State Normal School 1911,
after merger with Fresno Junior College. Became: Fresno State
Teachers College 1921; Fresno State College 1935. Adopted present
name 1972.

CALIFORNIA STATE UNIVERSITY, FULLERTON. Fullerton, Calif.
92631. State institution. Established as Orange County State College 1957. Became: Orange State College 1962; California State
College at Fullerton 1964; California State College, Fullerton 1969.
Adopted present name 1972.

California State University, Hayward 1972. See Hayward State
University, Hayward, Calif.

California State University, Humboldt. See Humboldt State University, Arcata, Calif.

CALIFORNIA STATE UNIVERSITY, LONG BEACH. Long Beach,
Calif. 90801. State institution. Established as Los Angeles-Orange
County State College 1949. Became: Long Beach State College 1950;
California State College, Long Beach 1968. Adopted present name
1972.

CALIFORNIA STATE UNIVERSITY, LOS ANGELES. Los Angeles,
Calif. 90032. State institution. Established as Los Angeles State
College 1947. Became: Los Angeles State College of Applied Arts
and Sciences 1949; California State College at Los Angeles 1964;
California State College, Los Angeles 1968. Adopted present name
1972.

CALIFORNIA STATE UNIVERSITY, NORTHRIDGE. Northridge,
Calif. 91324. State institution. Established as San Fernando Valley
Campus of Los Angeles State College of Applied Arts and Sciences
1956. Became: San Fernando Valley State College 1958, a separate
institution. Adopted present name 1972.

California State University, San Diego, 1972. <u>See</u> San Diego State University, San Diego, Calif.

CALIFORNIA STATE UNIVERSITY, SAN FRANCISCO. San Francisco, Calif. 94132. State institution. Established as San Francisco State Normal School 1899. Became: San Francisco State Teachers' College 1921; San Francisco State College 1935. Adopted present name 1972.

California State University, San Jose 1974. See San Jose State University, San Jose, Calif.

California Wesleyan University 1851. <u>See</u> University of the Pacific, Stockton, Calif.

California Western University 1952. <u>See</u> United States International University, San Diego, Calif.

Calumet Center, Gary, Ind. <u>See</u> Indiana University Northwest, Gary, Ind.

CALUMET COLLEGE. East Chicago, Ind. 46312. Non-public institution. Affiliated with the Society of the Precious Blood, Roman Catholic Church. Established as St. Joseph's College Calumet Center 1951. Became: St. Joseph's College Calumet Campus 1960; St. Joseph's Calumet College 1971. Adopted present name 1974.

CALVARY BIBLE COLLEGE. Kansas City, Mo. 64111. Non-public institution. Established as Kansas City Bible Institute 1932 by Dr. Walter L. Wilson. Merged with Midwest Bible and Missionary Institute 1961. Adopted present name 1961.

CALVIN COLLEGE. Grand Rapids, Mich. 49506. Non-public institution. Owned by the Christian Reformed Church. Established as Theological School 1876. Became: John Calvin Junior College 1906. Adopted present official name Calvin College and Seminary 1908.

Calvin College and Seminary 1908. <u>See</u> Calvin College, Grand Rapids, Mich.

Calvin Coolidge College, Boston, Mass. Closed June 1970.

Cameron State Agricultural College 1927. <u>See</u> Cameron University, Lawton, Okla.

Cameron State School of Agriculture 1909. <u>See</u> Cameron University, Lawton, Okla.

CAMERON UNIVERSITY. Lawton, Okla. 73501. State institution. Established as Cameron State School of Agriculture 1909. Became: Cameron State Agricultural College 1927. Adopted present name 1974.

CAMPBELL COLLEGE. Buie's Creek, N. C. 27506. Non-public
institution. Owned by the North Carolina Baptist State Convention
(Southern Baptist). Established as Buie's Creek Academy 1887, by
private group. Control passed to Baptist State Convention 1925.
Adopted present official name Campbell College, Inc. 1926.

CAMPBELLSVILLE COLLEGE. Campbellsville, Ky. 42718. Non-
public institution. Affiliated with the Kentucky Baptist Convention
(Southern Baptist). Established as Russell Creek Academy 1906.
Became: Campbellsville Junior College 1923. Adopted present name
1959.

Campbellsville Junior College 1923. See Campbellsville College,
Campbellsville, Ky.

Canaan College, Canaan, N. H. Closed June 1973.

Cane Hill College 1834. See The College of the Ozarks, Clarksville, Ark.

CAPITAL UNIVERSITY. Columbus, Oh. 43209. Non-public institution. Owned by The American Lutheran Church. Established as
Evangelical Lutheran Seminary 1830. Adopted present name 1850.

CAPITOL INSTITUTE OF TECHNOLOGY. Kensington, Md. 20795.
Non-public institution. Established as Residence Division, Capitol
Radio Engineering Institute 1932. Adopted present name after sep-
arating from Institute 1964.

Capuchin Theological Seminary, Garrison, N. Y. Closed June 1972.

Cardinal Cushing College, Brookline, Mass. Closed June 1972.

CARDINAL GLENNON COLLEGE. St. Louis, Mo. 63119. Non-
public institution. Owned by the Archdiocese of St. Louis, Roman
Catholic Church. Established as St. Mary's Seminary 1818. Adopted
present name 1959.

Cardinal O'Connell Seminary 1968. See St. John's Seminary,
Brighton, Mass.

CARDINAL STRITCH COLLEGE. Milwaukee, Wisc. 53217. Non-
public institution. Owned by the Sisters of St. Francis of Assisi,
Roman Catholic Church. Established as St. Clare College 1934.
Adopted present name 1946.

CARLETON COLLEGE. Northfield, Minn. 55057. Non-public institution. Established as Northfield College by the Congregational
Church 1866. Adopted present name 1872.

Carlisle Grammar School 1773. See Dickinson College, Carlisle,
Pa.

Carlisle Military Institute 1901. See University of Texas at Arlington, Arlington, Tex.

CARLOW COLLEGE. Pittsburgh, Pa. 15213. Non-public institution.
Owned by the Congregation of the Sisters of Mercy of Allegheny
County, Roman Catholic Church. Established as Mount Mercy Col-
lege 1929. Adopted present name 1969.

Carnegie Institute of Technology 1912. See Carnegie-Mellon University, Pittsburgh, Pa.

CARNEGIE-MELLON UNIVERSITY. Pittsburgh, Pa. 15213. Non-
public institution. Established as Carnegie Technical Schools 1900.
Became: Carnegie Institute of Technology 1912. Adopted present
name after merging with Mellon Institute 1967.

Carnegie Technical Schools 1900. See Carnegie-Mellon University,
Pittsburgh, Pa.

Carrier Seminary 1866. See Clarion State College, Clarion, Pa.

CARROLL COLLEGE. Helena, Mont. 59601. Non-public institution.
Affiliated with the Diocese of Helena, Roman Catholic Church. Established as Mount St. Charles College 1909. Adopted present name
1932.

CARROLL COLLEGE. Waukesha, Wisc. 53186. Non-public institution. Affiliated with The United Presbyterian Church in the U.S.A.
Established as Prairieville Academy 1840. Adopted present name
1846.

CARSON-NEWMAN COLLEGE. Jefferson City, Tenn. 37760. Non-
public institution. Affiliated with the Tennessee Baptist Convention,
Inc. Established as Mossy Creek Baptist Seminary 1851. Became:
Mossy Creek Baptist College 1856. Adopted present official name
Carson-Newman College of the Tennessee Baptist Convention, Inc.
1889.

Carson-Newman College of the Tennessee Baptist Convention, Inc.
1889. See Carson-Newman College, Jefferson City, Tenn.

CARTHAGE COLLEGE. Kenosha, Wisc. 53140. Non-public institution. Owned by the Wisconsin-Upper Michigan and Michigan Synods
of the Lutheran Church in America. Established as Hillsboro College, 1847 in Hillsboro, Ill. Became: Illinois State University 1852,
after moving to Springfield, Ill. Adopted present name 1870, after
moving to Carthage, Ill. Moved to present location 1962.

Cartoonist and Illustrator's School 1947. See School of Visual Arts,
New York, N.Y.

Cascade College, Portland, Ore. Closed June 1969.

Case Institute of Technology 1967. See Case Western Reserve University, Cleveland, Ohio.

CASE WESTERN RESERVE UNIVERSITY. Cleveland, Oh. 44106. Non-public institution. Established under present name by merger of Case Institute of Technology 1967 and Western Reserve University 1967.

Castleton Academy 1805. See Castleton State College, Castleton, Vt.

Castleton Academy and Female Seminary 1827. See Castleton State College, Castleton, Vt.

Castleton Normal School 1867. See Castleton State College, Castleton, Vt.

Castleton Seminary 1833. See Castleton State College, Castleton, Vt.

CASTLETON STATE COLLEGE. Castleton, Vt. 05735. State institution. Established as Rutland County Grammar School 1787. Became: Castleton Academy 1805; Castleton Academy and Female Seminary 1827; Vermont Classical High School 1828; Castleton Seminary 1833; Castleton Normal School 1867; Castleton Teachers College 1947. Adopted present name 1962.

Castleton Teachers College 1947. See Castleton State College, Castleton, Vt.

Cathedral College 1933. See Gannon College, Erie, Pa.

Catherine McAuley College, Rochester, N.Y. Closed June 1968.

Catherine Spalding College 1963. See Spalding College, Louisville, Ky.

Catholepistemiad University of Michigania 1817. See University of Michigan, Ann Arbor, Mich.

Catholic Junior College 1931. See Aquinas College, Grand Rapids, Mich.

Catholic Teachers College of New Mexico 1940. See University of Albuquerque, Albuquerque, N.M.

CEDAR CREST COLLEGE. Allentown, Pa. 18104. Non-public institution. Affiliated with the United Church of Christ. Established as Allentown Female College 1867. Became: Allentown College for Women 1893. Adopted present name 1913.

Cedar Rapids Collegiate Institute 1851. See Coe College, Cedar Rapids, Ia.

Centenary Biblical Institute 1867. See Morgan State University, Baltimore, Md.

CENTENARY COLLEGE. Hackettstown, N. J. 07840. Non-public institution. Established as Centenary Collegiate Institute 1867 by Newark Annual Conference of the Methodist Episcopal Church. Became: Centenary Junior College 1940; Centenary College for Women 1956. Adopted present name 1977.

Centenary College 1845. See Centenary College of Louisiana, Shreveport, La.

Centenary College for Women 1956. See Centenary College, Hackettstown, N. J.

CENTENARY COLLEGE OF LOUISIANA. Shreveport, La. 71104. Non-public institution. Affiliated with the Louisiana Conference of The United Methodist Church. Established as College of Louisiana, Jackson, La., 1825. Merged with Centenary College 1845, and became Centenary College, Shreveport 1908, after moving to that location. Adopted present name 1974.

Centenary College, Shreveport 1908. See Centenary College of Louisiana, Shreveport, La.

Centenary Collegiate Institute 1867. See Centenary College, Hackettstown, N. J.

Centenary Junior College 1940. See Centenary College, Hackettstown, N. J.

Central Christian College 1950. See Oklahoma Christian College, Oklahoma City, Okla.

Central College 1897. See Huntington College, Huntington, Ind.

Central College for Women. See Central Methodist College, Fayette, Mo.

Central Collegiate Institute, Altus, Ark., 1876. See Hendrix College, Conway, Ark.

CENTRAL CONNECTICUT STATE COLLEGE. New Britain, Conn. 06050. State institution. Established as New Britain Normal School 1849. Became: Teachers College of Connecticut 1933. Adopted present name 1959.

Central Mennonite College 1899. See Bluffton College, Bluffton, Ohio.

CENTRAL METHODIST COLLEGE. Fayette, Mo. 65448. Non-public institution. Owned by The United Methodist Church. Established as Central College 1854. Merged with Howard Payne College, Central

College for Women, Scarritt-Morrisville College and Marvin College
1922-25.   Adopted present name 1961.

Central Michigan College 1955. See Central Michigan University,
Mt. Pleasant, Mich.

Central Michigan College of Education 1940. See Central Michigan
University, Mount Pleasant, Mich.

Central Michigan Normal School 1895. See Central Michigan University, Mount Pleasant, Mich.

Central Michigan Normal School and Business Institute 1892. See
Central Michigan University, Mount Pleasant, Mich.

CENTRAL MICHIGAN UNIVERSITY.   Mount Pleasant, Mich. 48858.
State institution.   Established as Central Michigan Normal School
and Business Institute 1892.   Became: Central Michigan Normal
School 1895; Central State Teachers College 1927; Central Michigan
College of Education 1940; Central Michigan College 1955.   Adopted
present name 1959.

Central Missouri State College 1946. See Central Missouri State
University, Warrensburg, Mo.

Central Missouri State Teachers College 1919. See Central Missouri State University, Warrensburg, Mo.

CENTRAL MISSOURI STATE UNIVERSITY.   Warrensburg, Mo.
64093.   State institution.   Established as State Normal School for
Second Normal District of Missouri 1871.   Became: Central Missouri State Teachers College 1919; Central Missouri State College
1946.   Adopted present name 1972.

Central Pennsylvania College 1887. See Albright College, Reading,
Pa.

Central Pilgrim College 1959. See Bartlesville Wesleyan College,
Bartlesville, Okla.

Central State College 1939. See Central State University, Edmond,
Okla.

Central State College 1951. See Central State University, Wilberforce, Ohio.

Central State Normal School 1870. See Lock Haven State College,
Lock Haven, Pa.

Central State Normal School 1907. See Central State University,
Edmond, Okla.

Central State Teachers College 1919. See Central State University,
Edmond, Okla.

Central State Teachers College 1926. See University of Wisconsin-Stevens Point, Stevens Point, Wisc.

Central State Teachers College 1927. See Central Michigan University, Mount Pleasant, Mich.

CENTRAL STATE UNIVERSITY. Edmond, Okla. 73034. State institution. Established as The Normal School of the Territory of Oklahoma 1890. Became: Central State Normal School 1907; Central State Teachers College 1919; Central State College 1939. Adopted present name 1971.

CENTRAL STATE UNIVERSITY. Wilberforce, Oh. 45384. State institution. Established as Combined Normal and Industrial Department, Wilberforce University 1887. Became: College of Education and Industrial Arts 1941. Adopted present name 1965.

Central States College of Physiatrics 1976. See National College of Chiropractic, Lombard, Ill.

The Central University of Methodist Episcopal Church, South 1872. See The Vanderbilt University, Nashville, Tenn.

Central Washington College of Education 1937. See Central Washington State College, Ellensburg, Wash.

CENTRAL WASHINGTON STATE COLLEGE. Ellensburg, Wash. 98926. State institution. Established as Washington State Normal School 1890. Became: Central Washington College of Education 1937. Adopted present name 1961.

CENTRAL WESLEYAN COLLEGE. Central, S. C. 29630. Non-public institution. Owned and operated by the Wesleyan Church. Established as Wesleyan Methodist Bible Institute 1906. Became: Wesleyan Methodist College 1909. Adopted present name 1959.

CHADRON STATE COLLEGE. Chadron, Neb. 69337. State institution. Established as Nebraska State Normal College 1910. Became: Nebraska State Teachers College 1937. Adopted present name 1963.

CHAMINADE COLLEGE OF HONOLULU. Honolulu, Haw. 96816. Non-public institution. Affiliated with the Society of Mary, Roman Catholic Church. Established as St. Louis Junior College 1955. Adopted present name 1957.

CHAPMAN COLLEGE. Orange, Calif. 92666. Non-public institution. Affiliated with the Christian Church (Disciples of Christ). Established as Hesperian College, at Woodland, Calif. 1861. Became: Berkeley Bible Seminary 1896; California School of Christianity 1921; California Christian College 1923. Adopted present name 1934. Moved to present location 1954.

Charles City College 1914. See Morningside College, Sioux City, Ia.

Charlotte Center of the University of N. C. 1946. See University of North Carolina at Charlotte, Charlotte, N. C.

Charlotte College 1949. See University of North Carolina at Charlotte, Charlotte, N. C.

Charlotte Female Institute 1857. See Queens College, Charlotte, N. C.

The Chase School 1896. See Parsons School of Design, New York, N. Y.

CHATHAM COLLEGE. Pittsburgh, Pa. 15232. Non-public institution. Established as Pennsylvania Female College 1869. Became: Pennsylvania College for Women 1890. Adopted present name 1955.

Chattanooga City College 1969. See The University of Tennessee at Chattanooga, Chattanooga, Tenn.

Chattanooga University 1886. See The University of Tennessee at Chattanooga, Chattanooga, Tenn.

Cherokee Baptist Female College 1873. See Shorter College, Rome, Ga.

Cherokee Female Seminary 1846. See Northeastern Oklahoma University, Tahlequah, Okla.

Chesborough Seminary 1885. See Roberts Wesleyan College, Rochester, N. Y.

CHESTNUT HILL COLLEGE. Philadelphia, Pa. 19118. Non-public institution. Conducted by the Sisters of St. Joseph, Roman Catholic Church. Established as Mount St. Joseph Academy 1858. Adopted present name 1938.

CHEYNEY STATE COLLEGE. Cheyney, Pa. 19319. State institution. Established as Institute for Colored Youth 1842, in Philadelphia, by Quakers. Moved to present location 1902. Became: Cheyney Training School for Teachers 1914; State Normal School 1920, Cheyney, Pa. after purchase by state; Cheyney State Teachers College 1951. Adopted present name 1959.

Cheyney State Teachers College 1951. See Cheyney State College, Cheyney, Pa.

Cheyney Training School for Teachers 1914. See Cheyney State College, Cheyney, Pa.

Chicago Academy of Design 1866. See Art Institute of Chicago, Chicago, Ill.

Chicago Academy of Fine Arts 1879. See Art Institute of Chicago, Chicago, Ill.

Chicago College of Optometry. See Illinois College of Optometry, Chicago, Ill.

The Chicago Hospital College of Medicine 1912. See The University of Health Sciences/The Chicago Medical School, Chicago, Ill.

Chicago-Kent College of Law 1969. See Illinois Institute of Technology, Chicago, Ill.

Chicago Kindergarten College 1893. See National College of Education, Evanston, Ill.

Chicago Kindergarten Training School 1886. See National College of Education, Evanston, Ill.

The Chicago Medical School 1919. See The University of Health Sciences/The Chicago Medical School, Chicago, Ill.

The Chicago Medical School/University of Health Sciences 1967. See The University of Health Sciences/The Chicago Medical School, Chicago, Ill.

Chicago Normal College 1913. See Chicago State University, Chicago, Ill.

Chicago Normal School 1896. See Chicago State University, Chicago, Ill.

Chicago School of Nursing, Chicago, Ill. Closed Dec. 1968.

Chicago State College 1967. See Chicago State University, Chicago, Ill.

CHICAGO STATE UNIVERSITY. Chicago, Ill. 60621. State institution. Established as Cook County Normal School 1869. Became: Chicago Normal School 1896; Chicago Teachers College 1910; Chicago Normal College 1913; Chicago Teachers College 1938; Illinois Teachers College Chicago-South 1965; Chicago State College 1967. Adopted present name 1971.

Chicago Teachers College 1910. See Chicago State University, Chicago, Ill.

Chicago Teachers College 1938. See Chicago State University, Chicago, Ill.

Chicago Undergraduate Division of the University of Illinois 1946. See University of Illinois at Chicago Circle, Chicago, Ill.

Chico State College 1935. See California State University, Chico., Chico, Calif.

Chico State Normal School 1887. See California State University,
Chico, Chico, Calif.

Chico State Teachers College 1921. See California State University,
Chico. , Chico, Calif.

Childers Classical Institute 1906. See Abilene Christian University,
Abilene, Tex.

Chili Seminary 1866. See Roberts Wesleyan College, Rochester,
N. Y.

Chiropractic Institute of New York 1968. See National College of
Chiropractic, Lombard, Ill.

Christian College 1929. See Columbia College, Columbia, Mo.

Christian College 1965. See Oregon College of Education, Monmouth, Ore.

Christian College of the Southwest, Dallas. See Abilene Christian
University, Abilene, Tex.

Christian Female College 1851. See Columbia College, Columbia,
Mo.

Christian University 1853. See Culver-Stockton College, Canton,
Mo.

Christian Workers Training School 1892. See Malone College, Canton, Ohio.

Christopher College, Corpus Christi, Tex.   Closed May 1968.

Cincinnati Astronomical Society 1872. See University of Cincinnati,
Cincinnati, Oh.

Cincinnati College 1819. See University of Cincinnati, Cincinnati,
Oh.

Cincinnati College of Pharmacy 1954. See University of Cincinnati,
Cincinnati, Oh.

THE CITADEL. Charleston, S. C. 29409. State institution. Es-
tablished as The Citadel 1842. Became: South Carolina Military
Academy 1887. Adopted present official name The Citadel, The
Military College of South Carolina 1910.

The Citadel, The Military College of South Carolina 1910. See The
Citadel, Charleston, S. C.

Citrus Experiment Station 1907. See University of California,
Riverside, Riverside, Calif.

THE CITY COLLEGE. New York, N.Y. 10031. Municipal institution. Established as the Free Academy 1847. Adopted present name 1929, then adopted present official name The City College of the City University of New York 1961.

The City College of the City University of New York 1961. See The City College, New York, N.Y.

City University of New York Richmond College 1976. See City University of New York College of Staten Island.

CITY UNIVERSITY OF NEW YORK COLLEGE OF STATEN ISLAND. Staten Island, N.Y. 10301. Municipal institution. Established with the merger of City University of New York Richmond College 1976 and City University of New York Staten Island Community College 1976. Adopted present name 1976.

City University of New York Staten Island Community College 1976. See City University of New York College of Staten Island.

CLAFIN COLLEGE. Orangeburg, S.C. 29115. Non-public institution. Owned by The United Methodist Church. Established under present name 1869. Merged with Baker Theological Institute 1870.

Claremont College 1944. See Claremont University Center and Claremont Graduate School, Claremont, Calif.

Claremont College Undergraduate School for Men 1946. See Claremont Men's College, Claremont, Calif.

Claremont Colleges 1925. See Claremont University Center and Claremont Graduate School, Claremont, Calif.

Claremont Graduate School 1971. See Claremont University Center and Claremont Graduate School, Claremont, Calif.

Claremont Graduate School and University Center 1963. See Claremont University Center and Claremont Graduate School, Claremont, Calif.

CLAREMONT MEN'S COLLEGE. Claremont, Calif. 91711. Non-public institution. Established as Claremont College Undergraduate School for Men 1946. Adopted present name 1947.

Claremont University Center 1967. See Claremont University Center and Claremont Graduate School, Claremont, Calif.

CLAREMONT UNIVERSITY CENTER AND CLAREMONT GRADUATE SCHOOL. Claremont, Calif. 91711. Non-public institution. Established as Claremont Colleges 1925. Became: Claremont College 1944; Claremont University College 1961; Claremont Graduate School and University Center 1963; Claremont University Center 1967; Claremont Graduate School 1971. Adopted present name 1976.

Claremont University College 1961. See Claremont University Center and Claremont Graduate School, Claremont, Calif.

CLARION STATE COLLEGE. Clarion, Pa. 16214. State institution. Established as Carrier Seminary 1866. Became: Clarion State Normal School 1887; Clarion State Teachers College 1929. Adopted present name 1960.

Clarion State Normal School 1887. See Clarion State College, Clarion, Pa.

Clarion State Teachers College 1929. See Clarion State College, Clarion, Pa.

Clark and Erskine Seminary 1837. See Erskine College, Due West, S. C.

CLARK COLLEGE. Atlanta, Ga. 30314. Non-public institution. Affiliated with The United Methodist Church. Established as Clark University 1869. Adopted present name 1940.

Clark College 1902. See Clark University, Worcester, Mass.

CLARK UNIVERSITY. Worcester, Mass. 01610. Non-public institution. Established as Trustees of Clark University 1887, a graduate school. Established Clark College 1902, an undergraduate school. Adopted present name 1920, with merger of two schools.

Clark University 1869. See Clark College, Atlanta, Ga.

CLARKE COLLEGE. Dubuque, Ia. 52001. Non-public institution. Owned by the Sisters of Charity of the Blessed Virgin, Roman Catholic Church. Established as St. Mary's Academy 1843. Became: St. Joseph Academy 1846; Mount St. Joseph Academy 1879; Mount St. Joseph College 1901. Adopted present name 1928.

CLARKSON COLLEGE OF TECHNOLOGY. Potsdam, N. Y. 13676. Non-public institution. Established under present official name Thomas S. Clarkson Memorial College of Technology 1896.

Cleary Business College 1891. See Cleary College, Ypsilanti, Mich.

CLEARY COLLEGE. Ypsilanti, Mich. 48197. Non-public institution. Established as Cleary School of Penmanship 1883 by Patrick R. Cleary. Became: Cleary Business College 1891. Adopted present name 1933.

Cleary School of Penmanship 1883. See Cleary College, Ypsilanti, Mich.

Clemson College 1889. See Clemson University, Clemson, S. C.

CLEMSON UNIVERSITY. Clemson, S. C. 29631. State institution. Established as Clemson College 1889. Adopted present name 1964.

Cleveland Bible College 1937. See Malone College, Canton, Ohio.

Cleveland Bible Institute 1911. See Malone College, Canton, Ohio.

THE CLEVELAND INSTITUTE OF ART. Cleveland, Oh. 44106.
Non-public institution. Established as The Cleveland School of Art
1882. Adopted present name 1949.

Cleveland-Marshall School of Law 1969. See The Cleveland State
University, Cleveland, Oh.

The Cleveland School of Art 1882. See The Cleveland Institute of
Art, Cleveland, Oh.

THE CLEVELAND STATE UNIVERSITY. Cleveland, Oh. 44115.
State institution. Established as YMCA Educational Branch 1881.
Became: Cleveland YMCA School of Technology 1921; Fenn College
of the Cleveland YMCA School of Technology 1930; Fenn College 1936.
Became independent of YMCA 1951, adopted present name 1965.
Merged with Cleveland-Marshall School of Law 1969.

Cleveland University 1923. See John Carroll University, Cleveland,
Oh.

Cleveland YMCA School of Technology 1921. See The Cleveland
State University, Cleveland, Oh.

Clifton College 1954. See Texas Lutheran College, Seguin, Tex.

Clinton College 1880. See Presbyterian College, Clinton, S. C.

Coalition of Religious Seminaries 1968. See Washington Theological
Coalition, Silver Spring, Md.

COE COLLEGE. Cedar Rapids, Ia. 52402. Non-public institution.
Affiliated with The United Presbyterian Church in the U. S. Established as Cedar Rapids Collegiate Institute 1851. Became: Parsons
Seminary 1866; Coe Collegiate Institute 1875. Adopted present name
1881. Absorbed Leander Clark College 1919.

Coe Collegiate Institute 1875. See Coe College, Cedar Rapids, Ia.
52402.

COKER COLLEGE. Hartsville, S. C. 29550. Non-public institution.
Established as Welsh Neck Academy 1896. Became: Coker College
for Women 1908. Adopted present name 1970.

Coker College for Women 1908. See Coker College, Hartsville,
S. C.

COLBY COLLEGE. Waterville, Me. 04901. Non-public institution.
Established as Maine Literary and Theological Institution 1813. Became: Waterville College 1820; Colby University 1867. Adopted
present name 1899.

Colegio del Sagrado Corazon 1880. See College of the Sacred Heart, Santurce, P. R.

Colegio Universitario del Sagrado Corazon 1954. See College of the Sacred Heart, Santurce, P. R.

COLGATE UNIVERSITY. Hamilton, N. Y. 13346. Non-public institution. Established as Hamilton Literary and Theological Institution 1819. Became: Madison University 1846. Adopted present name 1890.

College and Academy of Philadelphia 1755. See University of Pennsylvania, Philadelphia, Pa.

College and Seminary of Our Lady of the Angels 1856. See Niagara University, Niagara University, N. Y.

College Center 1946. See University of North Carolina at Wilmington, Wilmington, N. C.

College Conservatory of Music 1962. See University of Cincinnati, Cincinnati, Oh.

College Del Rey, Phoenix, Ariz. Closed May 1973.

College of Agricultural Branch at Davis 1922. See University of California, Davis, Davis, Calif.

College of Agriculture 1923. See University of California, Davis, Davis, Calif.

College of Agriculture and Mechanical Arts 1880. See University of South Carolina, Columbia, S. C.

College of Agriculture and Mechanical Arts 1913. See Montana State University, Bozeman, Mont.

College of Artesia, Artesia, N. M. Closed June 1972.

College of California 1855. See University of California, Berkeley, Berkeley, Calif.

College of Education and Industrial Arts 1941. See Central State University, Wilberforce, Oh.

College of Emporia, Emporia, Kan. Closed Dec. 1973.

COLLEGE OF GREAT FALLS. Great Falls, Mont. 59405. Non-public institution. Owned by the Sisters of Providence, Roman Catholic Church. Established as Great Falls Normal College 1932. Became: Great Falls College of Education 1949. Adopted present name 1950.

College of Guam 1960. See University of Guam, Agana, Guam.

College of Hawaii 1907. See University of Hawaii, Honolulu, Haw.

College of Industrial Arts 1905. See Texas Woman's University, Denton, Tex.

THE COLLEGE OF INSURANCE. New York, N.Y. 10038. Non-public institution. Established as School of Insurance 1947. Adopted present name 1962.

College of Jewish Studies 1925. See Spertus College of Judaica, Chicago, Ill.

College of Louisiana, Jackson, La. 1825. See Centenary College of Louisiana, Shreveport, La.

College of Marshall 1917. See East Texas Baptist College, Marshall, Tex.

College of Medical Evangelists 1909. See Loma Linda University, Loma Linda, Calif.

COLLEGE OF MEDICINE AND DENTISTRY OF NEW JERSEY AT NEWARK. Newark, N.J. 07103. State institution. Established as Seton Hall College of Medicine and Dentistry 1954, under private auspices. Became state school and adopted present name 1965.

College of Medicine of Maryland 1807. See University of Maryland, College Park, Md.

College of Montana 1878. See Rocky Mountain College, Billings, Mont.

COLLEGE OF MOUNT ST. JOSEPH ON THE OHIO. Mount St. Joseph, Oh. 45051. Non-public institution. Affiliated with the Sisters of Charity, Roman Catholic Church. Established as Academy of Mount St. Joseph 1906. Adopted present name 1920.

COLLEGE OF MOUNT ST. VINCENT. Riverdale, N.Y. 10471. Non-public institution. Established as Academy of Mount Saint Vincent 1847. Adopted present name 1911.

College of New Jersey 1746. See Princeton University, Princeton, N.J.

THE COLLEGE OF NEW ROCHELLE. New Rochelle, N.Y. 10801. Non-public institution. Established as The College of St. Angela 1904. Adopted present name 1910.

COLLEGE OF NOTRE DAME OF MARYLAND. Baltimore, Md. 21210. Non-public institution. Owned by the School Sisters of Notre Dame, Roman Catholic Church. Established as Notre Dame of Maryland Collegiate Institute for Young Ladies 1873. Adopted present name 1895.

College of Notre Dame of Wilton, Wilton, Conn.   Closed June 1972.

College of Orlando, Orlando, Fla.   Closed 1973/74 School Year.

COLLEGE OF OSTEOPATHIC MEDICINE AND SURGERY.   Des
Moines, Ia. 50509.   Non-public institution.   Established as Dr. S.
S. Still College of Osteopathy 1898, by Dr. S. S. Still and others.
Became: Still College of Osteopathy 1906; Des Moines Still College
of Osteopathy 1911.   Adopted present name 1958.

College of Our Lady of Mercy 1948.   See   St. Joseph College,
North Windham, Me.

COLLEGE OF OUR LADY OF THE ELMS.   Chicopee, Mass. 01013.
Non-public institution.   Conducted by the Sisters of St. Joseph,
Roman Catholic Church.   Established as the Academy of Our Lady
of the Elms 1897, Pittsfield, Mass.   Became: St. Joseph's Normal
College and moved to present location 1899.   Adopted present name
1928.

College of Pharmaceutical Science, New York, N.Y.   Closed June
1976.

College of Police Science 1964.   See   John Jay College of Criminal
Justice, New York, N.Y.

College of Puget Sound 1914.   See   University of Puget Sound,
Tacoma, Wash.

College of Racine, Racine, Wisc.   Closed June 1973.

College of Sacred Heart 1917.   See   Manhattanville College, Purchase, N.Y.

The College of St. Angela 1904.   See   The College of New Rochelle,
New Rochelle, N.Y.

COLLEGE OF ST. BENEDICT.   St. Joseph, Minn. 56374.   Non-
public institution.   Sponsored by the Sisters of the Order of St. Benedict, Roman Catholic Church.   Established as St. Benedict's Academy 1887.   Became: St. Benedict's College and Academy 1913.
Adopted present name 1927.

COLLEGE OF ST. FRANCIS.   Joliet, Ill. 60435.   Non-public institution.   Affiliated with the Roman Catholic Church.   Established as
Assisi Junior College 1925.   Adopted present name 1930.

College of St. Francis Solano 1860.   See   Quincy College, Quincy, Ill.

College of St. Joseph on the Rio Grande 1951.   See   University of
Albuquerque, Albuquerque, N.M.

THE COLLEGE OF ST. JOSEPH THE PROVIDER.   Rutland, Vt.

05701. Non-public institution. Owned by the Sisters of St. Joseph, Roman Catholic Church. Established as St. Joseph's Teacher College 1954. Adopted present name 1960.

College of St. Mary of the Springs 1911. See Ohio Dominican College, Columbus, Oh.

COLLEGE OF ST. TERESA. Winona, Minn. 55987. Non-public institution. Sponsored by the Sisters of St. Francis, Roman Catholic Church. Established as Winona Seminary 1907. Adopted present name 1912.

College of St. Teresa 1916. See Avila College, Kansas City, Mo.

COLLEGE OF ST. THOMAS. St. Paul, Minn. 55105. Non-public institution. Affiliated with the Archdiocese of St. Paul and Minneapolis, Roman Catholic Church. Established as St. Thomas Aquinas Seminary 1885. Adopted present name 1894.

College of St. Thomas Aquinas in River Forest, Ill. 1939. See Aquinas Institute of Theology, Dubuque, Ia.

COLLEGE OF SANTE FE. Sante Fe, N.M. 87501. Non-public institution. Conducted by the Brothers of Christian Schools, Roman Catholic Church. Established as St. Michael's College 1874. Adopted present official name, College of the Christian Brothers of New Mexico 1966.

College of Southern Utah 1953. See Southern Utah State College, Cedar City, Ut.

College of the Christian Brothers of New Mexico 1966. See College of Sante Fe, Sante Fe, N.M.

College of the City of Detroit 1933. See Wayne State University, Detroit, Mich.

College of the Dayton Art Institute, Dayton, Oh. Closed May 1974.

College of the Holy Names 1956. See Holy Names College, Oakland, Calif.

THE COLLEGE OF THE OZARKS. Clarksville, Ark. 72830. Non-public institution. Owned by the Board of National Missions, United Presbyterian Church in the U.S. Established as Cane Hill College 1834. Became: Arkansas Cumberland College in Clarksville 1891. Adopted present name 1920.

College of the Pacific 1911. See University of the Pacific, Stockton, Calif.

College of the Potomac, Washington, D.C. Closed 1972/73 School Year.

COLLEGE OF THE SACRED HEART.   Santurce, P. R.   00908.   Non-public institution.   Affiliated with the Roman Catholic Church.   Established as Colegio del Sagrado Corazon 1880.   Adopted present official name Colegio Universitario del Sagrado Corazon 1954.

College of the Sacred Heart 1884.   See   Regis College, Denver, Colo.

College of the Sacred Heart 1921.   See   Lone Mountain College, San Francisco, Calif.

The College of the San Francisco Art Institute 1961.   See   San Francisco Art Institute, San Francisco, Calif.

COLLEGE OF THE SOUTHWEST.   Hobbs, N. M.   88240.   Non-public institution.   Affiliated with the Baptist Church until 1961.   Established as Hobbs Baptist College 1956 by B. Clarence Evans and others.   Became: New Mexico Baptist College 1958.   Adopted present name 1961, after becoming independent.

College of White Plains 1974.   See   Pace University White Plains Campus, White Plains, N. Y.

College of William and Mary in Norfolk 1956.   See   Old Dominion University, Norfolk, Va.

THE COLLEGE OF WOOSTER.   Wooster, Oh.   44691.   Non-public institution.   Affiliated with The United Presbyterian Church in the U. S. A.   Established as University of Wooster 1866.   Adopted present name 1914.

Collegiate Institute of Louisville 1937.   See   University of Louisville, Louisville, Ky.

The Collegiate School 1701.   See   Yale University, New Haven, Conn.

Colorado Agricultural and Mechanical College 1951.   See   Colorado State University, Fort Collins, Colo.

COLORADO SCHOOL OF MINES.   Golden, Colo.   80401.   State institution.   Established as Jarvis Hall by the Episcopal Church 1869.   Control assumed by territory of Colorado and adopted present name 1874.

Colorado Seminary 1864.   See   University of Denver, Denver, Colo.

Colorado State College 1957.   See   University of Northern Colorado, Greeley, Colo.

The Colorado State College of Agriculture and Mechanic Arts 1935.   See   Colorado State University, Fort Collins, Colo.

Colorado State College of Education 1935.   See   University of Northern Colorado, Greeley, Colo.

Colorado State Normal School 1901. See Western State College of
Colorado, Gunnison, Colo.

Colorado State Teachers College 1911. See University of Northern
Colorado, Greeley, Colo.

COLORADO STATE UNIVERSITY. Fort Collins, Colo. 80521. State
institution. Established as Agricultural College of Colorado 1870.
Became: The Colorado State College of Agriculture and Mechanic
Arts 1935; Colorado Agricultural and Mechanical College 1951.
Adopted present name 1957.

Colorado Woman's College 1888. See Colorado Woman's College,
Denver, Colo.

COLORADO WOMEN'S COLLEGE. Denver, Colo. 80220. Non-
public institution. Established as Colorado Woman's College 1888
by the American Baptist Convention. Became: Temple Buell College 1967. Adopted present name 1974.

Colored Agricultural and Normal University 1897. See Langston
University, Langston, Okla.

Colored Industrial and Agricultural School 1901. See Grambling
State University, Grambling, La.

Colored Methodist Episcopal High School 1882. See Lane College,
Jackson, Tenn.

Colored Normal, Industrial, Agricultural and Mechanical College of
South Carolina 1895. See South Carolina State College, Orangeburg,
S. C.

COLUMBIA BIBLE COLLEGE. Columbia, S. C. 29203. Non-public
institution. Established as Columbia Bible School 1923 by Miss
Emily Dick and others. Adopted present name 1930.

Columbia Bible School 1923. See Columbia Bible College, Columbia, S. C.

Columbia Bible School 1947. See Columbia Christian College,
Portland, Ore.

COLUMBIA CHRISTIAN COLLEGE. Portland, Ore. 97220. Non-
public institution. Established as Columbia Bible School 1947 by
L. D. Webb and others. Adopted present name 1956.

COLUMBIA COLLEGE. Columbia, Mo. 65201. Non-public institution. Affiliated with the Disciples of Christ. Established as Christian Female College 1851. Became: Christian College 1929. Adopted
present name 1970.

COLUMBIA COLLEGE. Columbia, S. C. 29203. Non-public insti-

tution. Affiliated with The United Methodist Church. Established as
The Columbia Female College 1854. Adopted present name 1905.

Columbia College 1784. See Columbia University, New York, N.Y.

Columbia College 1920. See Loras College, Dubuque, Ia.

Columbia College of Chiropractic, Baltimore, Md. 1954. See Columbia Institute of Chiropractic, Glen Head, N.Y.

Columbia Female Academy 1833. See Stephens College, Columbia,
Mo.

The Columbia Female College 1854. See Columbia College, Columbia, S.C.

COLUMBIA INSTITUTE OF CHIROPRACTIC. Glen Head, N.Y.
11545. Non-public institution. Established under present name in
1919 by Dr. Frank E. Dean. Merged with Columbia College of
Chiropractic, Baltimore, Md. 1954 and Atlantic States Chiropractic
Institute of Brooklyn, N.Y. 1964.

Columbia Institution for the Instruction of the Deaf and Dumb and
Blind 1857. See Gallaudet College, Washington, D.C.

Columbia Institution for the Instruction of the Deaf and Dumb 1865.
See Gallaudet College, Washington, D.C.

COLUMBIA UNION COLLEGE. Takoma Park, Md. 20012. Non-
public institution. Owned by the Seventh-day Adventists. Established as Washington Training College 1904. Became: Washington
Foreign Mission Seminary 1907; Washington Missionary College 1913.
Adopted present name 1961.

COLUMBIA UNIVERSITY. New York, N.Y. 10027. Non-public institution. Established as King's College 1754. Became: Columbia
College 1784. Adopted present official name Columbia University in
the City of New York 1912.

Columbia University 1901. See University of Portland, Portland,
Ore.

Columbia University 1928. See Bard College, Annandale-on-Hudson,
N.Y.

Columbia University in the City of New York 1912. See Columbia
University, New York, N.Y.

The Columbian College 1821. See The George Washington University, Washington, D.C.

Columbian University 1873. See The George Washington University,
Washington, D.C.

Combined Normal and Industrial Department, Wilberforce University 1887. See Central State University, Wilberforce, Oh.

CONCORD COLLEGE. Athens, W. Va. 24712. State institution. Established as Concord State Normal School 1872. Became: Concord State Teachers College 1931. Adopted present name 1943.

Concord State Normal School 1872. See Concord College, Athens, W. Va.

Concord State Teachers College 1931. See Concord College, Athens, W. Va.

CONCORDIA COLLEGE. Bronxville, N.Y. 10708. Non-public institution. Established as Concordia Collegiate Institute 1881 by John H. Sieker. Adopted present name 1969.

CONCORDIA COLLEGE. Moorhead, Minn. 56560. Non-public institution. Affiliated with The American Lutheran Church. Established under present name 1891. Merged with Park Region College of Fergus Falls 1912.

Concordia College 1839. See Concordia Senior College, Fort Wayne, Ind.

Concordia Collegiate Institute 1881. See Concordia College, Bronxville, N.Y.

CONCORDIA SENIOR COLLEGE. Fort Wayne, Ind. 46825. Non-public institution. Owned and controlled by The Lutheran Church - Missouri Synod. Established as Concordia College 1839. Adopted present name 1957.

CONCORDIA TEACHERS COLLEGE. Seward, Neb. 68434. Non-public institution. Owned by The Lutheran Church - Missouri Synod. Established as The Lutheran Seminary 1894. Adopted present name 1924.

Connecticut Agricultural College 1899. See University of Connecticut, Storrs, Conn.

CONNECTICUT COLLEGE. New London, Conn. 06320. Non-public institution. Established as Thames College 1911. Became: Connecticut College for Women 1911. Adopted present name 1969.

Connecticut College for Women 1911. See Connecticut College, New London, Conn.

Connecticut College of Commerce 1929. See Quinnipiac College, Hamden, Conn.

Connecticut State College 1933. See University of Connecticut, Storrs, Conn.

Convent and College of the Holy Names 1908. See Holy Names
College, Oakland, Calif.

Convent of Our Lady of the Sacred Heart 1868. See Holy Names
College, Oakland, Calif.

Convent of the Sacred Heart 1827. See Maryville College, St.
Louis, Mo.

Cook County Normal School 1869. See Chicago State University,
Chicago, Ill.

Cooper College 1909. See Sterling College, Sterling, Kan.

Cooper-Limestone Institute 1881. See Limestone College, Gaffney,
S. C.

Cooper Memorial College 1886. See Sterling College, Sterling,
Kan.

THE COOPER UNION. New York, N. Y. 10003. Non-public institution. Established under present official name The Cooper Union for
the Advancement of Science and Art 1859.

The Cooper Union for the Advancement of Science and Art 1859.
See The Cooper Union, New York, N. Y.

COPPIN STATE COLLEGE. Baltimore, Md. 21216. State institution. Established as High and Training School 1900. Became:
Fannie Jackson Coppin Normal School 1926; Coppin Teachers College
1938; Coppin State Teachers College 1950. Adopted present name
1963.

Coppin State Teachers College 1950. See Coppin State College,
Baltimore, Md.

Coppin Teachers College 1938. See Coppin State College, Baltimore, Md.

CORNELL COLLEGE. Mount Vernon, Ia. 52314. Non-public institution. Affiliated with The United Methodist Church. Established
as Iowa Conference Seminary 1852. Adopted present name 1855.

Cornell University 1865. See Cornell University Endowed Colleges,
Ithaca, N. Y.

CORNELL UNIVERSITY ENDOWED COLLEGES. Ithaca, N. Y. 14850.
Non-public institution. Established as Cornell University 1865.
Adopted present name 1973.

CORNISH INSTITUTE OF THE ALLIED ARTS. Seattle, Wash. 98102.
Non-public institution. Established as Cornish School of Allied Arts
1914, by Nellie Cornish. Adopted present name 1976.

Cornish School of Allied Arts 1914. See Cornish Institute of the Allied Arts, Seattle, Wash.

Cortland State Normal School 1868. See State University of New York College at Cortland, Cortland, N. Y.

Cortland State Teachers College 1941. See State University of New York College at Cortland, Cortland, N. Y.

Corvallis College 1858. See Oregon State University, Corvallis, Ore.

Crance Normal Institute of Music 1926. See State University of New York College at Potsdam, Potsdam, N. Y.

Creighton College 1878. See Creighton University, Omaha, Neb.

CREIGHTON UNIVERSITY. Omaha, Neb. 68131. Non-public institution. Traditionally associated with the Society of Jesus, Roman Catholic Church. Established as Creighton College 1878. Became: The Creighton University 1879. Adopted present name 1968.

The Creighton University 1879. See Creighton University, Omaha, Neb.

Croatan Normal School 1887. See Pembroke State University, Pembroke, N. C.

Cullman College 1976. See Southern Benedictine College, St. Bernard, Ala.

Cullowhee High School 1889. See Western Carolina University, Cullowhee, N. C.

Cullowhee Normal and Industrial School 1905. See Western Carolina University, Cullowhee, N. C.

Cullowhee State Normal School 1925. See Western Carolina University, Cullowhee, N. C.

CULVER-STOCKTON COLLEGE. Canton, Mo. 63435. Non-public institution. Affiliated with the Christian Church (Disciples of Christ). Established as Christian University 1853. Adopted present name 1917.

CUMBERLAND COLLEGE. Williamsburg, Ky. 40769. Non-public institution. Affiliated with the Kentucky Convention of the Southern Baptist Association. Established as Williamsburg Institute 1889. Adopted present name 1913.

Cumberland College 1806. See George Peabody College for Teachers, Nashville, Tenn.

Cumberland Valley State Normal School 1871. See Shippensburg
State College, Shippensburg, Pa.

CURRY COLLEGE.   Milton, Mass. 02186.   Non-public institution.
Established as School of Expression 1879.   Adopted present name
1943.

- D -

DAEMEN COLLEGE.   Buffalo, N.Y. 14226.   Non-public institution.
Established as Rosary Hill College 1947, by the Franciscan Sisters,
Roman Catholic Church.   Adopted present name 1976.

Dakota Collegiate Institute 1883.   See Sioux Falls College, Sioux
Falls, S.D.

Dakota School of Mines 1885.   See South Dakota School of Mines
and Technology, Rapid City, S.D.

DAKOTA STATE COLLEGE.   Madison, S.D. 57042.   State institution.
Established as Madison Normal School 1881.   Became: Eastern State
Normal School 1921; General Beadle State Teachers College 1947;
General Beadle State College 1964.   Adopted present name 1969.

Dakota Territorial Normal School 1883.   See Black Hills State College, Spearfish, S.D.

Dakota University 1882.   See Dakota Wesleyan University, Mitchell,
S.D.

DAKOTA WESLEYAN UNIVERSITY.   Mitchell, S.D. 57301.   Non-
public institution.   Affiliated with The United Methodist Church.
Established as Dakota University 1882.   Adopted present name 1904.

DALLAS BAPTIST COLLEGE.   Dallas, Tex. 75211.   Non-public
institution.   Controlled by the Baptist General Convention.   Established as Decatur Baptist College 1897.   Adopted present name 1965.

Dallas Institute of Vocal and Dramatic Art 1947.   See McMurry
College, Abilene, Tex.

DANA COLLEGE.   Blair, Neb. 68008.   Non-public institution.
Owned by The American Lutheran Church.   Established as Trinity
Seminary 1884.   Became: Trinity Seminary and Blair College after
merging with Danish College 1899; Dana College and Trinity Seminary 1903.   Adopted present name 1960 after Trinity Seminary
moved to campus of Wartburg Seminary in Dubuque, Ia.

Dana College and Trinity Seminary 1903.   See Dana College, Blair,
Neb.

Danbury State College 1959. See Western Connecticut State College, Danbury, Conn.

Danbury State Normal School 1903. See Western Connecticut State College, Danbury, Conn.

Danbury State Teachers College 1937. See Western Connecticut State College, Danbury, Conn.

DANIEL PAYNE COLLEGE, INC. Birmingham, Ala. 35214. Non-public institution. Affiliated with the African Methodist Episcopal Church. Established as Payne Institute 1889, by Dr. M. E. Bryant and others. Became: Payne University 1903; Greater Payne University 1926; Daniel Payne College 1940. Adopted present name 1971.

Danish College 1899. See Dana College, Blair, Neb.

Danville Female Institute 1854. See Averett College, Danville, Va.

Daughters College of the Christian Church of Missouri 1890. See William Woods College, Fulton, Mo.

DAVID LIPSCOMB COLLEGE. Nashville, Tenn. 37203. Non-public institution. Affiliated with the Church of Christ. Established as Nashville Bible School 1891. Adopted present name 1918.

Davidson Academy 1785. See George Peabody College for Teachers, Nashville, Tenn.

Dayton Westminister Choir School, Ohio, 1926. See Westminister Choir College, Princeton, N. J.

Daytona Cookman Collegiate Institute 1923. See Bethune-Cookman College, Daytona Beach, Fla.

Decatur Baptist College 1897. See Dallas Baptist College, Dallas, Tex.

The Decatur College and Industrial School of the James Millikin University 1901. See Millikin University, Decatur, Ill.

Decatur Female Seminary 1889. See Agnes Scott College, Decatur, Ga.

THE DEFIANCE COLLEGE. Defiance, Oh. 43512. Non-public institution. Affiliated with the United Church of Christ. Established as Defiance Female Seminary 1850. Adopted present name 1903.

Defiance Female Seminary 1850. See The Defiance College, Defiance, Oh.

DeLand Academy 1883. See Stetson University, DeLand, Fla.

DeLand Academy and College 1885. See Stetson University, De-Land, Fla.

DeLand University 1887. See Stetson University, DeLand, Fla.

Delaware College 1843. See University of Delaware, Newark, Del.

Delaware Conference Academy 1886. See University of Maryland, Eastern Shore, Princess Anne, Md.

Delaware Military Academy 1859. See Widener College, Chester, Pa.

DELAWARE STATE COLLEGE. Dover, Del. 19901. State institution. Established as State College for Colored Students 1891. Adopted present name 1947.

DELAWARE VALLEY COLLEGE OF SCIENCE AND AGRICULTURE. Doylestown, Pa. 18901. Non-public institution, receiving state aid. Established as The National Farm School 1896. Became: The National Farm School and Junior College 1946; National Agricultural College 1948. Adopted present name 1960.

Delta State College 1955. See Delta State University, Cleveland, Miss.

Delta State Teachers College 1924. See Delta State University, Cleveland, Miss.

DELTA STATE UNIVERSITY. Cleveland, Miss. 38732. State institution. Established as Delta State Teachers College 1924. Became: Delta State College 1955. Adopted present name 1974.

DeMazenod Scholasticate 1927. See Oblate College of the Southwest, San Antonio, Tex.

DENISON UNIVERSITY. Granville, Oh. 43023. Non-public institution. Established as Granville Literary and Theological Institution 1831, by Baptist Laymen. Became: Granville College 1845. Adopted present name 1856. Merged with Shepardson College 1897.

Denmark Industrial School 1897. See Voorhees College, Denmark, S. C.

DEPAUL UNIVERSITY. Chicago, Ill. Non-public institution. Affiliated with the Congregation of the Mission, Roman Catholic Church. Established as St. Vincent's College 1898. Adopted present name 1907.

DEPAUW UNIVERSITY. Greencastle, Ind. 46135. Non-public institution. Affiliated with The United Methodist Church. Established as Indiana Asbury University 1837. Adopted present name 1884.

DeSales Preparatory Seminary 1963. See Saint Francis de Sales
College, Milwaukee, Wisc.

Des Moines Still College of Osteopathy 1911. See College of Osteopathic Medicine and Surgery, Des Moines, Ia.

DETROIT BIBLE COLLEGE. Detroit, Mich. 48235. Non-public institution. Established as Detroit Bible Institute 1945, by Christian
Business Men's Committee of Detroit. Adopted present name 1960.

Detroit Bible Institute 1945. See Detroit Bible College, Detroit,
Mich.

Detroit Business Institute, Dearborn Campus 1962. See Detroit
College of Business, Dearborn, Mich.

Detroit Chiropractic College 1969. See National College of Chiropractic, Lombard, Ill.

Detroit College 1877. See University of Detroit, Detroit, Mich.

DETROIT COLLEGE OF BUSINESS. Dearborn, Mich. 48126. Non-
public institution. Established as Detroit Business Institute, Dearborn Campus 1962 by R. W. Sneden and H. F. Long. Adopted
present name 1964.

Detroit College of Medicine 1868. See Wayne State University,
Detroit, Mich.

THE DETROIT INSTITUTE OF TECHNOLOGY. Detroit, Mich.
48201. Non-public institution. Established as Detroit Technical
Institute 1891. Adopted present name 1918.

Detroit Technical Institute 1891. See The Detroit Institute of Technology, Detroit, Mich.

DICKINSON COLLEGE. Carlisle, Pa. 17013. Non-public institution.
Related to The United Methodist Church. Established as Carlisle
Grammar School 1773. Adopted present name 1783.

DICKINSON STATE COLLEGE. Dickinson, N.D. 58601. State institution. Established as Dickinson State Normal School 1918. Became: Dickinson State Teachers College 1931. Adopted present
name 1963.

Dickinson State Normal School 1918. See Dickinson State College,
Dickinson, N.D.

Dickinson State Teachers College 1931. See Dickinson State College,
Dickinson, N.D.

DILLARD UNIVERSITY. New Orleans, La. 70122. Non-public institution. Affiliated with The United Methodist Church and United

Church of Christ. Established through merger of New Orleans University 1930 and Straight College 1930. Adopted present name 1930.

Diocesan Sisters College, Bloomfield Branch, Bloomfield, Conn. Closed Sept. 1969.

District of Columbia Teachers College 1977. See University of the District of Columbia, Washington, D. C.

Divine Word Seminary, Techny, Ill. Closed May 1972.

Division of Graduate Studies of The City University of New York 1962. See Graduate School and University Center, New York, N. Y.

DOANE COLLEGE. Crete, Neb. 68333. Non-public institution. Established as Nebraska University, Fontenelle 1858. Moved to present location and adopted present name 1872.

Dr. S. S. Still College of Osteopathy 1898. See College of Osteopathic Medicine and Surgery, Des Moines, Ia.

Dominican College, Houston, Tex. Closed May 1975.

The Dominican College of St. Rose of Lima 1950. See Aquinas Institute of Theology, Dubuque, Ia.

DON BOSCO COLLEGE. Newton, N. J. 07860. Non-public institution. Owned by the Salesian Society, Roman Catholic Church. Established as St. Joseph House of Studies 1928. Became: Don Bosco Seminary 1931. Adopted present name 1937.

Don Bosco Seminary 1931. See Don Bosco College, Newton, N. J.

DORDT COLLEGE. Sioux Center, Ia. 51250. Non-public institution. Affiliated with the Christian Reformed Church. Established as Midwest Christian Junior College 1953. Adopted present name 1956.

Dorland-Bell School 1942. See Warren Wilson College, Swannanoa, N. C.

DOWLING COLLEGE. Oakdale, N. Y. 11769. Non-public institution. Established as Adelphi Suffolk College of Adelphi University 1959. Adopted present name 1968.

Drew Theological Seminary 1866. See Drew University, Madison, N. J.

DREW UNIVERSITY. Madison, N. J. 07940. Non-public institution. Affiliated with The United Methodist Church. Established as Drew Theological Seminary 1866. Adopted present name 1928.

Drexel Institute of Arts, Sciences and Industry 1891. See Drexel University, Philadelphia, Pa.

Drexel Institute of Technology 1936. See Drexel University, Philadelphia, Pa.

DREXEL UNIVERSITY. Philadelphia, Pa. 19104. Non-public institution, receiving state aid. Established as Drexel Institute of Arts, Sciences and Industry 1891. Became: Drexel Institute of Technology 1936. Adopted present name 1970.

The Dropsie College for Hebrew and Cognate Learning 1907. See The Dropsie University, Philadelphia, Pa.

THE DROPSIE UNIVERSITY. Philadelphia, Pa. 19132. Non-public institution. Established as The Dropsie College for Hebrew and Cognate Learning 1907. Adopted present name 1969.

DRURY COLLEGE. Springfield, Mo. 65802. Non-public institution. Established as Springfield College 1873 by the Congregational Church. Adopted present name 1873.

Dubuque College 1914. See Loras College, Dubuque, Ia.

Dubuque German College and Seminary 1911. See University of Dubuque, Dubuque, Ia.

Duchesne College of the Sacred Heart, Omaha, Neb. Closed June 1968.

Due West Female College 1927. See Erskine College, Due West, S.C.

DUKE UNIVERSITY. Durham, N.C. 27706. Non-public institution. Affiliated with The United Methodist Church. Established as Brown's Schoolhouse 1838. Became: Union Institute 1839; Normal College 1851; Trinity College 1859. Adopted present name 1924.

Du Lac Academy 1844. See Milton College, Milton, Wisc.

Duluth State Normal School 1905. See University of Minnesota Duluth, Duluth, Minn.

Duluth State Teachers College 1921. See University of Minnesota, Duluth, Duluth, Minn.

Dunbarton College of Holy Cross, Washington, D.C. Closed 1972/73 School Year.

Dunlora Academy 1830. See University of Richmond, Richmond, Va.

Duquesne University 1935. See Duquesne University of the Holy Ghost, Pittsburgh, Pa.

DUQUESNE UNIVERSITY OF THE HOLY GHOST. Pittsburgh, Pa. 15219. Non-public institution. Owned by the Congregation of the

Holy Ghost, Roman Catholic Church.   Established as Pittsburgh
Catholic College of the Holy Ghost 1878.   Became: University of
the Holy Ghost 1911; Duquesne University of the Holy Ghost 1911;
Duquesne University 1935.   Adopted present name 1960.

Durham State Normal School 1923.   See   North Carolina Central
University, Durham, N.C.

Dyke and Spencerian College 1942.   See   Dyke College, Cleveland,
Oh.

DYKE COLLEGE.   Cleveland, Oh. 44114.   Non-public institution.
Established as Folsom's Business College 1848.   Became: Bryant,
Lusk and Stratton Business College 1853; Union Business College
1874; Spencerian Business College 1877; Dyke and Spencerian College
1942, after merger with Dyke School of Commerce 1942.   Adopted
present name 1959.

Dyke School of Commerce 1942.   See   Dyke College, Cleveland, Oh.

- E -

EARLHAM COLLEGE.   Richmond, Ind. 47374.   Non-public institution.   Owned by the Indiana and Western Yearly Meetings of the Society of Friends.   Established as Friends Boarding School 1847.
Adopted present name 1859.

East Alabama Male College 1856.   See   Auburn University, Auburn,
Ala.

East Carolina College 1951.   See   East Carolina University, Greenville, N.C.

East Carolina Teacher Training School 1907.   See   East Carolina
University, Greenville, N.C.

East Carolina Teachers College 1921.   See   East Carolina University,
Greenville, N.C.

EAST CAROLINA UNIVERSITY.   Greenville, N.C. 27834.   State institution.   Established as East Carolina Teacher Training School
1907.   Became: East Carolina Teachers College 1921; East Carolina College 1951.   Adopted present name 1967.

EAST CENTRAL OKLAHOMA STATE UNIVERSITY.   Ada, Okla.
74820.   State institution.   Established as East Central State Normal
School 1909.   Became: East Central State Teachers College 1920;
East Central State College 1939.   Adopted present name 1975.

East Central State College 1939.   See   East Central Oklahoma State
University, Ada, Okla.

East Central State Normal School 1909. See East Central Oklahoma
State University, Ada, Okla.

East Central State Teachers College 1920. See East Central Oklahoma State University, Ada, Okla.

East Florida Seminary 1853. See University of Florida, Gainesville,
Fla.

East Stroudsburg Normal School 1893. See East Stroudsburg State
College, East Stroudsburg, Pa.

EAST STROUDSBURG STATE COLLEGE. East Stroudsburg, Pa.
18301. State institution. Established as East Stroudsburg Normal
School 1893. Became: East Stroudsburg State Normal School 1920;
East Stroudsburg State Teachers College 1927. Adopted present
name 1960.

East Stroudsburg State Normal School 1920. See East Stroudsburg
State College, East Stroudsburg, Pa.

East Stroudsburg State Teachers College 1927. See East Stroudsburg State College, East Stroudsburg, Pa.

East Tennessee College 1807. See The University of Tennessee,
Knoxville; Knoxville, Tenn.

East Tennessee State College 1944. See East Tennessee State University, Johnson City, Tenn.

East Tennessee State Normal School 1911. See East Tennessee
State University, Johnson City, Tenn.

East Tennessee State Teachers College 1925. See East Tennessee
State University, Johnson City, Tenn.

EAST TENNESSEE STATE UNIVERSITY. Johnson City, Tenn. 37601.
State institution. Established as East Tennessee State Normal School
1911. Became: East Tennessee State Teachers College 1925; East
Tennessee State College 1944. Adopted present name 1963.

East Tennessee University 1840. See The University of Tennessee,
Knoxville; Knoxville, Tenn.

East Tennessee University 1867. See Tennessee Wesleyan College,
Athens, Tenn.

East Tennessee Wesleyan College 1866. See Tennessee Wesleyan
College, Athens, Tenn.

EAST TEXAS BAPTIST COLLEGE. Marshall, Tex. 75670. Non-
public institution. Owned by the Baptist General Convention of Texas.
Established as College of Marshall 1917. Adopted present name 1944.

East Texas Normal College 1889. See East Texas State University, Commerce, Tex.

East Texas State College 1957. See East Texas State University, Commerce, Tex.

East Texas State Normal College 1917. See East Texas State University, Commerce, Tex.

East Texas State Teachers College 1923. See East Texas State University, Commerce, Tex.

EAST TEXAS STATE UNIVERSITY. Commerce, Tex. 75428. State institution. Established as East Texas Normal College 1889. Became: East Texas State Normal College 1917; East Texas State Teachers College 1923; East Texas State College 1957. Adopted present name 1965.

Eastern Baptist College 1932. See Eastern College, St. Davids, Pa.

Eastern Branch of the Maryland Agricultural College 1919. See University of Maryland, Eastern Shore, Princess Anne, Md.

EASTERN COLLEGE. St. Davids, Pa. 19087. Non-public institution. Affiliated with the American Baptist Convention. Established as Eastern Baptist College 1932 as the collegiate division of Eastern Baptist Theological Seminary. Became separate institution 1952, adopted present name 1972.

Eastern College of Chiropractic 1968. See National College of Chiropractic, Lombard, Ill.

EASTERN CONNECTICUT STATE COLLEGE. Willimantic, Conn. 06226. State institution. Established as Willimantic Normal School 1889. Became: Willimantic State Teachers College 1937. Adopted present name 1967.

Eastern Illinois State College 1947. See Eastern Illinois University, Charleston, Ill.

Eastern Illinois State Normal School 1895. See Eastern Illinois University, Charleston, Ill.

Eastern Illinois State Teachers College 1921. See Eastern Illinois University, Charleston, Ill.

EASTERN ILLINOIS UNIVERSITY. Charleston, Ill. 61920. State institution. Established as Eastern Illinois State Normal School 1895. Became: Eastern Illinois State Teachers College 1921; Eastern Illinois State College 1947. Adopted present name 1957.

Eastern Indiana Normal University 1898. See Ball State University, Muncie, Ind.

Eastern Kentucky State College 1948. See Eastern Kentucky University, Richmond, Ky.

Eastern Kentucky State Normal School 1906. See Eastern Kentucky University, Richmond, Ky.

Eastern Kentucky State Normal School and Teachers College 1922. See Eastern Kentucky University, Richmond, Ky.

Eastern Kentucky State Teachers College 1930. See Eastern Kentucky University, Richmond, Ky.

EASTERN KENTUCKY UNIVERSITY. Richmond, Ky. 40475. State institution. Established as Eastern Kentucky State Normal School 1906. Became: Eastern Kentucky State Normal School and Teachers College 1922; Eastern Kentucky State Teachers College 1930; Eastern Kentucky State College 1948. Adopted present name 1966.

EASTERN MENNONITE COLLEGE. Harrisonberg, Va. 22801. Non-public institution. Owned by The Mennonite Church. Established as Eastern Mennonite School 1917. Adopted present name 1948.

Eastern Mennonite School 1917. See Eastern Mennonite College, Harrisonberg, Va.

Eastern Michigan College 1955. See Eastern Michigan University, Ypsilanti, Mich.

EASTERN MICHIGAN UNIVERSITY. Ypsilanti, Mich. 48197. State institution. Established as Michigan State Normal School 1849. Became: Michigan State Normal College 1899; Eastern Michigan College 1955. Adopted present name 1959.

EASTERN MONTANA COLLEGE. Billings, Mont. 59101. State institution. Established as Eastern Montana State Normal School 1927. Became: Eastern Montana College of Education 1949. Adopted present name 1966.

Eastern Montana College of Education 1949. See Eastern Montana College, Billings, Mont.

Eastern Montana State Normal School 1927. See Eastern Montana College, Billings, Mont.

EASTERN NAZARENE COLLEGE. Quincy, Mass. 02170. Non-public institution. Controlled by the Church of Nazarene. Established as the Pentecostal Collegiate Institute 1900, Saratoga Springs, N.Y. Adopted present name 1918; moved to present location 1919.

Eastern New Mexico College 1940. See Eastern New Mexico University, Portales, N.M.

Eastern New Mexico Junior College 1927. See Eastern New Mexico University, Portales, N.M.

EASTERN NEW MEXICO UNIVERSITY. Portales, N. M. 88130.
State institution. Established as Eastern New Mexico Junior College
1927. Became: Eastern New Mexico College 1940. Adopted present name 1949.

Eastern Oregon College 1956. See Eastern Oregon State College,
La Grande, Ore.

Eastern Oregon College of Education 1939. See Eastern Oregon
State College, La Grande, Ore.

Eastern Oregon Normal School 1929. See Eastern Oregon State
College, La Grande, Ore.

EASTERN OREGON STATE COLLEGE. La Grande, Ore. 97850.
State institution. Established as Eastern Oregon Normal School 1929.
Became: Eastern Oregon College of Education 1939; Eastern Oregon
College 1956. Adopted present name 1974.

Eastern Pilgrim College 1954. See United Wesleyan College,
Allentown, Pa.

Eastern State Normal School 1921. See Dakota State College,
Madison, S. D.

EASTERN VIRGINIA MEDICAL AUTHORITY. Norfolk, Va. 23501.
Non-public institution. Established as Eastern Virginia Medical
School 1964. Adopted present name 1976.

Eastern Virginia Medical School 1964. See Eastern Virginia Medical Authority, Norfolk, Va.

Eastern Washington College of Education 1939. See Eastern Washington State College, Cheney, Wash.

EASTERN WASHINGTON STATE COLLEGE. Cheney, Wash. 99004.
State institution. Established as State Normal School at Cheney
1890. Became: Eastern Washington College of Education 1939.
Adopted present name 1961.

Eau Claire State Normal School 1916. See University of Wisconsin-Eau Claire, Eau Claire, Wisc.

Eau Claire State Teachers College 1927. See University of Wisconsin-Eau Claire, Eau Claire, Wisc.

ECKERD COLLEGE. St. Petersburg, Fla. 33733. Non-public institution. Affiliated with The United Presbyterian Church in the U. S.
Established as Florida Presbyterian College 1958. Adopted present
name 1972.

EDGECLIFF COLLEGE. Cincinnati, Oh. 45206. Non-public institution. Owned by The Sisters of Mercy of the Union in the U. S.,

Roman Catholic Church.   Established as Our Lady of Cincinnati
College 1935.   Adopted present name 1969.

EDGEWOOD COLLEGE.   Madison, Wisc. 53711.   Non-public institution.   Affiliated with the Dominican Sisters of Sinsiawa, Wisc.
Established as St. Regina Academy 1881.   Adopted present name 1941.

Edinboro Academy 1856.   See   Edinboro State College, Edinboro, Pa.

Edinboro Normal School 1857.   See   Edinboro State College, Edinboro,
Pa.

EDINBORO STATE COLLEGE.   Edinboro, Pa. 16412.   State institu-
tion.   Established as Edinboro Academy 1856.   Became: Edinboro
Normal School 1857; Edinboro State Normal School 1861; Edinboro
State Teachers College 1926.   Adopted present name 1960.

Edinboro State Normal School 1861.   See   Edinboro State College,
Edinboro, Pa.

Edinboro State Teachers College 1926.   See   Edinboro State College,
Edinboro, Pa.

Edinburg Junior College 1927.   See   Pan American University,
Edinburg, Tex.

Edinburg Regional College 1948.   See   Pan American University,
Edinburg, Tex.

Eliot Seminary 1853.   See   Washington University, St. Louis, Mo.

Elizabeth City State College 1963.   See   Elizabeth City State University, Elizabeth City, N. C.

Elizabeth City State Teachers College 1939.   See   Elizabeth City
State University, Elizabeth City, N. C.

ELIZABETH CITY STATE UNIVERSITY.   Elizabeth City, N. C. 27909.
State institution.   Established as Elizabeth State Colored Normal
School 1891.   Became: Elizabeth City State Teachers College 1939;
Elizabeth City State College 1963.   Adopted present name 1969.

Elizabeth State Colored Normal School 1891.   See   Elizabeth City
State University, Elizabeth City, N. C.

Elkhart Institute 1894.   See   Goshen College, Goshen, Ind.

Elmhurst Academy and Junior College 1919.   See   Elmhurst College,
Elmhurst, Ill.

ELMHURST COLLEGE.   Elmhurst, Ill. 60126.   Non-public institu-
tion.   Affiliated with the United Church of Christ.   Established as
Elmhurst Pro-Seminary and Academy 1871.   Became: Elmhurst
Academy and Junior College 1919.   Adopted present name 1924.

Elmhurst Pro-Seminary and Academy 1871.   See   Elmhurst College,
Elmhurst, Ill.

ELMIRA COLLEGE.   Elmira, N.Y.   14901.   Non-public institution.
Established as Elmira Female College 1855.   Adopted present name
1890.

Elmira Female College 1855.   See   Elmira College, Elmira, N.Y.

Embry-Riddle Aeronautical Institute 1952.   See   Embry-Riddle Aeronautical University, Daytona Beach, Fla.

EMBRY-RIDDLE AERONAUTICAL UNIVERSITY.   Daytona Beach,
Fla. 32015.   Non-public institution.   Established as a flying school
by Embry-Riddle Corporation 1926.   Became: Embry-Riddle International School of Aviation 1940; Embry-Riddle Aeronautical Institute
1952.   Adopted present name 1971.

Embry-Riddle International School of Aviation 1940.   See   Embry-
Riddle Aeronautical University, Daytona Beach, Fla.

EMERSON COLLEGE.   Boston, Mass. 02116.   Non-public institution.
Established as Boston Conservatory of Oratory 1880.   Became:
Monroe College of Oratory 1881; Emerson College of Oratory 1890.
Adopted present name 1939.

Emerson College of Oratory 1890.   See   Emerson College, Boston,
Mass.

Emmanuel Missionary College 1901.   See   Andrews University,
Berrien Springs, Mich.

Emory College 1836.   See   Emory University, Atlanta, Ga.

EMORY UNIVERSITY.   Atlanta, Ga. 30322.   Non-public institution.
Owned by The United Methodist Church.   Established as Emory College 1936.   Adopted present name 1915.

EMPORIA KANSAS STATE COLLEGE.   Emporia, Kan. 66801.   State
institution.   Established as Kansas State Normal School 1863.   Became: Kansas State Teachers College of Emporia 1923.   Adopted
present name 1974.

Epworth University 1904.   See   Oklahoma City University, Oklahoma
City, Okla.

ERSKINE COLLEGE.   Due West, S.C. 29639.   Non-public institution.
Affiliated with the Associate Reformed Presbyterian Church.   Es-
tablished as The Academy at Due West 1835.   Became: Clark and
Erskine Seminary 1837.   Adopted present name 1842.   Merged with
Erskine Theological Seminary 1926 and with Due West Female Col-
lege 1927.

Erskine Theological Seminary 1926. See Erskine College, Due West, S. C.

Eugene Bible College 1930. See Northwest Christian College, Eugene, Ore.

Eugene Bible University 1908. See Northwest Christian College, Eugene, Ore.

Eugene Divinity School 1895. See Northwest Christian College, Eugene, Ore.

EUREKA COLLEGE. Eureka, Ill. 61530. Non-public institution. Affiliated with the Christian Church, Disciples of Christ. Established as Walnut Grove Academy 1848. Adopted present name 1855.

Evangelical Free Church Seminary 1946. See Trinity College, Deerfield, Ill.

Evangelical Lutheran College 1891. See Texas Lutheran College, Seguin, Tex.

Evangelical Lutheran Seminary 1830. See Capital University, Columbus, Ohio.

Evansville College 1919. See University of Evansville, Evansville, Ind.

The Extension Center of the College of William and Mary 1919. See Old Dominion University, Norfolk, Va.

Extension Division of the University of Hawaii 1947. See University of Hawaii at Hilo, Hilo, Haw.

- F -

Fairfield College Preparatory 1942. See Fairfield University, Fairfield, Conn.

FAIRFIELD UNIVERSITY. Fairfield, Conn. 06430. Non-public institution. Conducted by the Society of Jesus, Roman Catholic Church. Established as Fairfield College Preparatory School 1942. Became: college unit of Fairfield University of St. Robert Bellarmine 1945. Adopted present name 1969.

Fairfield University of St. Robert Bellarmine 1945. See Fairfield University, Fairfield, Conn.

Fairleigh Dickinson College 1948. See Fairleigh Dickinson University, Rutherford, N. J.

Fairleigh Dickinson Junior College 1941. See Fairleigh Dickinson
University, Rutherford, N. J.

FAIRLEIGH DICKINSON UNIVERSITY. Rutherford, N. J. 07070. Non-
public institution. Established as Fairleigh Dickinson Junior College
1941. Became: Fairleigh Dickinson College 1948. Adopted present
name 1956.

FAIRMONT STATE COLLEGE. Fairmont, W. Va. 26554. State institution. Established as The Regency of West Virginia Normal
School at Fairmont 1865. Became: Fairmont State Normal School
1867; Fairmont State Teachers College 1931. Adopted present name
1943.

Fairmont State Normal School 1867. See Fairmont State College,
Fairmont, W. Va.

Fairmont State Teachers College 1931. See Fairmont State College,
Fairmont, W. Va.

Fairmount College 1887. See Wichita State University, Wichita, Kan.

Fairmount Institute 1892. See Wichita State University, Wichita,
Kan.

FAITH BAPTIST BIBLE COLLEGE. Ankeny, Ia. 50021. Non-public
institution. Affiliated with the General Association of Regular Baptist Churches. Established as Omaha Bible Institute 1921 by W. H.
Jordan and J. L. Patten. Became: Omaha Baptist Bible Institute
1952; Omaha Baptist Bible College 1960. Adopted present name 1967.

Falls City Center, Jeffersonville, Ind. 1941. See Indiana University-
Southeast, New Albany, Ind.

Fannie Jackson Coppin Normal School 1926. See Coppin State College, Baltimore, Md.

Farmer's High School 1855. See The Pennsylvania State University,
University Park, Pa.

Farmington State College 1965. See University of Maine at Farmington, Farmington, Me.

Farmington State College of the University of Maine 1968. See University of Maine at Farmington, Farmington, Me.

Farmington State Normal School 1868. See University of Maine at
Farmington, Farmington, Me.

Farmington State Teachers College 1945. See University of Maine
at Farmington, Farmington, Me.

Farmville Female College 1839. See Longwood College, Farmville,
Va.

Father Judge Mission Seminary, Monroe, Va.   Closed June 1971.

The Fayette Seminary of the Upper Iowa Conference 1850. See
Upper Iowa College, Fayette, Ia.

Fayetteville State College 1963. See Fayetteville State University,
Fayetteville, N. C.

Fayetteville State Teachers College 1939. See Fayetteville State
University, Fayetteville, N. C.

FAYETTEVILLE STATE UNIVERSITY. Fayetteville, N. C. 28301.
State university. Established as Howard School 1867. Became:
State Colored Normal School 1877; State Colored Normal and Indus-
trial School 1916; State Normal School for the Negro Race 1921;
State Normal School 1926; Fayetteville State Teachers College 1939;
Fayetteville State College 1963. Adopted present name 1969.

Federal City College 1977. See University of the District of Columbia, Washington, D. C.

FELICIAN COLLEGE. Lodi, N. J. 07644. Non-public institution.
Founded by the Felician Sisters of the Lodi, New Jersey Province.
Established as Immaculate Conception Normal School 1935. Became: Immaculate Conception Junior College 1942. Adopted present
name 1967.

Female Institute of the Tennessee Annual Conference 1843. See
Athens State College, Athens, Ala.

Female Medical College of Pennsylvania 1850. See The Medical
College of Pennsylvania, Philadelphia, Pa.

Female Normal and High School 1870. See Hunter College, New
York, N. Y.

Female Orphans School of the Christian Church of Missouri 1870.
See William Woods College, Fulton, Mo.

Fenn College 1923. See The Cleveland State University, Cleveland,
Oh.

Fenn College of the Cleveland YMCA School of Technology 1930.
See The Cleveland State University, Cleveland, Oh.

Ferris Industrial School 1885. See Ferris State College, Big Rapids, Mich.

FERRIS STATE COLLEGE. Big Rapids, Mich. 49307. State institution. Established as Big Rapids Industrial School 1884. Became:
Ferris Industrial School 1885. Adopted present name 1963.

Fifth Normal School District 1905. See Northwest Missouri State
University, Maryville, Mo.

Finch College, New York, N.Y.   Closed June 1975.

Fine Arts Institute of Kansas City 1907.   See   Kansas City Art Institute, Kansas City, Mo.

First District Agricultural and Mechanical High School 1906.   See
Georgia Southern College, Statesboro, Ga.

First District Agricultural School 1909.   See   Arkansas State University, State University, Ark.

First District Normal School 1870.   See   Northeast Missouri State
University, Kirksville, Mo.

The First Institute of Podiatry 1919.   See   New York College of
Podiatric Medicine, New York, N.Y.

First State Normal School at Winona 1858.   See   Winona State University, Winona, Minn.

FITCHBURG STATE COLLEGE.   Fitchburg, Mass. 01420.   State
institution.   Established as State Normal School 1894.   Became:
State Teachers College 1933; State College at Fitchburg 1962. Adopted
present name 1967.

Flint College of University of Michigan 1956.   See   University of
Michigan-Flint, Flint, Mich.

Flint Institute of Technology 1923.   See   General Motors Institute,
Flint, Mich.

Flora Macdonald College.   See   St. Andrews Presbyterian College,
Laurinburg, N.C.

Florence Normal School 1872.   See   University of North Alabama,
Florence, Ala.

Florence State College 1957.   See   University of North Alabama,
Florence, Ala.

Florence State Teachers College 1929.   See   University of North
Alabama, Florence, Ala.

Florence State University 1968.   See   University of North Alabama,
Florence, Ala.

Florida Agricultural and Mechanical College 1909.   See   Florida
Agricultural and Mechanical University, Tallahassee, Fla.

FLORIDA AGRICULTURAL AND MECHANCIAL UNIVERSITY.   Tallahassee, Fla. 32307.   State institution.   Established as The State
Normal College for Colored Students 1887.   Became: Florida Agricultural and Mechanical College 1909.   Adopted present name 1953.

Florida Baptist Academy 1892. See Florida Memorial College,
Miami, Fla.

Florida Baptist Academy in Jacksonville 1892. See Florida Memorial College, Miami, Fla.

Florida Baptist Institute 1941. See Florida Memorial College,
Miami, Fla.

Florida Conference College 1885. See Florida Southern College,
Lakeland, Fla.

FLORIDA INSTITUTE OF TECHNOLOGY. Melbourne, Fla. 32901.
Non-public institution. Established as Brevard Engineering College
1958. Adopted present name 1966.

FLORIDA MEMORIAL COLLEGE. Miami, Fla. 33054. Non-public
institution. Affiliated with three Florida Baptist conventions. Established as Florida Baptist Academy in Jacksonville 1892. Became:
Florida Baptist Academy 1892 after moving to St. Augustine; Florida
Normal College 1941 after merger with Florida Baptist Institute;
Florida Normal and Industrial Memorial College 1950. Adopted
present name 1963; moved to present location 1968.

Florida Normal and Industrial Memorial College 1950. See Florida
Memorial College, Miami, Fla.

Florida Normal College 1941. See Florida Memorial College,
Miami, Fla.

Florida Presbyterian College 1958. See Eckerd College, St. Petersburg, Fla.

Florida Seminary 1902. See Florida Southern College, Lakeland,
Fla.

FLORIDA SOUTHERN COLLEGE. Lakeland, Fla. 33802. Non-public institution. Owned by the Florida Annual Conference of the United
Methodist Church. Established as Florida Conference College 1885.
Became: Florida Seminary 1902; Southern College 1906. Adopted
present name 1935.

FLORIDA STATE UNIVERSITY. Tallahassee, Fla. 32306. State
institution. Established as Seminary West of the Suwannee 1851.
Adopted present name 1947.

Folsom's Business College 1848. See Dyke College, Cleveland, Oh.

FORDHAM UNIVERSITY. Bronx, N.Y. 10458. Non-public institution. Established as St. John's College 1841 by the Archbishop of
New York. Control transferred to Society of Jesus, Roman Catholic
Church 1846. Adopted present name 1907. Control transferred to
lay board of trustees 1969.

Forsyth Female Collegiate Institute 1849. See Tift College, Forsyth, Ga.

FORT HAYES KANSAS STATE COLLEGE. Hayes, Kan. 67601. State institution. Established as Western Branch of Kansas Normal School of Emporia 1901. Became: Fort Hayes Kansas State Normal School 1913. Adopted present name 1931.

Fort Hayes Kansas State Normal School 1913. See Fort Hayes Kansas State College, Hayes, Kan.

Fort Kent State College 1965. See University of Maine at Fort Kent, Fort Kent, Me.

Fort Kent State College of the University of Maine 1968. See University of Fort Kent, Fort Kent, Me.

Fort Kent State Normal School 1955. See University of Maine at Fort Kent, Fort Kent, Me.

Fort Kent State Teachers College 1961. See University of Maine at Fort Kent, Fort Kent, Me.

FORT LAUDERDALE COLLEGE. Fort Lauderdale, Fla. 33301. Non-public institution. Established as Fort Lauderdale College of Business and Finance 1940. Adopted present name 1976.

Fort Lauderdale College of Business and Finance 1940. See Fort Lauderdale College, Fort Lauderdale, Fla.

Fort Lewis A & M College 1948. See Fort Lewis College, Durango, Colo.

FORT LEWIS COLLEGE. Durango, Colo. 81301. State institution. Established as Fort Lewis School, a branch of Colorado A & M College 1911. Became: Fort Lewis A & M College 1948, after acquiring independence. Adopted present name 1964.

Fort Lewis School 1911. See Fort Lewis College, Durango, Colo.

Fort Valley Normal and Industrial School 1895. See Fort Valley State College, Fort Valley, Ga.

FORT VALLEY STATE COLLEGE. Fort Valley, Ga. 31030. State institution. Established as Fort Valley Normal and Industrial School 1895. Adopted present name after merger with State Teachers and Agricultural College at Forsyth 1939.

Fort Wayne Art Institute of Fine Arts and Museum of Fine Arts 1962. See Indiana University-Purdue University, Fort Wayne, Ind.

Fort Wayne Art School Museum 1922. See Indiana University-Purdue University. Dept. of Fine Arts. Fort Wayne, Ind.

Fort Wayne Center of Indiana University 1917. See Indiana University-Purdue University at Fort Wayne. Fort Wayne, Ind.

Fort Wayne College 1855. See Taylor University, Upland, Ind.

Fort Wayne Female College 1846. See Taylor University, Upland, Ind.

Fort Worth Christian College 1971. See Abilene Christian University, Abilene, Tex.

FORT WRIGHT COLLEGE. Spokane, Wash. 99204. Non-public institution. Established as Holy Names Normal School 1907. Became: Holy Names College at Fort Wright 1939. Adopted present official name Fort Wright College of the Holy Names 1963.

Fort Wright College of the Holy Names 1963. See Fort Wright College, Spokane, Wash.

Fourth District Agricultural School 1909. See University of Arkansas at Monticello, Monticello, Ark.

FRAMINGHAM STATE COLLEGE. Framingham, Mass. 01701. State institution. Established as State Normal School, Lexington, Mass. 1839. Became: State Normal School at Framingham 1853; Framingham State Teachers College 1932; State College at Framingham 1960. Adopted present name 1968.

Framingham State Teachers College 1932. See Framingham State College, Framingham, Mass.

Frances Shimer Academy and Junior College 1908. See Shimer College, Mt. Carroll, Ill.

Frances Shimer Academy of the University of Chicago 1896. See Shimer College, Mt. Carroll, Ill.

Frances Shimer College 1942. See Shimer College, Mt. Carroll, Ill.

Frances Shimer Junior College 1932. See Shimer College, Mt. Carroll, Ill.

Frances Shimer School 1910. See Shimer College, Mt. Carroll, Ill.

Francis T. Nicholls Junior College of La. State University 1948. See Nicholls State University, Thibodaux, La.

Francis T. Nicholls State College 1956. See Nicholls State University, Thibodaux, La.

FRANKLIN AND MARSHALL COLLEGE. Lancaster, Pa. 17604.

Non-public institution. Related to the United Church of Christ. Established as Franklin College 1787. Merged with Marshall College 1853. Adopted present name 1853.

Franklin College 1787. See Franklin and Marshall College, Lancaster, Pa.

Franklin College 1863. See Wilmington College, Wilmington, Oh.

FRANKLIN COLLEGE OF INDIANA. Franklin, Ind. 46131. Non-public institution. Affiliated with the American Baptist Convention. Established as Indiana Baptist Manual Labor Institute 1834. Adopted present name 1844.

Fredericksburg Normal and Industrial School for Women 1908. See Mary Washington College, Fredericksburg, Va.

Free Academy 1847. See The City College, New York, N.Y.

FREED-HARDEMAN COLLEGE. Henderson, Tenn. 38340. Non-public institution. Affiliated with Churches of Christ. Established as Henderson Male and Female Institute 1869 by A. S. Sayles and Helen Post. Became: Henderson Masonic Male and Female Institute 1877; West Tennessee Christian College 1885; Georgie Robertson Christian College 1897; National Teachers Normal and Business College 1907. Adopted present name 1919.

Fremont College 1919. See Midland Lutheran College, Fremont, Neb.

French-American College 1894. See American International College, Springfield, Mass.

French Broad Baptist Institute 1856. See Mars Hill College, Mars Hill, N.C.

French-Protestant College, Lowell, Mass. 1885. See American International College, Springfield, Mass.

Fresno Junior College 1911. See California State University, Fresno. Fresno, Calif.

Fresno State College 1935. See California State University, Fresno, Calif.

Fresno State Normal School 1911. See California State University, Fresno. Fresno, Calif.

Fresno State Teachers College 1921. See California State University, Fresno. Fresno, Calif.

Friends Bible Institute and Training School 1899. See Malone College, Canton, Oh.

Friends Boarding School 1847.   See   Earlham College, Richmond,
Ind.

Friends Pacific Academy 1885.   See   George Fox College, Newberg,
Ore.

FRIENDS WORLD COLLEGE.   Huntington, N. Y. 11743.   Non-public
institution.   Affiliated with the Religious Society of Friends (Quakers).   Established as Friends World Institute 1965.   Adopted present
name 1967.

Friends World Institute 1965.   See   Friends World College, Huntington, N. Y.

FROSTBURG STATE COLLEGE.   Frostburg, Md. 21532.   State institution.   Established as State Normal School at Frostburg 1898.
Became: State Teachers College at Frostburg 1935.   Adopted present name 1963.

Furman Academy and Theological Institution 1825.   See   Furman
University, Greenville, S. C.

Furman Theological Institution 1833.   See   Furman University,
Greenville, S. C.

FURMAN UNIVERSITY.   Greenville, S. C. 29613.   Non-public institution.   Affiliated with the Southern Baptist Church.   Established
as Furman Academy and Theological Institution 1825.   Became:
Furman Theological Institution 1833.   Adopted present name 1850.
Merged with Greenville Women's College 1938.

- G -

GALLAUDET COLLEGE.   Washington, D. C. 20002.   Non-public institution.   Receives federal government support.   Established as
Kendall School 1856.   Became: Columbia Institution for the Instruction of the Deaf and Dumb and Blind 1857; National Deaf Mute College 1864; Columbia Institution for the Instruction of the Deaf and
Dumb 1865.   Adopted present name 1954.

Galloway Women's College 1933.   See   Hendrix College, Conway,
Ark.

GANNON COLLEGE.   Erie, Pa. 16501.   Non-public institution.
Affiliated with the Catholic Diocese of Erie, Roman Catholic Church.
Established as Cathedral College 1933.   Became: Gannon School of
Arts and Sciences 1941.   Adopted present name 1944.

Gannon School of Arts and Sciences 1941.   See   Gannon College,
Erie, Pa.

GARDNER-WEBB COLLEGE. Boiling Springs, N.C. 28017. Non-public institution. Owned by the Baptist State Convention of N.C. (Southern Baptist). Established as Boiling Springs High School 1905. Became: Gardner-Webb Junior College 1928. Adopted present name 1969.

Gardner-Webb Junior College 1928. See Gardner-Webb College, Boiling Springs, N.C.

Garland Junior College 1976. See Simmons College, Boston, Mass.

Gary College 1948. See Indiana University Northwest, Gary, Ind.

General Beadle State College 1964. See Dakota State College, Madison, S.D.

General Beadle State Teachers College 1947. See Dakota State College, Madison, S.D.

GENERAL MOTORS INSTITUTE. Flint, Mich. 48502. Non-public institution. Established as educational program of Industrial Fellowship League 1919. Became: School of Automotive Trades 1920; Flint Institute of Technology 1923; General Motors Institute of Technology 1926. Adopted present name 1932.

General Motors Institute of Technology 1926. See General Motors Institute, Flint, Mich.

Geneseo Normal and Training School 1867. See State University of New York College at Geneseo, Geneseo, N.Y.

Geneseo Teachers College 1942. See State University of New York College at Geneseo, Geneseo, N.Y.

GENEVA COLLEGE. Beaver Falls, Pa. 15010. Non-public institution. Controlled by the Reformed Presbyterian Church of North America. Established as Geneva Hall 1848. Adopted present name 1873.

Geneva College Medical Division 1834. See State University of New York Upstate Medical Center, Syracuse, N.Y.

Geneva Hall 1848. See Geneva College, Beaver Falls, Pa.

GEORGE FOX COLLEGE. Newberg, Ore. 97132. Non-public institution. Controlled by the Northwest Yearly Meeting of Friends Church. Established as Friends Pacific Academy 1885. Became: Pacific College 1891. Adopted present name 1949.

GEORGE MASON UNIVERSITY. Fairfax, Va. 22030. State institution. Established as The University College 1957, a branch of the University of Virginia. Adopted present name 1972, after becoming independent.

GEORGE PEABODY COLLEGE FOR TEACHERS. Nashville, Tenn.
37203. Non-public institution. Established as Davidson Academy
1785. Became: Cumberland College 1806; University of Nashville
1826; State Normal College 1875; Peabody Normal College 1889.
Adopted present name 1909.

George Pepperdine College 1937. See Pepperdine University, Los
Angeles, Calif.

THE GEORGE WASHINGTON UNIVERSITY. Washington, D. C. 20006.
Non-public institution. Established as The Columbian College 1821.
Became: Columbian University 1873. Adopted present name 1904.

GEORGE WILLIAMS COLLEGE. Downers Grove, Ill. 60515. Non-
public institution. Established as Young Men's Christian Association
Training School 1884. Became: Secretarial Institute and Training
School 1896; Institute and Training School of the YMCA 1903; Young
Men's Christian Association College 1913. Adopted present name
1933.

Georgetown College 1789. See Georgetown University, Washington,
D. C.

GEORGETOWN UNIVERSITY. Washington, D. C. 20007. Non-public
institution. Conducted by the Society of Jesus, Roman Catholic
Church. Established as Georgetown College 1789. Adopted present
name 1815.

Georgia Baptist Female Seminary 1878. See Brenau College,
Gainesville, Ga.

GEORGIA COLLEGE. Milledgeville, Ga. 31061. State institution.
Established as Georgia Normal and Industrial College 1889. Became: Georgia State College for Women 1922; The Woman's College
of Georgia 1961; Georgia College at Milledgeville 1967. Adopted
present name 1971.

Georgia College at Milledgeville 1967. See Georgia College, Milledgeville, Ga.

The Georgia Female College 1836. See Wesleyan College, Macon,
Ga.

GEORGIA INSTITUTE OF TECHNOLOGY. Atlanta, Ga. 30332. State
institution. Established as Georgia School of Technology 1885.
Adopted present name 1948.

Georgia Institute of Technology Evening School of Commerce 1913.
See Georgia State University, Atlanta, Ga.

Georgia Normal and Agricultural College 1917. See Albany State
College, Albany, Ga.

Georgia Normal and Industrial College 1889. See Georgia College, Milledgeville, Ga.

Georgia Normal School 1924. See Georgia Southern College, Statesboro, Ga.

Georgia Robertson Christian College 1897. See Freed-Hardeman College, Henderson, Tenn.

Georgia School of Technology 1885. See Georgia Institute of Technology, Atlanta, Ga.

GEORGIA SOUTHERN COLLEGE. Statesboro, Ga. 30458. State institution. Established as First District Agricultural and Mechanical High School 1906. Became: Georgia Normal School 1924; South Georgia Teachers College 1929; Georgia Teachers College 1939. Adopted present name 1959.

GEORGIA SOUTHWESTERN COLLEGE. Americus, Ga. 31709. State institution. Established as Third District Agricultural and Mechanical School 1908. Became: Third District Agricultural and Mechanical College 1926. Adopted present name 1932.

Georgia State College 1931. See Savannah State College, Savannah, Ga.

Georgia State College 1962. See Georgia State University, Atlanta, Ga.

Georgia State College for Women 1922. See Georgia College, Milledgeville, Ga.

Georgia State College of Business Administration 1955. See Georgia State University, Atlanta, Ga.

Georgia State Industrial College for Colored Youth 1890. See Savannah State College, Savannah, Ga.

GEORGIA STATE UNIVERSITY. Atlanta, Ga. 30303. State institution. Established as Georgia Institute of Technology Evening School of Commerce 1913. Became: University System Center 1932; Atlanta Division, University of Georgia 1947; Georgia State College of Business Administration 1955; Georgia State College 1962. Adopted present name 1969.

Georgia State Womans College 1922. See Valdosta State College, Valdosta, Ga.

Georgia Teachers College 1939. See Georgia Southern College, Statesboro, Ga.

GEORGIAN COURT COLLEGE. Lakewood, N.J. 08701. Non-public institution. Owned by the Sisters of Mercy, Roman Catholic Church.

Established as Mount St. Mary College 1905. Adopted present name
1924.

German Presbyterian Theological School of the Northwest 1891. See
University of Dubuque, Dubuque, Ia.

German Theological School 1868. See Bloomfield College, Bloomfield, N. J.

German Theological School of the Northwest 1852. See University
of Dubuque, Dubuque, Ia.

German Wallace College 1863. See Baldwin-Wallace College,
Berea, Oh.

Girls High and Normal School 1854. See Boston State College,
Boston, Mass.

Girls' Industrial College 1901. See Texas Woman's University,
Denton, Tex.

Glad Tidings Bible Institute 1924. See Bethany Bible College, Santa
Cruz, Calif.

Glad Tidings Bible Training School, San Francisco. See Bethany
Bible College, Santa Cruz, Calif.

GLASSBORO STATE COLLEGE. Glassboro, N. J. 08028. State institution. Established as Glassboro State Normal School 1921. Became: Glassboro State Teachers College 1935. Adopted present
name 1966.

Glassboro State Normal School 1921. See Glassboro State College,
Glassboro, N. J.

Glassboro State Teachers College 1935. See Glassboro State College, Glassboro, N. J.

Glenville Branch, State Normal School of West Virginia 1872. See
Glenville State College, Glenville, W. Va.

GLENVILLE STATE COLLEGE. Glenville, W. Va. 26351. State in-
stitution. Established as Glenville Branch, State Normal School of
West Virginia 1872. Became: Glenville State Normal School 1898;
Glenville State Teachers College 1931. Adopted present name 1943.

Glenville State Normal School 1898. See Glenville State College,
Glenville, W. Va.

Glenville State Teachers College 1931. See Glenville State College,
Glenville, W. Va.

GODDARD COLLEGE. Plainfield, Vt. 05667. Non-public institution.

Established as Green Mountain Central Institute 1863, Barre, Vt.
Became: Goddard Seminary 1870; Goddard Seminary and Junior College 1935. Adopted present name and moved to present location 1938.

Goddard Seminary 1870. See Goddard College, Plainfield, Vt.

Goddard Seminary and Junior College 1935. See Goddard College, Plainfield, Vt.

Golden Gate Baptist Theological Seminary, Mill Valley, Calif. Closed 1974.

Golden Gate College 1923. See Golden Gate University, San Francisco, Calif.

GOLDEN GATE UNIVERSITY. San Francisco, Calif. 94105. Non-public institution. Established as Golden Gate College 1923. Adopted present name 1974.

Gonzaga College 1887. See Gonzaga University, Spokane, Wash.

GONZAGA UNIVERSITY. Spokane, Wash. 99202. Non-public institution. Sponsored by the Society of Jesus, Roman Catholic Church. Established as Gonzaga College 1887. Adopted present name 1912.

Gordon Bible College 1916. See Gordon College, Wenham, Mass.

Gordon Bible Institute 1889. See Gordon College, Wenham, Mass.

GORDON COLLEGE. Wenham, Mass. 01984. Non-public institution. Established as Gordon Bible Institute 1889. Became: Gordon Bible College 1916; Gordon College of Theology and Missions 1921; Gordon College and Gordon Divinity School 1962. Adopted present name 1970, after separating from Divinity School.

Gordon College and Gordon Divinity School 1962. See Gordon College, Wenham, Mass.

Gordon College of Theology and Missions 1921. See Gordon College, Wenham, Mass.

Gorham State College 1878. See University of Maine at Portland-Gorham, Gorham, Me.

GOSHEN COLLEGE. Goshen, Ind. 46526. Non-public institution. Owned by the Mennonite Church Board of Education. Established as Elkhart Institute 1894. Adopted present name 1903.

GOUCHER COLLEGE. Towson, Md. 21204. Non-public institution. Established as Woman's College of Baltimore City 1885. Became: Woman's College of Baltimore 1890. Adopted present name 1910.

Grace Bible Institute 1943. <u>See</u> Grace College of the Bible, Omaha, Neb.

GRACE COLLEGE OF THE BIBLE. Omaha, Neb. 68108. Non-public institution. Established as Grace Bible Institute 1943 by J. R. Barkman and others. Adopted present name 1976.

GRADUATE SCHOOL AND UNIVERSITY CENTER. New York, N.Y. 10036. Municipal institution. Established as Division of Graduate Studies of The City University of New York 1962. Adopted present name 1968.

GRAMBLING STATE UNIVERSITY. Grambling, La. 71245. State institution. Established as Colored Industrial and Agricultural School 1901. Became: Lincoln Parish Training School 1918; Louisiana Normal and Industrial Institute 1928; Grambling College 1947. Adopted present name 1974.

GRAND CANYON COLLEGE. Phoenix, Ariz. 85017. Non-public institution. Owned by the Arizona Southern Baptist Convention. Established as Grand Canyon College, Prescott, Ariz. 1949. Moved to present location 1951.

Grand Canyon College, Prescott, Ariz. <u>See</u> Grand Canyon College, Phoenix, Ariz.

Grand Island College of Nebraska 1931. <u>See</u> Sioux Falls College, Sioux Falls, S.D.

Grant Memorial University 1886. <u>See</u> Tennessee Wesleyan College, Athens, Tenn.

Grant University 1889. <u>See</u> The University of Tennessee at Chattanooga, Chattanooga, Tenn.

Granville College 1845. <u>See</u> Denison University, Granville, Oh.

Granville Literary and Theological Institution 1831. <u>See</u> Denison University, Granville, Oh.

Graysville Academy 1892. <u>See</u> Southern Missionary College, Collegedale, Tenn.

Great Falls College of Education 1949. <u>See</u> College of Great Falls, Great Falls, Mont.

Great Falls Normal College 1932. <u>See</u> College of Great Falls, Great Falls, Mont.

Greater Payne University 1926. <u>See</u> Daniel Payne College, Inc., Birmingham, Ala.

Green County Teachers College, Monroe, Wisc. Closed June 1967.

81   Green Mountain

Green Mountain Central Institute 1863, Barre, Vt. See Goddard
College, Plainfield, Vt.

Greenbrier College, Lewisburg, W. Va.   Closed June 1972.

Greenbrier College of Osteopathic Medicine 1974. See West Virginia School of Osteopathic Medicine.

Greence Academy 1849. See Waynesburg College, Waynesburg, Pa.

GREENSBORO COLLEGE. Greensboro, N. C. 27420.   Non-public
institution. Affiliated with The United Methodist Church. Established
as Greensboro Female College 1838. Became: Greensboro College
for Women 1913. Adopted present official name Greensboro College,
Inc. 1921.

Greensboro College for Women 1913. See Greensboro College,
Greensboro, N. C.

Greensboro College, Inc. 1921. See Greensboro College, Greensboro, N. C.

Greensboro Evening College 1953. See Guilford College, Greensboro, N. C.

Greensboro Female College 1838. See Greensboro College, Greensboro, N. C.

GREENVILLE COLLEGE. Greenville, Ill. 62246.   Non-public institution. Affiliated with the Free Methodist Church of North America.
Established as Almira College 1855. Adopted present name 1892.

Greenville Women's College 1938. See Furman University, Greenville, S. C.

GRINNELL COLLEGE. Grinnell, Ia. 50112.   Non-public institution.
Established under present official name Iowa College 1846. Adopted
present name 1909.

GROVE CITY COLLEGE. Grove City, Pa. 16127.   Non-public insti-
tution. Affiliated with The United Presbyterian Church in the U. S. A.
Established as Select School at Pine Grove 1858. Became: Pine
Grove Normal Academy 1879. Adopted present name 1884.

Grubbs Vocational College 1917. See University of Texas at Arlington, Arlington, Tex.

GUILFORD COLLEGE. Greensboro, N. C. 27410.   Non-public institution. Established as New Garden Boarding School 1837. Adopted
present name 1889. Merged with Greensboro Evening College 1953.

GUSTAVUS ADOLPHUS COLLEGE. St. Peter, Minn. 56082.   Non-
public institution. Owned by The Lutheran Church in America. Es-

tablished as Academy at Red Wing, Minn. 1862. Became: St.
Ansgar's Academy 1863, after moving to East Union, Minn. Adopted
present name 1876, after moving to present location.

GWYNEDD-MERCY COLLEGE. Gwynedd Valley, Pa. 19437. Non-
public institution. Sponsored by the Sisters of Mercy, Roman Catholic Church. Established as Gwynedd-Mercy Junior College 1948.
Adopted present name 1963.

Gwynedd-Mercy Junior College 1948. See Gwynedd-Mercy College,
Gwynedd Valley, Pa.

- H -

Hall-Moody Institute 1900. See The University of Tennessee at
Martin, Martin, Tenn.

Hall-Moody Junior College 1917. See The University of Tennessee
at Martin, Martin, Tenn.

Hall-Moody Normal School 1905. See The University of Tennessee
at Martin, Martin, Tenn.

HAMILTON COLLEGE. Clinton, N. Y. 13323. Non-public institution.
Established as Hamilton-Oneida Academy 1793. Adopted present name
1812.

Hamilton Literary and Theological Institution 1819. See Colgate
University, Hamilton, N. Y.

Hamilton-Oneida Academy 1793. See Hamilton College, Clinton,
N. Y.

Hammond Junior College 1925. See Southeastern Louisiana University, Hammond, La.

Hampstead Academy 1826. See Mississippi College, Clinton, Miss.

HAMPTON INSTITUTE. Hampton, Va. 23368. Non-public institution.
Established as Hampton Normal and Agricultural Institute 1868.
Adopted present name 1930.

Hampton Normal and Agricultural Institute 1868. See Hampton Institute, Hampton, Va.

Hanover Academy 1827. See Hanover College, Hanover, Ind.

HANOVER COLLEGE. Hanover, Ind. 47143. Non-public institution.
Related to the Board of Christian Education of the United Presbyterian
Church in the U. S. and the Synod of Indiana. Established as Hanover
Academy 1827. Adopted present name 1833. Established Henry C.
Long College for Women 1947.

Hardin College 1946. <u>See</u> Midwestern State University, Wichita Falls, Tex.

Hardin Junior College 1937. <u>See</u> Midwestern State University, Wichita Falls, Tex.

HARDIN-SIMMONS UNIVERSITY. Abilene, Tex. 79601. Non-public institution. Owned by the Southern Baptist Convention. Established as Abilene Baptist College 1891. Became: Simmons College 1891; Simmons University 1925. Adopted present name 1934.

HARDING COLLEGE. Searcy, Ark. 72143. Non-public institution. Affiliated with the Church of Christ. Established as Arkansas Christian College, Morrilton, Ark. 1919. Purchased assets of Harper College of Kansas 1924. Adopted present name 1924. Moved to present location 1934.

Harper College (of Kansas) 1924. <u>See</u> Harding College, Searcy, Ark.

Harper College 1950. <u>See</u> State University of New York at Binghampton, Binghampton, N.Y.

HARRIS TEACHERS COLLEGE. St. Louis, Mo. 63103. Municipal institution. Established as St. Louis Normal School 1857. Became: Teachers College 1904. Adopted present name 1910. Merged with Stowe Teachers College 1954.

HARTFORD GRADUATE CENTER. Hartford, Conn. 06120. Non-public institution. Established as Hartford Graduate Center 1955. Became: Rensselaer Polytechnic Institute of Connecticut 1961. Re-adopted present name 1975.

Hartford School of Religious Education 1925. <u>See</u> The Hartford Seminary, Hartford, Conn.

Hartford School of Religious Pedagogy 1903. <u>See</u> The Hartford Seminary, Hartford, Conn.

THE HARTFORD SEMINARY. Hartford, Conn. 06105. Non-public institution. Established as Theological Institute of Connecticut 1834. Became: Hartford Theological Seminary 1885; Hartford School of Religious Pedagogy 1903; Hartford School of Religious Education 1925. Adopted present name 1961.

Hartford Theological Seminary 1885. <u>See</u> The Hartford Seminary, Hartford, Conn.

Hartsville Academy 1850. <u>See</u> Huntington College, Huntington, Ind.

Hartsville College 1883. <u>See</u> Huntington College, Huntington, Ind.

Hartsville University 1851. <u>See</u> Huntington College, Huntington, Ind.

HARTWICK COLLEGE. Oneonta, N. Y. 13820. Non-public institution. Established as Hartwick Seminary 1797. Adopted present name 1928.

Hartwick Seminary 1797. See Hartwick College, Oneonta, N. Y.

HAVERFORD COLLEGE. Haverford, Pa. 19041. Non-public institution. Established as Haverford School 1833, by The Society of Friends. Adopted present name 1856.

Haverford School 1833. See Haverford College, Haverford, Pa.

HAYWARD STATE UNIVERSITY. Hayward, Calif. 94542. State institution. Established as State College for Alameda County 1957. Became: California State College at Hayward 1963; California State College, Hayward 1968; California State University, Hayward 1972. Adopted present name 1974.

Healdsburg College, Healdsburg, Calif. 1882. See Pacific Union College, Angwin, Calif.

HEBREW COLLEGE. Brookline, Mass. 02146. Non-public institution. Established as Hebrew Teachers College 1921. Adopted present name 1969.

Hebrew Teachers College 1921. See Hebrew College, Brookline, Mass.

Hebrew Union College 1875. See Hebrew Union College--Jewish Institute of Religion, Cincinnati, Oh.

HEBREW UNION COLLEGE--JEWISH INSTITUTE OF RELIGION. Cincinnati, Oh. 45220. Non-public institution. Affiliated with the Union of American Hebrew Congregations. Established as Hebrew Union College 1875. Merged with Jewish Institute of Religion, New York 1950. Adopted present name 1950.

HEIDELBERG COLLEGE. Tiffin, Oh. 44883. Non-public institution. Affiliated with The United Church of Christ. Established as Heidelberg University 1850. Adopted present name 1926.

Heidelberg University 1850. See Heidelberg College, Tiffin, Oh.

Hellenic College 1968. See Hellenic College-Holy Cross Greek Orthodox School of Theology, Brookline, Mass.

HELLENIC COLLEGE-HOLY CROSS GREEK ORTHODOX SCHOOL OF THEOLOGY. Brookline, Mass. 02146. Non-public institution. Owned by the Greek Orthodox Archdiocese of North and South America. Established as Holy Cross Greek Orthodox Theological School 1937. Became: Hellenic College 1968. Adopted present name 1974.

Henderson-Brown College 1909. See Henderson State University, Arkadelphia, Ark.

Henderson-Brown College 1929. See Hendrix College, Conway, Ark.

Henderson College 1904. See Henderson State University, Arkadelphia, Ark.

Henderson Male and Female Institute 1869. See Freed-Hardeman College, Henderson, Tenn.

Henderson Masonic Male and Female Institute 1877. See Freed-Hardeman College, Henderson, Tenn.

Henderson State College 1972. See Henderson State University, Arkadelphia, Ark.

Henderson State Teachers College 1929. See Henderson State University, Arkadelphia, Ark.

HENDERSON STATE UNIVERSITY. Arkadelphia, Ark. 71923. State institution. Established as Arkadelphia Methodist College by Methodist Conferences of Arkansas 1890. Became: Henderson College 1904; Henderson-Brown College 1909. Control assumed by state and merged with Hendrix College 1929 becoming Henderson State Teachers College 1929; Henderson State College 1972. Adopted present name 1975.

HENDRIX COLLEGE. Conway, Ark. 72032. Non-public institution. Owned by The United Methodist Church. Established as Central Collegiate Institute, Altus, Ark. 1876. Became: Hendrix College 1889 and moved to Conway, Ark. 1890; merged with Henderson-Brown College and became Hendrix-Henderson College 1929; merged with Galloway Women's College and adopted present name 1933.

Hendrix College 1889. See Hendrix College, Conway, Ark.

Hendrix College 1929. See Henderson State University, Arkadelphia, Ark.

Hendrix-Henderson College 1929. See Hendrix College, Conway, Ark.

Henry C. Long College for Women 1947. See Hanover College, Hanover, Ind.

Henry Kendall College 1894. See The University of Tulsa, Tulsa, Okla.

HERBERT H. LEHMAN COLLEGE. New York, N.Y. 10468. Municipal institution. Established as Hunter College in the Bronx, 1931. Adopted present official name Herbert H. Lehman College of The City University of New York 1968, after becoming an autonomous unit of CUNY.

Herbert H. Lehman College of The City University of New York 1968. See Herbert H. Lehman College, New York, N.Y.

Hesperian College, Woodland, Calif. 1861. See Chapman College, Orange, Calif.

High and Training School 1900. See Coppin State College, Baltimore, Md.

High Museum School of Art 1928. See Atlanta College of Art, Atlanta, Ga.

Highland College 1891. See Lenoir Rhyne College, Hickory, N.C.

Highland College, Pasadena, Calif. Closed May 1974.

Hillman College for Women 1942. See Mississippi College, Clinton, Miss.

Hillsboro College 1847. See Carthage College, Kenosha, Wisc.

HILLSDALE COLLEGE. Hillsdale, Mich. 49242. Non-public institution. Established as Michigan Central College at Spring Arbor, Mich. 1844. Adopted present name 1853.

HIRAM COLLEGE. Hiram, Oh. 44234. Non-public institution. Affiliated with the Christian Church, Disciples of Christ. Established as Western Reserve Eclectic Institute 1850. Adopted present name 1867.

Hiram Scott College, Scottsbluff, Neb. Closed July 1971.

Hobbs Baptist College 1956. See College of the Southwest, Hobbs, N.M.

Hofstra College 1939. See Hofstra University, Hempstead, N.Y.

HOFSTRA UNIVERSITY. Hempstead, N.Y. 11550. Non-public institution. Established as Nassau-Hofstra Memorial 1935. Became: Hofstra College 1939. Adopted present name 1963.

HOLLINS COLLEGE. Hollins College, Va. 24020. Non-public institution. Established as Valley Union Seminary 1842. Became: Hollins Institute 1855. Adopted present name 1911.

Hollins Institute 1855. See Hollins College, Hollins College, Va.

Hollywood College, Hollywood, Fla. Closed 1973/74 School Year.

Holy Cross College, Washington, D.C. Closed 1968/69 School Year.

Holy Cross Greek Orthodox Theological School 1937. Hellenic College-Holy Cross Greek Orthodox School of Theology, Brookline, Mass.

Holy Cross Normal College 1931. See Our Lady of Holy Cross College, New Orleans, La.

Holy Family College 1935. See Silver Lake College, Manitowoc, Wisc.

Holy Family Normal School 1869. See Silver Lake College, Manitowoc, Wisc.

Holy Family Seminary, West Hartford, Conn. Closed June 1968.

Holy Name Technical School 1930. See Lewis University, Lockport, Ill.

HOLY NAMES COLLEGE. Oakland, Calif. 94619. Non-public institution. Conducted by the Sisters of the Holy Name, Roman Catholic Church. Established as Convent of Our Lady of the Sacred Heart 1868. Became: Convent and College of the Holy Names 1908; College of the Holy Names 1956. Adopted present name 1971.

Holy Names College at Fort Wright 1939. See Fort Wright College, Spokane, Wash.

Holy Names Normal School 1907. See Fort Wright College, Spokane, Wash.

The Homeopathic Medical College of the State of New York in New York City 1860. See New York Medical College, New York, N.Y.

HOOD COLLEGE OF FREDERICK: MARYLAND. Frederick, Md. 21701. Non-public institution. Affiliated with the United Church of Christ. Established as Woman's College of Frederick, Md. 1893. Adopted present name 1913.

HOPE COLLEGE. Holland, Mich. 49423. Non-public institution. Affiliated with the Reformed Church in America. Established as Pioneer School 1851. Adopted present name 1866.

HOUGHTON COLLEGE. Houghton, N.Y. 14744. Non-public institution. Controlled by The Wesleyan Church. Established as Houghton Wesleyan Methodist Seminary 1883. Adopted present name 1923.

Houghton Wesleyan Methodist Seminary 1883. See Houghton College, Houghton, N.Y.

Houlton Academy 1848. See Ricker College, Houlton, Me.

Houston Junior College 1927. See University of Houston, Houston, Tex.

HOUSTON-TILLOTSON COLLEGE. Austin, Tex. 78702. Non-public institution. Affiliated with the United Church of Christ and the United Methodist Church. Established as Tillotson Collegiate and Normal Institute 1875. Became: Tillotson College 1894. Merged with Samuel Houston College 1952. Adopted present name 1952.

Howard College 1841.   See   Sanford University, Birmingham, Ala.

Howard Payne College.   See   Central Methodist College, Fayette,
Mo.

Howard School 1867.   See   Fayetteville State University, Fayetteville,
N.C.

Humboldt State College 1935.   See   Humboldt State University, Arcata, Calif.

Humboldt State Normal School 1913.   See   Humboldt State University,
Arcata, Calif.

Humboldt State Teachers College 1921.   See   Humboldt State University, Arcata, Calif.

HUMBOLDT STATE UNIVERSITY.   Arcata, Calif. 95521.   State institution.   Established as Humboldt State Normal School 1913.   Became: Humboldt State Teachers College 1921.   Humboldt State College 1935; California State University at Humboldt 1972.   Adopted
present name 1974.

HUNTER COLLEGE.   New York, N.Y. 10021.   Municipal institution.
Established as Female Normal and High School 1870.   Became:
Hunter College 1914.   Adopted present official name Hunter College
of The City University of New York 1961.

Hunter College in the Bronx 1931.   See   Herbert H. Lehman College,
New York, N.Y.

Hunter College of The City University of New York 1961.   See
Hunter College, New York, N.Y.

HUNTINGDON COLLEGE.   Montgomery, Ala. 36106.   Non-public
institution.   Owned by The United Methodist Church.   Established
as Tuskegee Female College 1854.   Became: Alabama Conference
Female College 1872; Woman's College of Alabama 1909.   Adopted
present name 1935.

HUNTINGTON COLLEGE.   Huntington, Ind. 46750.   Non-public institution.   Owned by the Church of the United Brethren in Christ.
Established as Hartsville Academy 1850.   Became: Hartsville University 1851; Hartsville College 1883; Central College 1897.   Adopted present name 1917.

Huntsville Normal School 1875.   See   Alabama Agricultural and
Mechanical University, Normal, Ala.

HURON COLLEGE.   Huron, S.D. 57350.   Non-public institution.
Affiliated with The United Presbyterian Church in the U.S.   Established as Presbyterian University of Southern Dakota 1883.   Became: Pierre University 1883.   Adopted present name 1898, after
moving to present location.

HUSSON COLLEGE. Bangor, Me. 04401. Non-public institution.
Established as Shaw Business School 1898. Became: Bangor Maine
School of Commerce 1926. Adopted present name 1947.

Hyatt School 1853. See Widener College, Chester, Pa.

- I -

Idaho State College 1947. See Idaho State University, Pocatello,
Ida.

IDAHO STATE UNIVERSITY. Pocatello, Ida. 83201. State institution. Established as The Academy of Idaho, a secondary school,
1901. Became: The Idaho Technical Institute 1915; Southern Branch
of the University of Idaho 1927; Idaho State College 1947. Adopted
present name 1963.

The Idaho Technical Institute 1915. See Idaho State University,
Pocatello, Ida.

ILLINOIS BENEDICTINE COLLEGE. Lisle, Ill. 60532. Non-public
institution. Affiliated with the Benedictine Fathers, Roman Catholic
Church. Established as St. Procopius College 1887. Adopted present name 1971.

ILLINOIS COLLEGE OF OPTOMETRY. Chicago, Ill. 60616. Non-
public institution. Established as Northern Illinois College of Ophthalmology and Otology 1872. Became: Northern Illinois College
of Optometry 1926, after merger with Needles Institute of Optometry.
Adopted present name 1955 after merger with Chicago College of
Optometry.

Illinois Conference Female College 1851. See MacMurray College,
Jacksonville, Ill.

Illinois Female Academy 1846. See MacMurray College, Jacksonville, Ill.

Illinois Female College 1863. See MacMurray College, Jacksonville,
Ill.

Illinois Holiness University 1909. See Olivet Nazarene College,
Kankakee, Ill.

Illinois Institute 1853. See Wheaton College, Wheaton, Ill.

ILLINOIS INSTITUTE OF TECHNOLOGY. Chicago, Ill. 60616. Non-
public institution. Established under present name 1940 by merger
of Armour Institute of Technology and Lewis Institute. Merged with
Chicago-Kent College of Law 1969.

Illinois State Normal University 1857. See Illinois State University, Normal, Ill.

ILLINOIS STATE UNIVERSITY. Normal, Ill. 61761. State institution. Established as Illinois State Normal University 1857. Became: Illinois State University at Normal 1963. Adopted present name 1967.

Illinois State University 1852. See Carthage College, Kenosha, Wisc.

Illinois State University at Normal 1963. See Illinois State University, Normal, Ill.

Illinois Teachers College, Chicago-North 1965. See Northeastern Illinois University, Chicago, Ill.

Illinois Teachers College, Chicago-South 1965. See Chicago State University, Chicago, Ill.

Illinois Woman's College 1899. See MacMurray College, Jacksonville, Ill.

Immaculata College, Bartlett, Ill. Closed Aug. 1969.

IMMACULATA COLLEGE. Immaculata, Pa. 19345. Non-public institution. Owned by the Sisters Servants of the Immaculate Heart of Mary, Roman Catholic Church. Established as Villa Maria Academy for Girls 1914. Became: Villa Maria College 1920. Adopted present name 1928.

Immaculate Conception Junior College 1924. See Marian College, Indianapolis, Ind.

Immaculate Conception Junior College 1942. See Felician College, Lodi, N.J.

Immaculate Conception Normal School 1935. See Felician College, Lodi, N.J.

Indian Normal School of Robeson County 1911. See Pembroke State University, Pembroke, N.C.

Indiana Asbury University 1837. See DePauw University, Greencastle, Ind.

Indiana Baptist Manual Labor Institute 1834. See Franklin College of Indiana, Franklin, Ind.

Indiana Central College 1902. See Indiana Central University, Indianapolis, Ind.

INDIANA CENTRAL UNIVERSITY. Indianapolis, Ind. 46227. Non-public institution. Affiliated with the United Methodist Church.

Established as Indiana Central University 1902, but was known as
Indiana Central College. Adopted present name 1975.

Indiana College 1828. See Indiana University at Bloomington,
Bloomington, Ind.

INDIANA INSTITUTE OF TECHNOLOGY. Fort Wayne, Ind. 46803.
Non-public institution. Established as Indiana Technical College
1930. Adopted present name 1963.

Indiana Normal School 1871. See Indiana University of Pennsylvania, Indiana, Pa.

Indiana Normal School 1905. See Ball State University, Muncie, Ind.

INDIANA NORTHERN GRADUATE SCHOOL OF PROFESSIONAL MAN-
AGEMENT. Marion, Ind. 46952. Non-public institution. Established as Indiana Northern University, Inc. 1963. Adopted present
name 1975.

Indiana Northern University, Inc. 1963. See Indiana Northern
Graduate School of Professional Management, Marion, Ind.

Indiana State College 1959. See Indiana University of Pennsylvania,
Indiana, Pa.

Indiana State Normal School 1865. See Indiana State University,
Terre Haute, Ind.

Indiana State Normal School 1920. See Indiana University of Pennsylvania, Indiana, Pa.

Indiana State Normal School, Eastern Division 1918. See Ball
State University, Muncie, Ind.

Indiana State Seminary 1820. See Indiana University at Bloomington, Bloomington, Ind.

Indiana State Teachers College 1927. See Indiana University of
Pennsylvania, Indiana, Pa.

Indiana State Teacher's College 1929. See Indiana State University,
Terre Haute, Ind.

INDIANA STATE UNIVERSITY. Terre Haute, Ind. 47809. State
institution. Established as Indiana State Normal School 1865. Became: Indiana State Teacher's College 1929. Adopted present name
1965.

Indiana Technical College 1930. See Indiana Institute of Technology,
Fort Wayne, Ind.

INDIANA UNIVERSITY AT BLOOMINGTON. Bloomington, Ind. 47401.

State institution.   Established as Indiana State Seminary 1820.   Became: Indiana College 1828.   Adopted present name 1838.

INDIANA UNIVERSITY AT KOKOMO.   Kokomo, Ind. 46901.   State institution.   Established as Kokomo Center of Indiana University 1945.   Adopted present name 1970.

INDIANA UNIVERSITY AT SOUTHBEND.   South Bend, Ind. 46615. State institution.   Established as South Bend-Mishawaka Center of Indiana University 1933.   Adopted present name 1962.

INDIANA UNIVERSITY NORTHWEST.   Gary, Ind. 46408.   State institution.   Established as Indiana University 1922.   Assumed control of Gary College 1948.   Merged with Calumet Center 1963.   Adopted present name 1963.

INDIANA UNIVERSITY OF PENNSYLVANIA.   Indiana, Pa. 15701. State institution.   Established as Indiana Normal School 1871.   Became: Indiana State Normal School 1920; Indiana State Teachers College 1927; Indiana State College 1959.   Adopted present name 1965.

INDIANA UNIVERSITY-PURDUE UNIVERSITY AT FORT WAYNE. Fort Wayne, Ind. 46805.   State institution.   Established as Fort Wayne Center of Indiana University 1917.   Merged with Purdue University Fort Wayne Campus 1975.   Adopted present name 1975.

INDIANA UNIVERSITY-PURDUE UNIVERSITY. DEPT. OF FINE ARTS. Fort Wayne, Ind. 46805.   State institution.   Established as Fort Wayne Art School Museum 1922.   Became: Fort Wayne Art Institute of Fine Arts and Museum of Fine Arts 1962.   Adopted present name 1977, after merger with Indiana-Purdue University.

INDIANA UNIVERSITY-SOUTHEAST.   New Albany, Ind. 47150. State institution.   Established as Falls City Center 1941, Jeffersonville, Ind.   Adopted present name 1969.   Moved to present location 1974.

Indianola Seminary 1860.   See   Simpson College, Indianola, Ia.

Industrial Branch of Morgan State College 1935.   See   University of Maryland, Eastern Shore.   Princess Anne, Md.

Industrial Fellowship League 1919.   See   General Motors Institute, Flint, Mich.

Industrial Institute and College 1908.   See   University of Arts and Sciences of Oklahoma, Chickasha, Okla.

Industrial Institute and College of Louisiana 1894.   See   Louisiana Tech University, Ruston, La.

Industrial School for Colored Youth 1867.   See   Bowie State College, Bowie, Md.

Institute and Training School of the YMCA 1903. See George Williams College, Downers Grove, Ill.

Institute for Colored Youth 1842. See Cheyney State College, Cheyney, Pa.

The Institute of Musical Art 1905. See The Juilliard School, New York, N.Y.

Institute of the Sisters of St. Joseph 1892. See Medaille College, Buffalo, N.Y.

INTER-AMERICAN UNIVERSITY OF PUERTO RICO. San Germain, P.R. 00753. Non-public institution. Affiliated with The United Presbyterian Church in the U.S. Established as Polytechnic Institute of Puerto Rico 1912. Adopted present name 1956.

Intermountain Union College 1923. See Rocky Mountain College, Billings, Mont.

International College of Chiropractic 1971. See National College of Chiropractic, Lombard, Ill.

International YMCA College 1912. See Springfield College, Springfield, Mass.

International YMCA Training School 1890. See Springfield College, Springfield, Mass.

Iowa Agricultural College 1858. See Iowa State University of Science and Technology, Ames, Ia.

Iowa College 1846. See Grinnell College, Grinnell, Ia.

Iowa Conference Seminary 1852. See Cornell College, Mount Vernon, Ia.

Iowa State College of Agriculture and Mechanic Arts 1898. See Iowa State University of Science and Technology, Ames, Ia.

Iowa State Normal School 1876. See University of Northern Iowa, Cedar Falls, Ia.

Iowa State Teachers College 1909. See University of Northern Iowa, Cedar Falls, Ia.

IOWA STATE UNIVERSITY OF SCIENCE AND TECHNOLOGY. Ames, Ia. 50010. State institution. Established as Iowa Agricultural College 1858. Became: Iowa State College of Agriculture and Mechanic Arts 1898. Adopted present name 1959.

IOWA WESLEYAN COLLEGE. Mount Pleasant, Ia. 52641. Nonpublic institution. Affiliated with The United Methodist Church.

Established as Literary Institute 1842.   Became: Iowan Wesleyan
University 1855.   Adopted present name 1912.

Iowan Wesleyan University 1855.   See   Iowa Wesleyan College,
Mount Pleasant, Ia.

Ithaca College,   Ithaca, N.Y. 14850.   Non-public institution.   Established as Ithaca Conservatory of Music 1892.   Became: Ithaca Conservatory and Affiliated Schools 1926.   Adopted present name 1931.

Ithaca College 1929.   See   Westminster Choir College, Princeton,
N.J.

Ithaca Conservatory and Affiliated Schools 1926.   See   Ithaca College,
Ithaca, N.Y.

Ithaca Conservatory of Music 1892.   See   Ithaca College, Ithaca,
N.Y.

- J -

J. & S. Green Collegiate Institute 1897.   See   Piedmont College,
Demorest, Ga.

J. S. Green College 1899.   See   Piedmont College, Demorest, Ga.

Jackson College for Negro Teachers 1944.   See   Jackson State University, Jackson, Miss.

Jackson Male Academy 1825.   See   Union University, Jackson, Tenn.

Jackson State College 1956.   See   Jackson State University, Jackson,
Miss.

JACKSON STATE UNIVERSITY.   Jackson, Miss. 39217.   State insti-
tution.   Established as Natchez Seminary 1877 by American Baptist
Home Missionary Society.   Became: Mississippi Negro Training
School 1940, after transfer to state control; Jackson College for
Negro Teachers 1944; Jackson State College 1956.   Adopted present
name 1974.

Jacksonville Junior College 1934.   See   Jacksonville University,
Jacksonville, Fla.

Jacksonville State College 1957.   See   Jacksonville State University,
Jacksonville, Ala.

JACKSONVILLE STATE UNIVERSITY.   Jacksonville, Ala. 36265.
State institution.   Established as State Normal School 1883.   Be-
came: State Teachers College 1929; Jacksonville State College 1957.
Adopted present name 1966.

JACKSONVILLE UNIVERSITY. Jacksonville, Fla. 32211. Non-public institution. Established as Jacksonville Junior College 1934. Adopted present name 1956.

JARVIS CHRISTIAN COLLEGE. Hawkins, Tex. 75765. Non-public institution. Affiliated with the Disciples of Christ. Established as Jarvis Christian Institute 1912. Adopted present name 1921.

Jarvis Christian Institute 1912. See Jarvis Christian College, Hawkins, Tex.

Jarvis Hall 1869. See Colorado School of Mines, Golden, Colo.

Jasper County Junior College 1964. See Missouri Southern State College, Joplin, Mo.

Jefferson College 1865. See Washington and Jefferson College, Washington, Pa.

Jefferson Medical College 1838. See Thomas Jefferson University, Philadelphia, Pa.

Jefferson Medical College of the Jefferson College of Canonsburg, Pa. 1824. See Thomas Jefferson University, Philadelphia, Pa.

Jefferson Seminary 1798. See University of Louisville, Louisville, Ky.

JERSEY CITY STATE COLLEGE. Jersey City, N.J. 07305. State institution. Established as New Jersey State Normal School 1927. Became: New Jersey State Teachers College 1955. Adopted present name 1958.

Jesus College 1872. See Macalester College, St. Paul, Minn.

THE JESUIT SCHOOL OF THEOLOGY AT BERKELEY. Berkeley, Calif. 94709. Non-public institution. Conducted by the Society of Jesus, Roman Catholic Church. Established as Alma College, Los Gatos, Calif. 1934. Relocated in Berkeley and adopted present name 1969.

Jewish Institute of Religion, New York 1950. See Hebrew Union College-Institute of Religion, Cincinnati, Oh.

Jewish Theological Seminary Association 1886. See Jewish Theological Seminary of America, New York, N.Y.

JEWISH THEOLOGICAL SEMINARY OF AMERICA. New York, N.Y. 10027. Non-public institution. Affiliated with the Conservative Movement in American Judaism. Established as Jewish Theological Seminary Association 1886. Adopted present name 1901.

John B. Stetson University 1889. See Stetson University, DeLand, Fla.

JOHN BROWN UNIVERSITY. Siloam Springs, Ark. 72761. Non-public institution. Established as Southwestern Collegiate Institute 1919. Became: John E. Brown College 1920; joined the Siloam School of the Bible and John E. Brown Vocational College and adopted present name 1934. Divisions merged into single unit 1948.

John Calvin Junior College 1906. See Calvin College, Grand Rapids, Mich.

JOHN CARROLL UNIVERSITY. Cleveland, Oh. 44118. Non-public institution. Affiliated with the Society of Jesus, Roman Catholic Church. Established as St. Ignatius College 1886. Became: Cleveland University 1923. Adopted present name later in 1923.

John E. Brown College 1920. See John Brown University, Siloam Springs, Ark.

John E. Brown Vocational College 1934. See John Brown University, Siloam Springs, Ark.

John F. Kennedy College, Wahoo, Neb. Closed July 1975.

John J. Pershing College, Beatrice, Neb. Closed July 1971.

JOHN JAY COLLEGE OF CRIMINAL JUSTICE. New York, N.Y. 10010. Municipal institution. Established as College of Police Science 1964. Adopted present official name John Jay College of Criminal Justice of The City University of New York 1966.

John Jay College of Criminal Justice of The City University of New York 1966. See John Jay College of Criminal Justice, New York, N.Y.

John McNeese Junior College 1940. See McNeese State University, Lake Charles, La.

John Tarleton Agricultural College 1917. See Tarleton State University, Stephenville, Tex.

John Tarleton College 1899. See Tarleton State University, Stephenville, Tex.

JOHN WESLEY COLLEGE. Owosso, Mich. 48867. Non-public institution. Established as Owosso College 1909. Adopted present name 1972.

Johnson Academy 1828. See Johnson State College, Johnson, Vt.

JOHNSON C. SMITH UNIVERSITY. Charlotte, N.C. 28216. Non-public institution. Affiliated with The United Presbyterian Church in the U.S. Established as the Biddle Memorial Institute 1867. Became: Biddle University 1876. Adopted present name 1923.

Johnson Normal School 1866. See Johnson State College, Johnson, Vt.

JOHNSON STATE COLLEGE. Johnson, Vt. 05656. State institution. Established as Johnson Academy 1828. Became: Lamoile County Grammar School 1836; Johnson Normal School 1866; Johnson Teachers College 1947. Adopted present name 1962.

Johnson Teachers College 1947. See Johnson State College, Johnson, Vt.

Joplin Junior College 1937. See Missouri Southern State College, Joplin, Mo.

JUDSON COLLEGE. Marion, Ala. 36756. Non-public institution. Owned by the Alabama Baptist State Convention (Southern Baptist). Established as Judson Female Institute 1838. Adopted present name 1904.

Judson Female Institute 1838. See Judson College, Marion, Ala.

Juilliard Graduate School 1946. See The Juilliard School, New York, N. Y.

THE JUILLIARD SCHOOL. New York, N. Y. 10023. Non-public institution. Established as The Institute of Musical Art 1905. Became: Juilliard School of Music 1946, after combining with Juilliard Graduate School 1946. Adopted present name 1968.

Juilliard School of Music 1946. See The Juilliard School, New York, N. Y.

JUNIATA COLLEGE. Huntingdon, Pa. 16652. Non-public institution. Established as Brethren's Normal College 1876. Adopted present name 1894.

Junior College of Augusta 1925. See Augusta College, Augusta, Ga.

Junior College of Commerce 1935. See Quinnipiac College, Hamden, Conn.

Junior College of Connecticut 1927. See University of Bridgeport, Bridgeport, Conn.

- K -

Kalamazoo Branch of the University of Michigan 1840. See Kalamazoo College, Kalamazoo, Mich.

KALAMAZOO COLLEGE. Kalamazoo, Mich. 49001. Non-public institution. Affiliated with the American Baptist Convention. Es-

tablished as Michigan and Huron Institute 1833. Became: Kalamazoo
Literary Institute 1837; Kalamazoo Branch of the University of Michigan 1840; readopted name Kalamazoo Literary Institute 1850. Adopted present name 1855.

Kalamazoo Literary Institute 1837. See Kalamazoo College, Kalamazoo, Mich.

KANSAS CITY ART INSTITUTE. Kansas City, Mo. 64111. Non-
public institution. Established as Kansas City Art Institute and
School of Design 1887. Became: Fine Arts Institute of Kansas City
1907; Kansas City Art Institute 1920; Kansas City Art Institute and
School of Design 1945. Adopted present name 1965.

Kansas City Art Institute and School of Design 1887. See Kansas
City Art Institute, Kansas City, Mo.

Kansas City Bible Institute 1932. See Calvary Bible College,
Kansas City, Mo.

KANSAS NEWMAN COLLEGE. Wichita, Kan. 67213. Non-public
institution. Owned and operated by Sisters Adorers of the Most
Precious Blood, Wichita Province, Roman Catholic Church. Established as Sacred Heart College 1933 by the Rev. Leon A. McNeill
and Mother M. Beata Netemeyer. Adopted present name 1973.

Kansas State Agricultural College 1863. See Kansas State University, Manhattan, Kan.

Kansas State Chiropractic College 1974. See National College of
Chiropractic, Lombard, Ill.

Kansas State College of Agriculture and Applied Science 1931. See
Kansas State University, Manhattan, Kan.

KANSAS STATE COLLEGE OF PITTSBURG. Pittsburg, Kan. 66762.
State institution. Established as Kansas State Manual Training Normal School 1903. Became: Kansas State Teachers College of Pittsburg 1925. Adopted present name 1959.

Kansas State Manual Training Normal School 1903. See Kansas
State College of Pittsburg, Pittsburg, Kan.

Kansas State Normal School 1863. See Emporia Kansas State College, Emporia, Kan.

Kansas State Teachers College of Emporia 1923. See Emporia
Kansas State College, Emporia, Kan.

Kansas State Teachers College of Pittsburg 1925. See Kansas
State College of Pittsburg, Pittsburg, Kan.

KANSAS STATE UNIVERSITY. Manhattan, Kan. 66502. State insti-

tution.   Established as Kansas State Agricultural College 1863.   Became: Kansas State College of Agriculture and Applied Science 1931.
Adopted present name 1959.

KANSAS WESLEYAN.   Salina, Kan. 67401.   Non-public institution.
Owned by The United Methodist Church.   Established as Kansas Wesleyan University 1885.   Adopted present name 1969.

Kansas Wesleyan University 1885.   See Kansas Wesleyan, Salina,
Kan.

KEAN COLLEGE OF NEW JERSEY.   Union, N. J. 07083.   State institution.   Established as Newark Normal School 1855.   Became:
New Jersey State Normal School at Newark 1913; Newark State
Teachers College 1935; Newark State College 1958.   Adopted present
name 1974.

KEARNEY STATE COLLEGE.   Kearney, Neb. 68847.   State institution.   Established as Nebraska State Normal School 1905.   Became:
Nebraska State Teachers College 1921.   Adopted present name 1963.

Keene Academy 1893.   See Southwestern Union College, Keene, Tex.

Keene Normal School 1909.   See Keene State College, Keene, N. H.

KEENE STATE COLLEGE.   Keene, N. H. 03431.   State institution.
Established as Keene Normal School 1909.   Became: Keene Teachers College 1939.   Adopted present name 1963, after becoming a
division of The University of New Hampshire.

Keene Teachers College 1939.   See Keene State College, Keene,
N. H.

Kendall School 1856.   See Gallaudet College, Washington, D. C.

Kent County School 1718.   See Washington College, Chestertown,
Md.

Kent State College 1929.   See Kent State University, Kent, Oh.

Kent State Normal College 1915.   See Kent State University, Kent,
Oh.

Kent State Normal School 1910.   See Kent State University, Kent,
Oh.

KENT STATE UNIVERSITY.   Kent, Oh. 44242.   State institution.
Established as Kent State Normal School 1910.   Became: Kent State
Normal College 1915; Kent State College 1929.   Adopted present
name 1935.

Kentucky Industrial College for Colored Persons 1926.   See Kentucky State College, Frankfort, Ky.

Kentucky Normal and Industrial Institute for Colored Persons 1902.
See Kentucky State College, Frankfort, Ky.

Kentucky Normal Institute 1886. See Kentucky State College, Frankfort, Ky.

Kentucky Southern College, Louisville, Ky. Closed Aug. 1969.

KENTUCKY STATE COLLEGE. Frankfort, Ky. 40601. State institution. Established as Kentucky Normal Institute 1886. Became: Kentucky Normal and Industrial Institute for Colored Persons 1902; Kentucky Industrial College for Colored Persons 1926; Kentucky State College for Negroes 1938. Adopted present name 1952.

Kentucky State College for Negroes 1938. See Kentucky State College, Frankfort, Ky.

Kentucky University 1865. See Transylvania University, Lexington, Ky.

KENYON COLLEGE. Gambier, Oh. 43022. Non-public institution. Affiliated with the Protestant Episcopal Church. Established as The Theological Seminary of the Protestant Episcopal Church 1824. Adopted present name 1891.

Ker-Anna Junior College 1941. See Annhurst College, Woodstock, Conn.

Keystone Normal School 1866. See Kutztown State College, Kutztown, Pa.

King William's School 1696. See St. John's College, Annapolis, Md.

King's College 1754. See Columbia University, New York, N.Y.

KIRKSVILLE COLLEGE OF OSTEOPATHIC MEDICINE. Kirksville, Mo. 65101. Non-public institution. Established as the American School of Osteopathy and Surgery 1926, after merger with Andrew Taylor Still College of Osteopathy and Surgery 1926. Adopted present name 1971.

Kirksville College of Osteopathy and Surgery 1926. See Kirksville College of Osteopathic Medicine, Kirksville, Mo.

Klein School of Optics 1894. See New England College of Optometry, Boston, Mass.

KNOX COLLEGE. Galesburg, Ill. 61401. Non-public institution. Established as Prairie College 1836. Became: Knox Manual Labor College 1837. Adopted present name 1857.

Knox Manual Labor College 1837. See Knox College, Galesburg, Ill.

KNOXVILLE COLLEGE. Knoxville, Tenn. 37921. Non-public institution. Affiliated with The United Presbyterian Church in the U.S.A.
Established as McKee School for Negro Youth 1863. Adopted present name 1875.

Kokomo Center of Indiana University 1945. See Indiana University
at Kokomo, Kokomo, Ind.

KUTZTOWN STATE COLLEGE. Kutztown, Pa. 19530. State institution. Established as Keystone Normal School 1866. Became:
Kutztown State Teachers College 1926. Adopted present name 1960.

Kutztown State Teachers College 1926. See Kutztown State College,
Kutztown, Pa.

- L -

La Sierra College 1967. See Loma Linda University, Loma Linda,
Calif.

LAGRANGE COLLEGE. LaGrange, Ga. 30240. Non-public institution. Affiliated with the North Georgia Annual Conference of The
United Methodist Church. Established as LaGrange Female Academy
1831. Became: LaGrange Female Institute 1847; LaGrange Female
College 1851. Adopted present name 1934.

LaGrange College 1830. See University of North Alabama, Florence,
Ala.

LaGrange Female Academy 1831. See LaGrange College, LaGrange,
Ga.

LaGrange Female College 1851. See LaGrange College, LaGrange,
Ga.

LaGrange Female Institute 1847. See LaGrange College, LaGrange,
Ga.

Lake Charles Junior College 1939. See McNeese State University,
Lake Charles, La.

LAKE ERIE COLLEGE. Painesville, Oh. 44077. Non-public institution. Established as Lake Erie Seminary 1856. Adopted present
name 1908.

Lake Erie Seminary 1856. See Lake Erie College, Painesville, Oh.

LAKE FOREST COLLEGE. Lake Forest, Ill. 60045. Non-public
institution. Established as Lind University 1857. Became: Lake
Forest University 1865. Adopted present name 1965.

Lake Forest University 1865. See Lake Forest College, Lake Forest, Ill.

LAKE SUPERIOR STATE COLLEGE. Sault Sainte Marie, Mich. 49783. State institution. Established as Sault Sainte Marie Branch of Michigan Technological University 1946. Adopted present name 1966.

LAKELAND COLLEGE. Sheboygan, Wisc. 53081. Non-public institution. Affiliated with the United Church of Christ. Established as Mission House 1862. Adopted present name 1956.

Lamar College 1932. See Lamar University, Beaumont, Tex.

Lamar State College of Technology 1951. See Lamar University, Beaumont, Tex.

Lamar Union Junior College 1940. See Lamar University, Beaumont, Tex.

LAMAR UNIVERSITY. Beaumont, Tex. 77710. State institution. Established as South Park Junior College 1923. Became: Lamar College 1932; Lamar Union Junior College 1940; Lamar State College of Technology 1951. Adopted present name 1971.

LAMBUTH COLLEGE. Jackson, Tenn. 38301. Non-public institution. Owned by the Memphis Annual Conference of The United Methodist Church. Established as Memphis Conference Female Institute 1843. Adopted present name 1923.

Lamoile County Grammar School 1836. See Johnson State College, Johnson, Vt.

Lancaster County Normal Institute 1855. See Millersville State College, Millersville, Pa.

Lancaster Junior College 1918. See Atlantic Union College, South Lancaster, Mass.

LANDER COLLEGE. Greenwood, S. C. 29646. Non-public institution. Receives financial support from Greenwood County. Established as Williamston Female College 1872. Became part of the South Carolina Conference of Methodist Episcopal Church South 1898. Adopted present name 1904. Control assumed by Greenwood County 1951.

LANE COLLEGE. Jackson, Tenn. 38301. Non-public institution. Affiliated with the Christian Methodist Episcopal Church. Established as Colored Methodist Episcopal High School 1882. Became: Lane Institute 1883. Adopted present name 1895.

Lane Institute 1883. See Lane College, Jackson, Tenn.

LANGSTON UNIVERSITY.   Langston, Okla. 73050.   State institution.
Established as Colored Agricultural and Normal University 1897.
Adopted present name 1941.

Las Cruces College 1888.   See   New Mexico State University, Las
Cruces, N. M.

Las Vegas College in New Mexico Territory 1877.   See   Regis College, Denver, Colo.

LAVERNE COLLEGE.   LaVerne, Calif. 91750.   Non-public institution.   Affiliated with the Church of the Brethren.   Established as
Lordsburg Academy 1891.   Adopted present name 1917.

Lawrence College 1913.   See   Lawrence University, Appleton, Wisc.

Lawrence Institute 1847.   See   Lawrence University, Appleton, Wisc.

LAWRENCE UNIVERSITY.   Appleton, Wisc. 54911.   Non-public institution.   Established as Lawrence Institute 1847.   Became: Lawrence University 1849; Lawrence College 1913.   Merged with Milwaukee-Downer College 1964.   Adopted present name 1964.

Layton School of Art and Design, Milwaukee, Wisc.   Closed May
1974.

Lea College, Albert Lea, Minn.   Closed August 1973.

Leander Clark College 1919.   See   Coe College, Cedar Rapids, Ia.

Lebanon Seminary 1828.   See   McKendree College, Lebanon, Ill.

LEE COLLEGE.   Cleveland, Tenn. 37311.   Non-public institution.
Owned by the Church of God.   Established as Bible Training School
1918.   Merged with Murphy Collegiate Institute 1938 and moved to
Sevierville, Tenn.   Adopted present name 1947 after moving back to
present location.

LeMoyne College 1932.   See   LeMoyne-Owen College, Memphis,
Tenn.

LeMoyne Junior College 1928.   See   LeMoyne-Owen College, Memphis, Tenn.

LeMoyne Normal Institute 1870.   See   LeMoyne-Owen College, Memphis, Tenn.

LEMOYNE-OWEN COLLEGE.   Memphis, Tenn. 38126.   Non-public
institution.   Affiliated with the American Missionary Association
and the Tennessee Baptist Missionary and Educational Convention.
Established as LeMoyne Normal Institute 1870.   Became: LeMoyne
Junior College 1928; LeMoyne College 1932.   Merged with Owen College 1968.   Adopted present name 1968.

LENOIR RHYNE COLLEGE. Hickory, N.C. 28601. Non-public institution. Owned by the North Carolina Synod of The Lutheran Church in America. Established as Highland College 1891. Adopted present name 1923.

LESLEY COLLEGE. Cambridge, Mass. 02138. Non-public institution. Established as Lesley Normal School 1909. Became: The Lesley School 1936. Adopted present name 1943.

Lesley Normal School 1909. See Lesley College, Cambridge, Mass.

Lesley School 1936. See Lesley College, Cambridge, Mass.

LeTOURNEAU COLLEGE. Longview, Tex. 75601. Non-public institution. Established as LeTourneau Technical Institute 1946. Adopted present name 1961.

LeTourneau Technical Institute 1946. See LeTourneau College, Longview, Tex.

LEWIS AND CLARK COLLEGE. Portland, Ore. 97219. Non-public institution. Affiliated with the regional synod of The United Presbyterian Church in the U.S. Established as Albany College 1867. Adopted present name 1942.

Lewis-Clark Normal School 1955. See Lewis-Clark State College, Lewiston, Id.

LEWIS-CLARK STATE COLLEGE. Lewiston, Id. 83501. State institution. Established as Lewiston State Normal School 1893. Became: Northern Idaho College of Education 1947; Lewis-Clark Normal School 1955. Adopted present name 1971.

Lewis College 1961. See Lewis University, Lockport, Ill.

Lewis College of Science and Technology 1946. See Lewis University, Lockport, Ill.

Lewis Holy Name School of Aeronautics 1934. See Lewis University, Lockport, Ill.

Lewis Institute. See Illinois Institute of Technology, Chicago, Ill.

Lewis School of Aeronautics 1940. See Lewis University, Lockport, Ill.

LEWIS UNIVERSITY. Lockport, Ill. 60441. Non-public institution. Affiliated with the Christian Brothers, Roman Catholic Church. Established as Holy Name Technical School 1930. Became: Lewis Holy Name School of Aeronautics 1934; Lewis School of Aeronautics 1940; Lewis College of Science and Technology 1946; Lewis College 1961. Adopted present name 1974.

Lewiston State Normal School 1893. See Lewis-Clark State College, Lewiston, Id.

LIBERTY BAPTIST COLLEGE. Lynchburg, Va. 24505. Non-public institution. Established as Lynchburg Baptist College 1971 by Dr. Jerry Falwell. Adopted present name 1975.

Liberty Hall 1776. See Washington and Lee University, Lexington, Va.

Liberty Hall Academy 1782. See Washington and Lee University, Lexington, Va.

LIMESTONE COLLEGE. Gaffney, S. C. 29340. Non-public institution. Established as Limestone Springs School 1845. Became: Cooper-Limestone Institute 1881. Adopted present name 1899. Control assumed by State Convention of the Baptist Denomination of South Carolina 1921. Private control assumed 1942.

Limestone Springs School 1845. See Limestone College, Gaffney, S. C.

Lincoln Chiropractic College 1971. See National College of Chiropractic, Lombard, Ill.

Lincoln College 1865. See Washburn University of Topeka, Kan.

Lincoln County Teachers College, Merrill, Wisc. Closed June 1967.

Lincoln Institute 1866. See Lincoln University, Jefferson City, Mo.

Lincoln Open University, Lombard, Ill. Closed May 1975.

Lincoln Parish Training School 1918. See Grambling State University, Grambling, La.

LINCOLN UNIVERSITY. Jefferson City, Mo. 65101. State institution. Established as Lincoln Institute, a private institution, 1866. Became state institution 1879. Adopted present name 1921.

LINCOLN UNIVERSITY. Lincoln University, Pa. 19352. Non-public institution, receiving state aid. Established as Ashmun Institute 1854. Adopted present name 1866.

Lind University 1857. See Lake Forest College, Lake Forest, Ill.

Linden Wood 1827. See The Lindenwood Colleges, St. Charles, Mo.

Linden Wood Female College 1853. See The Lindenwood Colleges, St. Charles, Mo.

Lindenwood College 1870. See The Lindenwood Colleges, St. Charles, Mo.

Lindenwood College II for Men 1969. See The Lindenwood Colleges, St. Charles, Mo.

THE LINDENWOOD COLLEGES. St. Charles, Mo. 63301. Non-public institution. Established as Linden Wood 1827. Became: Linden Wood Female College 1853; Lindenwood College 1870. Established Lindenwood College II for Men 1969. Adopted present name 1970.

LINFIELD COLLEGE. McMinnville, Ore. 97128. Non-public institution. Affiliated with the American Baptist Convention. Established as Oregon City College 1849. Became: Baptist College at McMinnville 1854, after moving from Oregon City; McMinnville College 1890. Adopted present name 1922.

Literary Institute 1842. See Iowa Wesleyan College, Mount Pleasant, Ia.

Little Rock Junior College 1929. See University of Arkansas at Little Rock, Ark.

Livingston Collegiate Institute 1840. See Livingston University, Livingston, Ala.

Livingston Female Academy 1835. See Livingston University, Livingston, Ala.

Livingston State College 1957. See Livingston University, Livingston, Ala.

LIVINGSTON UNIVERSITY. Livingston, Ala. 35470. State institution. Established as Livingston Female Academy 1835 by citizens' group. Became: Livingston Collegiate Institute 1840; Alabama Normal College 1882. Control transferred to state, 1907. Became: State Teachers College 1929; Livingston State College 1957. Adopted present name 1968.

LIVINGSTONE COLLEGE. Salisbury, N.C. 28144. Non-public institution. Affiliated with the African Methodist Episcopal Zion Church. Established as Zion Wesley Institute 1879. Became: Zion Wesley College 1885. Adopted present name 1887.

LOCK HAVEN STATE COLLEGE. Lock Haven, Pa. 17745. State institution. Established as Central State Normal School 1870. Became: State Teachers College, Lock Haven, Pa. 1927. Adopted present name 1960.

Logan Basic College of Chiropractic, Inc. 1935. See Logan College of Chiropractic, Inc. St. Louis, Mo.

LOGAN COLLEGE OF CHIROPRACTIC, INC. St. Louis, Mo. 63017. Non-public institution. Established as Logan Basic College of Chiropractic, Inc. 1935 by Dr. Hugh B. Logan. Adopted present name 1976.

Loma Linda Sanitarium School of Nursing 1905. <u>See</u> Loma Linda University, Loma Linda, Calif.

LOMA LINDA UNIVERSITY. Loma Linda, Calif. 92354. Non-public institution. Owned by the Seventh-day Adventists. Established as Loma Linda Sanitarium School of Nursing 1905. Became: College of Medical Evangelists 1909. Adopted present name 1961. Merged with La Sierra College 1967.

LONE MOUNTAIN COLLEGE. San Francisco, Calif. 94118. Non-public institution. Affiliated with the Religious of the Sacred Heart, Roman Catholic Church. Established as Sacred Heart Academy in Menlo Park 1898. Became: College of the Sacred Heart 1921; San Francisco College for Women 1930. Relocated in San Francisco 1930. Adopted present name 1970.

Long Beach State College 1950. <u>See</u> California State University, Long Beach; Long Beach, Calif.

The Long Island College Hospital Teaching Division 1860. <u>See</u> State University of New York Downstate Medical Center, Brooklyn, N. Y.

Long Island College of Medicine 1930. <u>See</u> State University of New York Downstate Medical Center, Brooklyn, N. Y.

LONG ISLAND UNIVERSITY ARNOLD AND MARIE SCHWARTZ COLLEGE OF PHARMACY AND HEALTH SCIENCES. Brooklyn, N. Y. 11216. State institution. Established as Long Island University Brooklyn College of Pharmacy 1929, after merger with Brooklyn College of Pharmacy 1929. Adopted present name 1976.

Long Island University College of Podiatry 1939. <u>See</u> New York College of Podiatric Medicine, New York, N. Y.

Longview College, Enfield, Conn. Closed June 1972.

LONGWOOD COLLEGE. Farmville, Va. 23901. State institution. Established as Farmville Female College 1839. Became: State Female Normal School 1884; State Normal School for Women 1914; State Teachers College at Farmville 1924. Adopted present name 1949.

LORAS COLLEGE. Dubuque, Ia. 52001. Non-public institution. Affiliated with the Archdiocese of Dubuque, Roman Catholic Church. Established as St. Raphael's Seminary 1839. Became: Mount St. Bernard 1850; St. Joseph College 1873; Dubuque College 1914; Columbia College 1920. Adopted present name 1939.

Lordsburg Academy 1891. <u>See</u> Laverne College, LaVerne, Calif.

Loretto Academy 1891. <u>See</u> Loretto Heights College, Denver, Colo.

Loretto College 1915. See Webster College, St. Louis, Mo.

LORETTO HEIGHTS COLLEGE. Denver, Colo. 80236. Non-public
institution. Owned by the Sisters of Loretto, Roman Catholic Church.
Established as Loretto Academy, a secondary school, 1891. Adopted
present name 1918.

LOS ANGELES BAPTIST COLLEGE. Newhall, Calif. 91321. Non-
public institution. Affiliated with the General Association of Regular
Baptist Churches. Established as Los Angeles Baptist Theological
Seminary 1927. Adopted present name 1959.

Los Angeles Baptist Theological Seminary 1927. See Los Angeles
Baptist College, Newhall, Calif.

Los Angeles College 1911. See Loyola Marymount University, Los
Angeles, Calif.

Los Angeles College of Optometry 1950. See Southern California
College of Optometry.

Los Angeles County Art Institute 1947. See Otis Art Institute of
Los Angeles County, Los Angeles, Calif.

Los Angeles Medical School of Ophthalmology and Optometry 1904.
See Southern California College of Optometry, Fullerton, Calif.

Los Angeles-Orange County State College 1949. See California State
University, Long Beach; Long Beach, Calif.

Los Angeles Pacific College 1965. See Azusa Pacific College,
Azusa, Calif.

Los Angeles School of Optometry 1922. See Southern California
College of Optometry, Fullerton, Calif.

Los Angeles State 1947. See California State University, Los
Angeles, Los Angeles, Calif.

Los Angeles State College of Applied Arts and Sciences 1949. See
California State University, Los Angeles, Los Angeles, Calif.

Louisiana Normal and Industrial Institute 1928. See Grambling
State University, Grambling, La.

Louisiana Normal School 1884. See Northwestern State University
of Louisiana, Natchitoches, La.

Louisiana Polytechnic Institute 1921. See Louisiana Tech University, Ruston, La.

Louisiana State Normal College 1918. See Northwestern State University of Louisiana, Natchitoches, La.

Louisiana State Seminary of Learning and Military Academy, Pineville, La. 1860. See Louisiana State University and Agricultural and Mechanical College at Baton Rouge, Baton Rouge, La.

Louisiana State University 1870. See Louisiana State University and Agricultural and Mechanical College at Baton Rouge, Baton Rouge, La.

LOUISIANA STATE UNIVERSITY AND AGRICULTURAL AND MECHANICAL COLLEGE AT BATON ROUGE. Baton Rouge, La. 70803. State institution. Established as Louisiana State Seminary of Learning and Military Academy, Pineville, La. 1860. Moved to present location 1869. Became: Louisiana State University 1870. Merged with Agricultural and Mechanical College of Louisiana 1877. Adopted present name 1976.

LOUISIANA TECH UNIVERSITY. Ruston, La. 71270. State institution. Established as Industrial Institute and College of Louisiana 1894. Became: Louisiana Polytechnic Institute 1921. Adopted present name 1970.

Lowell State College. See University of Lowell, Lowell, Mass.

Lowell Technological Institute 1953. See University of Lowell, Lowell, Mass.

Lowell Textile Institute 1928. See University of Lowell, Lowell, Mass.

Lowell Textile School 1895. See University of Lowell, Lowell, Mass.

LOYOLA COLLEGE. Baltimore, Md. 21210. Non-public institution. Affiliated with the Society of Jesus, Roman Catholic Church. Established under present name 1852. Merged with Mount Saint Agnes College of Women 1971.

Loyola College 1904. See Loyola University in New Orleans, New Orleans, La.

Loyola College of Los Angeles 1919. See Loyola Marymount University, Los Angeles, Calif.

LOYOLA MARYMOUNT UNIVERSITY. Los Angeles, Calif. 90045. Non-public institution. Conducted by the Society of Jesus, Roman Catholic Church. Established as St. Vincent's College 1865, by the Vincentian Fathers. Became: Los Angeles College 1911. Control assumed by the Society of Jesus; St. Vincent's College 1917; Loyola College of Los Angeles 1919; Loyola University of Los Angeles 1930. Became affiliated with Marymount College of Los Angeles 1968. Adopted present name 1974.

Loyola University, Chicago 1909. See Loyola University of Chicago, Chicago, Ill.

LOYOLA UNIVERSITY IN NEW ORLEANS. New Orleans, La. 70118. Non-public institution. Conducted by the Society of Jesus, Roman Catholic Church. Established as Preparatory College of Immaculate Conception 1847. Became: Loyola College 1904; Loyola University, New Orleans 1912. Adopted present name 1974.

Loyola University, New Orleans 1912. See Loyola University in New Orleans, New Orleans, La.

LOYOLA UNIVERSITY OF CHICAGO. Chicago, Ill. 60611. Non-public institution. Conducted by the Society of Jesus, Roman Catholic Church. Established as St. Ignatius College 1870. Became: Loyola University, Chicago 1909. Adopted present name 1976.

Loyola University of Los Angeles 1930. See Loyola Marymount University, Los Angeles, Calif.

Luther College 1962. See Midland Lutheran College, Fremont, Neb.

Lutheran College 1912. See Texas Lutheran College, Seguin, Tex.

Lutheran Normal School 1918. See Augustana College, Sioux Falls, S.D.

Lutheran Proseminary in Rochester 1885. See Wagner College, Staten Island, N.Y.

The Lutheran Seminary 1894. See Concordia Teachers College, Seward, Neb.

Lyceum of Ripon 1850. See Ripon College, Ripon, Wisc.

LYCOMING COLLEGE. Williamsport, Pa. 17701. Non-public institution. Affiliated with The United Methodist Church. Established as Williamsport Academy 1812. Became: Williamsport Dickinson Seminary 1848; Williamsport Dickinson Seminary and Junior College 1929. Adopted present name 1948.

Lynchburg Baptist College 1971. See Liberty Baptist College, Lynchburg, Va.

LYNCHBURG COLLEGE. Lynchburg, Va. 24504. Non-public institution. Affiliated with the Christian Church, Disciples of Christ. Established as Virginia Christian College 1903. Adopted present name 1919.

Lyndon Institute 1911. See Lyndon State College, Lyndonville, Vt.

LYNDON STATE COLLEGE. Lyndonville, Vt. 05851. State institution. Established as Lyndon Institute 1911. Became: Lyndon Teachers College 1940. Adopted present name 1962.

Lyndon Teachers College 1940. See Lyndon State College, Lyndonville, Vt.

- M -

M. J. Lewi College of Podiatry 1957. See New York College of
Podiatric Medicine, New York, N. Y.

MACALESTER COLLEGE. St. Paul, Minn. 55101. Non-public institution. Affiliated with The United Presbyterian Church in the U. S.
Established as the Baldwin School 1853. Became: Baldwin University 1864; Jesus College 1872. Adopted present name 1874.

McComb Female Institute 1910. See Belhaven College, Jackson,
Miss.

McKee School for Negro Youth 1863. See Knoxville College, Knoxville, Tenn.

McKENDREE COLLEGE. Lebanon, Ill. 62254. Non-public institution. Affiliated with the Southern Illinois Conference of The United
Methodist Church. Established as Lebanon Seminary 1828. Adopted
present name 1830.

McKenzie College 1873. See Southwestern University, Georgetown,
Tex.

The McKicken University 1859. See University of Cincinnati, Cincinnati, Oh.

Mackinac College, Mackinac Island, Mich. Closed June 1973.

Maclay College of Theology, San Fernando 1885. See School of
Theology At Claremont, Calif.

McMinville College 1890. See Linfield College, McMinnville, Ore.

MacMURRAY COLLEGE. Jacksonville, Ill. 62650. Non-public insti-
tution. Affiliated with the Central Illinois Conference of The United
Methodist Church. Established as Illinois Female Academy 1846.
Became: Illinois Conference Female College 1851; Illinois Female
College 1863; Illinois Woman's College 1899; MacMurray College for
Women 1930. Adopted present name 1953. Merged with MacMurray
College (for men) 1969.

MacMurray College for Women 1930. See MacMurray College,
Jacksonville, Ill.

McMURRY COLLEGE. Abilene, Tex. 79605. Non-public institution.
Affiliated with The United Methodist Church. Established under pres-
ent name 1922. Merged with Dallas Institute of Vocal and Dramatic
Art 1947.

McNeese State College 1950. See McNeese State University, Lake
Charles, La.

McNEESE STATE UNIVERSITY. Lake Charles, La. 70601. State
institution. Established as Lake Charles Junior College, a division
of La. State University 1939. Became: John McNeese Junior College 1940; McNeese State College 1950, after becoming independent.
Adopted present name 1970.

McPHERSON COLLEGE. McPherson, Kan. 67460. Non-public institution. Affiliated with the Church of the Brethren. Established as
McPherson College and Industrial Institute 1887. Adopted present
name 1898.

McPherson College and Industrial Institute 1887. See McPherson
College, McPherson, Kan.

Madawaska Training School 1878. See University of Maine at Fort
Kent, Fort Kent, Me.

MADISON COLLEGE. Harrisonburg, Va. 22801. State institution.
Established as Normal and Industrial School for Women 1908. Be-
came: State Normal School for Women at Harrisonburg 1914; State
Teachers College at Harrisonburg 1924. Adopted present name 1938.

Madison College 1849. See Waynesburg College, Waynesburg, Pa.

Madison Normal School 1881. See Dakota State College, Madison, S.D.

Madison University 1846. See Colgate University, Hamilton, N.Y.

MADONNA COLLEGE. Livonia, Mich. 48150. Non-public institution.
Owned and operated by the Felician Sisters, O.F.M. of Detroit, Roman Catholic Church. Established as Presentation Junior College
1937. Adopted present name 1947.

Maine Literary and Theological Institution 1813. See Colby College,
Waterville, Me.

MALONE COLLEGE. Canton, Oh. 44709. Non-public institution.
Controlled by The Evangelical Friends Church-Eastern Region. Es-
tablished as Christian Workers Training School 1892. Became:
Friends Bible Institute and Training School 1899; Cleveland Bible
Institute 1911; Cleveland Bible College 1937. Adopted present name
1957.

MANCHESTER COLLEGE. North Manchester, Ind. 46962. Non-
public institution. Affiliated with the Church of the Brethren. (Purchased 1895). Established as Roanoke Classical Seminary 1860.
Adopted present name 1889. Merged with Mount Morris College
1932.

MANHATTAN COLLEGE. Riverdale, Bronx, N.Y. 10471. Non-public institution.   Sponsored by the Christian Brothers, Roman Catholic Church.   Established as Academy of the Holy Infancy 1853. Adopted present name 1863.

Manhattanville Academy 1841.   See   Manhattanville College, Purchase, N. Y.

MANHATTANVILLE COLLEGE.   Purchase, N. Y. 10577.   Non-public institution.   Established as Manhattanville Academy 1841.   Became: College of Sacred Heart 1917; Manhattanville College of the Sacred Heart 1937.   Adopted present name 1966.

Manhattanville College of the Sacred Heart 1937.   See   Manhattanville College, Purchase, N. Y.

Mankato State College 1957.   See   Mankato State University, Mankato, Minn.

Mankato State Normal School 1867.   See   Mankato State University, Mankato, Minn.

MANKATO STATE UNIVERSITY.   Mankato, Minn. 56001.   State institution.   Established as Mankato State Normal School 1867.   Became: Mankato State College 1957.   Adopted present name 1975.

MANNES COLLEGE OF MUSIC.   New York, N. Y. 10021.   Non-public institution.   Established as Mannes Music School 1940 by David and Clara Mannes.   Adopted present name 1953.

Mannes Music School 1940.   See   Mannes College of Music, New York, N. Y.

Mansfield Classical Seminary 1854.   See   Mansfield State College, Mansfield, Pa.

MANSFIELD STATE COLLEGE.   Mansfield, Pa. 16933.   State institution.   Established as Mansfield Classical Seminary 1854.   Became: State Normal School, Mansfield, Pa. 1862; Mansfield State Normal School 1920; Mansfield State Teachers College 1927.   Adopted present name 1960.

Mansfield State Normal School 1920.   See   Mansfield State College, Mansfield, Pa.

Mansfield State Teachers College 1927.   See   Mansfield State College, Mansfield, Pa.

MARIAN COLLEGE.   Indianapolis, Ind. 46222.   Non-public institution.   Conducted by the Sisters of St. Francis, Oldenberg, Ind, Roman Catholic Church.   Established as St. Francis Normal School for Women 1851.   Became: Immaculate Conception Junior College 1924.   Adopted present name 1938.

Marian College 1936. See Marian College of Fond du Lac, Fond du Lac, Wisc.

Marian College 1946. See Marist College, Poughkeepsie, N.Y.

MARIAN COLLEGE OF FOND du LAC. Fond du Lac, Wisc. Non-public institution. Conducted by the Sisters of The Congregation of St. Agnes, Roman Catholic Church. Established as Marian College 1936. Adopted present name 1960.

Marillac College, St. Louis, Mo. Closed May 1975.

Marine Biological Station of San Diego 1903. See University of California, San Diego, LaJolla, Calif.

MARIST COLLEGE. Poughkeepsie, N.Y. 12601. Non-public institution. Established as Marist Training School 1930. Became: Marian College 1946. Adopted present name 1960.

Marist Training School 1930. See Marist College, Poughkeepsie, N.Y.

Mark Hopkins Institute 1893. See San Francisco Art Institute, San Francisco, Calif.

Marquette College 1864. See Marquette University, Milwaukee, Wisc.

Marquette School of Medicine 1967. See The Medical College of Wisconsin, Milwaukee, Wisc.

MARQUETTE UNIVERSITY. Milwaukee, Wisc. 53233. Non-public institution. Conducted under the auspices of the Society of Jesus, Roman Catholic Church. Established as St. Aloysius Academy 1857. Became: Marquette College 1864. Adopted present name 1907.

Marquette University School of Medicine 1918. See The Medical College of Wisconsin, Milwaukee, Wisc.

MARS HILL COLLEGE. Mars Hill, N.C. 28754. Non-public institution. Affiliated with the North Carolina Baptist State Convention (Southern Baptist). Established as French Broad Baptist Institute 1856. Adopted present name 1859.

Marshall Academy 1837. See Marshall University, Huntington, W.Va.

Marshall College 1853. See Franklin and Marshall College, Lancaster, Pa.

Marshall College 1858. See Marshall University, Huntington, W.Va.

MARSHALL UNIVERSITY. Huntington, W.Va. 25701. State institu-

tion. Established as Marshall Academy 1837. Became: Marshall
College 1858, under West Virginia Conference of Methodist Episcopal
Church; West Virginia State Normal School 1867, when state assumed
control. Adopted present name 1961.

Marvin College 1922-25. See Central Methodist College, Fayette,
Mo.

MARY BALDWIN COLLEGE. Staunton, Va. 24401. Non-public in-
stitution. Affiliated with the Synod of Virginia of the Presbyterian
Church in the U.S. Established as Augusta Female Academy 1842.
Became: Mary Baldwin Seminary 1895. Adopted present name 1923.

Mary Baldwin Seminary 1895. See Mary Baldwin College, Staunton,
Va.

MARY HARDIN-BAYLOR COLLEGE. Belton, Tex. 76513. Non-
public institution. Affiliated with the Southern Baptist Convention.
Established as Women's Division Baylor Female College 1866; Baylor College for Women 1924. Adopted present name 1934.

Mary Immaculate Seminary 1939. See Mary Immaculate Seminary
and College, Northampton, Pa.

MARY IMMACULATE SEMINARY AND COLLEGE. Northampton, Pa.
18067. Non-public institution. Owned by the Eastern Province of
the Congregation of the Mission, Roman Catholic Church. Established as Seminary of St. Mary of the Barrens, Perryville, Mo.
1818. Became: St. Vincent's Seminary 1862, after moving to St.
Louis, Mo.; Mary Immaculate Seminary 1939, after moving to Ger-
mantown, Pa. 1868, then to present location. Adopted present name
1955.

Mary Manse College, Toledo, Oh. Closed Aug. 1975.

MARY WASHINGTON COLLEGE. Fredericksburg, Va. 22401. Non-
public institution. Established as Fredericksburg Normal and Industrial School for Women 1908. Became: State Teachers College,
Fredericksburg 1924; Mary Washington College 1938; Mary Washington College of the University of Virginia 1944. Adopted present name
1972, after becoming independent.

Mary Washington College 1938. See Mary Washington College,
Fredericksburg, Va.

Mary Washington College of the University of Virginia 1944. See
Mary Washington College, Fredericksburg, Va.

MARYCREST COLLEGE. Davenport, Ia. 52804. Non-public institution. Owned by the Congregation of the Humility of Mary, Roman
Catholic Church. Established as Women's Division of St. Ambrose
College 1939. Incorporated as separate college, adopted present
name 1954.

Maryglade College, Memphis, Mich. Closed July 1974.

MARYGROVE COLLEGE. Detroit, Mich. 48221. Non-public institution. Owned by Sisters Servants of the Immaculate Heart of Mary,
Monroe, Mich. Roman Catholic Church. Established as Saint Mary's
College at Monroe, Mich. 1905. Adopted present name and moved
to present location 1927.

Maryknoll College, Glen Ellyn, Ill. Closed May, 1971.

Maryland State College 1948. See University of Maryland, Eastern
Shore, Princess Anne, Md.

Maryland State College of Agriculture 1920. See University of
Maryland, College Park, Md.

Maryland State Normal School 1865. See Towson State University,
Baltimore, Md.

Maryland State Normal School 1925. See Salisbury State College,
Salisbury, Md.

Maryland State Teachers College at Bowie 1938. See Bowie State
College, Bowie, Md.

Marylhurst College 1930. See Marylhurst Education Center, Marylhurst, Ore.

MARYLHURST EDUCATION CENTER. Marylhurst, Ore. 97036.
Non-public institution. Conducted by the Sisters of the Holy Names
of Jesus and Mary, Roman Catholic Church. Established as St.
Mary's Academy 1859. Became: St. Mary's Academy and College
1893; Marylhurst College 1930. Adopted present name 1974.

MARYMOUNT COLLEGE. Los Angeles, Calif. 90045. Non-public
institution. Conducted by the Religious Heart of Mary, Roman Catholic Church. Established 1933. Became affiliated with Loyola University of Los Angeles 1968.

Marymount College 1922. See Marymount College of Kansas, Salina, Kan.

Marymount College, City Campus, Marymount College, Tarrytown
1947. See Marymount Manhattan College, New York, N.Y.

MARYMOUNT COLLEGE OF KANSAS. Salina, Kan. 67401. Non-
public institution. Owned by the Sisters of St. Joseph of Concordia,
Roman Catholic Church. Established as Marymount College 1922.
Adopted present name 1970.

Marymount College of Los Angeles 1968. See Loyola Marymount
University, Los Angeles, Calif.

MARYMOUNT COLLEGE OF VIRGINIA. Arlington, Va. 22207. Non-public institution. Affiliated with the Religious of the Sacred Heart, Roman Catholic Church. Established as Marymount Junior College 1950 by Marymount College, Tarrytown, N.Y. Adopted present name 1960.

Marymount Junior College 1936. See Marymount Manhattan College, New York, N.Y.

Marymount Junior College 1950. See Marymount College of Virginia, Arlington, Va.

MARYMOUNT MANHATTAN COLLEGE. New York, N.Y. 10021. Non-public institution. Controlled by the Religious of the Sacred Heart of Mary, Roman Catholic Church. Established as Marymount Junior College 1936. Became: Marymount College, City Campus, Marymount College, Tarrytown 1947. Adopted present name 1961.

MARYVILLE COLLEGE. Maryville, Tenn. 37801. Non-public institution. Related to The United Presbyterian Church in the U.S.A. Established as Southern and Western Theological Seminary 1819. Adopted present name 1842.

MARYVILLE COLLEGE. St. Louis, Mo. 63141. Non-public institution. Sponsored by the St. Louis Province of the Society of the Sacred Heart of Jesus, Roman Catholic Church. Established as Convent of the Sacred Heart 1827. Became: Maryville College and Academy of the Sacred Heart 1920; Maryville College of the Sacred Heart 1929; Mercy Junior College 1970. Adopted present name 1972.

Maryville College and Academy of the Sacred Heart 1920. See Maryville College, St. Louis, Mo.

Maryville College of the Sacred Heart 1929. See Maryville College, St. Louis, Mo.

Marywood College 1923. See Aquinas College, Grand Rapids, Mich.

Massachusetts Agricultural College 1863. See University of Massachusetts-Amherst, Amherst, Mass.

MASSACHUSETTS COLLEGE OF ART. Boston, Mass. 02115. State institution. Established as Massachusetts Normal Art School 1873. Became: Massachusetts School of Art 1926. Adopted present name 1959.

Massachusetts College of Optometry 1950. See New England College of Optometry, Boston, Mass.

MASSACHUSETTS MARITIME ACADEMY. Buzzards Bay, Mass. 02532. State institution. Established as Massachusetts Nautical Training School 1891. Adopted present name 1942.

Massachusetts Nautical Training School 1891.   See   Massachusetts
Maritime Academy, Buzzards Bay, Mass.

Massachusetts Normal Art School 1873.   See   Massachusetts College
of Art, Boston, Mass.

Massachusetts School of Art 1926.   See   Massachusetts College of
Art, Boston, Mass.

Massachusetts School of Optometry 1909.   See   New England College
of Optometry, Boston, Mass.

Massachusetts State College 1931.   See   University of Massachusetts-
Amherst, Amherst, Mass.

Mater Christi Seminary, Albany, N.Y.   Closed June 1969.

Mauna Olu College of Maui, Paia, Haw.   1972.   See   United States
International University, San Diego, Calif.

MAYVILLE STATE COLLEGE.   Mayville, N.D. 58257.   State institution.   Established as State Normal School 1889.   Became: State
Teachers College 1925.   Adopted present name 1963.

Mechanics Institute 1891.   See   Rochester Institute of Technology,
Rochester, N.Y.

MEDAILLE COLLEGE.   Buffalo, N.Y. 14214.   Non-public institution.   Established as Institute of the Sisters of St. Joseph 1892.
Became: Mount St. Joseph Normal School 1927; Mount St. Joseph
Teachers College 1937; Mount St. Joseph College 1964.   Adopted
present name 1967.

Medical Academy of Georgia 1828.   See   Medical College of Georgia,
Augusta, Ga.

MEDICAL COLLEGE OF GEORGIA.   Augusta, Ga. 30902.   State
institution.   Established as Medical Academy of Georgia 1828 by
Dr. William R. Waring and others.   Became: Medical Institute of
Georgia 1829; Medical College of Georgia 1833; Medical Department
of the University of Georgia 1873, after state assumed control.
Adopted present name 1950.

Medical College of Ohio 1819.   See   University of Cincinnati, Cincinnati, Oh.

THE MEDICAL COLLEGE OF PENNSYLVANIA.   Philadelphia, Pa.
19129.   Non-public institution.   Established as Female Medical College of Pennsylvania 1850 by William J. Mullen, Joseph S. Long-
shore and others.   Became: Woman's Medical College of Pennsylvania 1867.   Adopted present name 1970.

Medical College of South Carolina 1824.   See   Medical University of
South Carolina, Charleston, S.C.

Medical College of University of Louisiana 1847. See Tulane University, New Orleans, La.

Medical College of Virginia 1968. See Virginia Commonwealth University, Richmond, Va.

THE MEDICAL COLLEGE OF WISCONSIN. Milwaukee, Wisc. 53233. Non-public institution, receiving state assistance. Established as School of Medicine, Marquette University 1913, after merger of Wisconsin College of Physicians and Surgeons 1913 and Milwaukee Medical College 1913. Became: Marquette University School of Medicine 1918; Marquette School of Medicine 1967, after becoming independent. Adopted present name 1970.

Medical Department of Central Tennessee College 1876. See Meharry Medical College, Nashville, Tenn.

Medical Department of the University of Georgia. See Medical College of Georgia, Augusta, Ga.

Medical Institute of Georgia 1829. See Medical College of Georgia, Augusta, Ga.

MEDICAL UNIVERSITY OF SOUTH CAROLINA. Charleston, S. C. 29401. State institution. Established as Medical College of South Carolina 1824. Adopted present name 1969.

MEHARRY MEDICAL COLLEGE. Nashville, Tenn. 37208. Non-public institution. Affiliated with the United Methodist Episcopal Church. Established as Medical Department of Central Tennessee College 1876 by the five Meharry brothers (Hugh, Alexander, Jesse, David, Samuel). Became: Meharry Medical College of Walden University 1900. Adopted present name 1915.

Meharry Medical College of Walden University 1900. See Meharry Medical College, Nashville, Tenn.

Mellon Institute 1967. See Carnegie-Mellon University, Pittsburgh, Pa.

THE MEMPHIS ACADEMY OF ARTS. Memphis, Tenn. 38112. Non-public institution partially supported by the City of Memphis. Established as Mid-South School of Fine Arts 1936. Adopted present name 1936.

Memphis Conference Female Institute 1843. See Lambuth College, Jackson, Tenn.

Memphis State College 1941. See Memphis State University, Memphis, Tenn.

MEMPHIS STATE UNIVERSITY. Memphis, Tenn. 38111. State institution. Established as West Tennessee State Normal School 1909.

Became: West Tennessee State Teachers College 1929; Memphis State College 1941. Adopted present name 1957.

Mendota College 1893. See Aurora College, Aurora, Ill.

MENLO COLLEGE SCHOOL OF BUSINESS ADMINISTRATION. Menlo Park, Calif. 94025. Non-public institution. Established as William Warren School 1915. Became: Menlo School and Junior College 1927. Adopted present name 1949.

Menlo School and Junior College 1927. See Menlo College School of Business Administration, Menlo Park, Calif.

Mercer Institute 1830. See Mercer University, Macon, Ga.

MERCER UNIVERSITY. Macon, Ga. 31207. Non-public institution. Owned by the Georgia Baptist Convention (Southern Baptist). Established as Mercer Institute 1830. Adopted present name 1838. Merged with Atlanta Baptist College, Atlanta, 1973.

MERCY COLLEGE. Dobbs Ferry, N.Y. 10522. Non-public institution. Established as Mercy Junior College 1950. Adopted present name 1952.

Mercy College 1941. See Mercy College of Detroit, Detroit, Mich.

MERCY COLLEGE OF DETROIT. Detroit, Mich. 48219. Non-public institution. Conducted by the Sisters of Mercy, Province of Detroit, Roman Catholic Church. Established as Mercy College 1941. Adopted present name 1963.

Mercy Junior College 1950. See Mercy College, Dobbs Ferry, N.Y.

Mercy Junior College 1970. See Maryville College, St. Louis, Mo.

MEREDITH COLLEGE. Raleigh, N.C. Non-public institution. Affiliated with the North Carolina Baptist State Convention (Southern Baptist). Established as Baptist Female University 1891. Became: Baptist University for Women 1905. Adopted present name 1909.

MERRIMACK COLLEGE. North Andover, Mass. 01845. Non-public institution. Conducted by the Order of St. Augustine, Roman Catholic Church. Established as Augustinian College of the Merrimack Valley 1947. Adopted present name 1969.

Merriweather Campus of Long Island University 1954. See C. W. Post Center, Greenvale, N.Y.

Messiah Bible College 1924. See Messiah College, Grantham, Pa.

Messiah Bible School and Missionary Training Home 1909. See Messiah College, Grantham, Pa.

MESSIAH COLLEGE. Grantham, Pa. 17027. Non-public institution.
Related to the Brethren in Christ Church. Established as Messiah
Bible School and Missionary Training Home 1909. Became: Messiah
Bible College 1924. Adopted present name 1951. Merged with Up-
land College 1965.

Methodist General Biblical Institute 1839, Newbury, Vt. See Boston University, Boston, Mass.

Methodist Protestant College, West Lafayette, Oh. 1916. See Adrian
College, Adrian, Mich.

Methodist University of Oklahoma 1911. See Oklahoma City University, Oklahoma City, Okla.

Metropolitan College of Chiropractic and Mechanotherapy 1973. See
National College of Chiropractic, Lombard, Ill.

METROPOLITAN STATE UNIVERSITY. St. Paul, Minn. 55101.
State institution. Established as Minnesota Metropolitan State College
1971. Adopted present name 1976.

Michigan Agricultural College 1909. See Michigan State University,
East Lansing, Mich.

Michigan and Huron Institute 1833. See Kalamazoo College, Kalamazoo, Mich.

Michigan Central College at Spring Arbor, Mich. 1844. See Hillsdale College, Hillsdale, Mich.

Michigan College of Mines 1897. See Michigan Technological University, Houghton, Mich.

Michigan College of Mining and Technology 1927. See Michigan
Technological University, Houghton, Mich.

Michigan Mining School 1885. See Michigan Technological University, Houghton, Mich.

Michigan State College of Agriculture and Applied Science 1925.
See Michigan State University, East Lansing, Mich.

Michigan State Normal College 1899. See Eastern Michigan University, Ypsilanti, Mich.

Michigan State Normal School 1849. See Eastern Michigan University, Ypsilanti, Mich.

MICHIGAN STATE UNIVERSITY. East Lansing, Mich. 48823. State
institution. Established as Agricultural College of State of Michigan
1855. Became: State Agricultural College 1861; Michigan Agricultural College 1909; Michigan State College of Agriculture and Applied

Science 1925; Michigan State University of Agriculture and Applied Science 1955. Adopted present name 1964.

Michigan State University at Oakland 1957. See Oakland University, Rochester, Mich.

Michigan State University of Agriculture and Applied Science 1955. See Michigan State University, East Lansing, Mich.

MICHIGAN TECHNOLOGICAL UNIVERSITY. Houghton, Mich. 49931. State institution. Established as Michigan Mining School 1885. Became: Michigan College of Mines 1897; Michigan College of Mining and Technology 1927. Adopted present name 1964.

Middle Tennessee State College 1943. See Middle Tennessee State University, Murfreesboro, Tenn.

Middle Tennessee State Normal School 1909. See Middle Tennessee State University, Murfreesboro, Tenn.

Middle Tennessee State Teachers College 1926. See Middle Tennessee State University, Murfreesboro, Tenn.

MIDDLE TENNESSEE STATE UNIVERSITY. Murfreesboro, Tenn. 37130. State institution. Established as Middle Tennessee State Normal School 1909. Became: Middle Tennessee State Teachers College 1926; State Teachers College, Murfreesboro 1929; Middle Tennessee State College 1943. Adopted present name 1965.

Midland College, Atchinson 1883. See Midland Lutheran College, Fremont, Neb.

MIDLAND LUTHERAN COLLEGE. Fremont, Neb. 68025. Non-public institution. Affiliated with the Nebraska and Rocky Mountain Synods of the Lutheran Church in America. Established as Midland College, Atchinson 1883; merged with Fremont College, moved to Fremont 1919; merged with Luther College and adopted present name 1962.

Mid-South School of Fine Arts 1936. See The Memphis Academy of Arts, Memphis, Tenn.

Midwest Bible and Missionary Institute 1961. See Calvary Bible College, Kansas City, Mo.

Midwest Christian Junior College 1953. See Dordt College, Sioux Center, Ia.

Midwestern College, Denison, Ia. Closed Oct. 1970.

MIDWESTERN STATE UNIVERSITY. Wichita Falls, Tex. 76308. State institution. Established as Wichita Falls Junior College 1922. Became: Hardin Junior College 1937; Hardin College 1946; Midwestern University 1950. Adopted present name 1975.

Midwestern University 1950. See Midwestern State University, Wichita Falls, Tex.

MILES COLLEGE. Birmingham, Ala. 35208. Non-public institution. Owned by the Christian Methodist Episcopal Church. Established as Miles Memorial College 1905. Adopted present name 1941.

Miles Memorial College 1905. See Miles College, Birmingham, Ala.

Millersville Academy 1854. See Millersville State College, Millersville, Pa.

MILLERSVILLE STATE COLLEGE. Millersville, Pa. 17551. State institution. Established as Millersville Academy 1854. Became: Lancaster County Normal Institute 1855; Millersville State Normal School 1859; State Teachers College, Millersville, Pa. 1927. Adopted present name 1959.

Millersville State Normal School 1859. See Millersville State College, Millersville, Pa.

MILLIGAN COLLEGE. Milligan College, Tenn. 37682. Non-public institution. Affiliated with the Christian Churches and Church of Christ. Established as Buffalo Male and Female Institute 1866. Adopted present name 1881.

MILLIKIN UNIVERSITY. Decatur, Ill. 62522. Non-public institution. Affiliated with The United Presbyterian Church in the U.S. Established as The Decatur College and Industrial School of the James Millikin University 1901. Adopted present name 1953.

MILLS COLLEGE. Oakland, Calif. 94613. Non-public institution. Established as Young Ladies Seminary, Benecia 1852. Moved to present location 1871. Became: Mills Seminary and College 1877. Adopted present name 1885.

Mills College of Education, New York, N.Y. Closed June 1974.

Mills Seminary and College 1877. See Mills College, Oakland, Calif.

Milton Academy 1856. See Milton College, Milton, Wisc.

MILTON COLLEGE. Milton, Wisc. 53563. Non-public institution. Established as Du Lac Academy 1844. Became: Milton Academy 1856. Adopted present name 1867.

Milwaukee-Downer College 1964. See Lawrence University, Appleton, Wisc.

Milwaukee Medical College 1913. See The Medical College of Wisconsin, Milwaukee, Wisc.

MILWAUKEE SCHOOL OF ENGINEERING. Milwaukee, Wisc. 53201.
Non-public institution. Established as School of Engineering of Milwaukee 1903. Adopted present name 1932.

MINNEAPOLIS COLLEGE OF ART AND DESIGN. Minneapolis, Minn.
55404. Non-public institution. Established as Minneapolis School of
Fine Art 1886. Became: Minneapolis School of Art 1912. Adopted
present name 1970.

Minneapolis-Minnesota College of Law 1956. See William Mitchell
College of Law, St. Paul, Minn.

Minneapolis School of Art 1912. See Minneapolis College of Art
and Design, Minneapolis, Minn.

Minneapolis School of Fine Art 1886. See Minneapolis College of
Art and Design, Minneapolis, Minn.

Minnesota Metropolitan State College 1971. See Metropolitan State
University, St. Paul, Minn.

Minn's Evening Normal School 1857. See San Jose State University,
San Jose, Calif.

MINOT STATE COLLEGE. Minot, S.D. 58701. State institution.
Established as Northwestern Normal School 1913. Became: Minot
State Teachers College 1924. Adopted present name 1964.

Minot State Teachers College 1924. See Minot State College,
Minot, S.D.

Mission House 1862. See Lakeland College, Sheboygan, Wisc.

Missionary Institute of the Evangelical Lutheran Church 1858. See
Susquehanna University, Selingsgrove, Pa.

Missionary Training Institute 1882. See Nyack College, Nyack,
N.Y.

Mississippi Academy 1827. See Mississippi College, Clinton, Miss.

Mississippi Agricultural and Mechanical College 1878. See Mississippi State University, Starkville, Miss.

MISSISSIPPI COLLEGE. Clinton, Miss. 39058. Non-public institution. Established as Hampstead Academy 1826. Became: Mississippi Academy 1827. Adopted present name 1830. Absorbed Hillman College for Women 1942.

Mississippi Industrial Institute and College 1884. See Mississippi
University for Women, Columbus, Miss.

Mississippi Negro Training School 1940. See Jackson State University, Jackson, Miss.

Mississippi Normal College 1910. See University of Southern Mississippi, Hattiesburg, Miss.

Mississippi Southern College 1940. See University of Southern Mississippi, Hattiesburg, Miss.

Mississippi State College 1932. See Mississippi State University, Starkville, Miss.

Mississippi State College for Women 1920. See Mississippi University for Women, Columbus, Miss.

MISSISSIPPI STATE UNIVERSITY. Starkville, Miss. 39762. State institution. Established as Mississippi Agricultural and Mechanical College 1878. Became: Mississippi State College 1932. Adopted present name 1958.

Mississippi Synodical College of Holly Springs 1939. See Belhaven College, Jackson, Miss.

MISSISSIPPI UNIVERSITY FOR WOMEN. Columbus, Miss. 39701. State institution. Established as Mississippi Industrial Institute and College 1884. Became: Mississippi State College for Women 1920. Adopted present name 1974.

MISSISSIPPI VALLEY STATE COLLEGE. Itta Bena, Miss. 38941. State institution. Established as Mississippi Vocational College 1946. Adopted present name 1964.

Mississippi Vocational College 1946. See Mississippi Valley State College, Itta Bena, Miss.

Mississippi Women's College 1911. See William Carey College, Hattiesburg, Miss.

MISSOURI BAPTIST COLLEGE. St. Louis, Mo. 63141. Non-public institution. Owned and supported by the Missouri Baptist Convention. Established as St. Louis Baptist College 1957 by the St. Louis Baptist Association and the Missouri Baptist Convention. Was unofficially known as the Hannibal-LaGrange Extension Center. Became: Missouri Baptist College of St. Louis 1963. Adopted present name 1973.

Missouri Baptist College of St. Louis 1963. See Missouri Baptist College, St. Louis, Mo.

MISSOURI SOUTHERN STATE COLLEGE. Joplin, Missouri 64801. State institution. Established as Joplin Junior College 1937. Became: Jasper County Junior College 1964. Adopted present name 1965.

Missouri State Normal School 1906. See Southwest Missouri State University, Springfield, Mo.

MISSOURI WESTERN COLLEGE. St. Joseph, Mo. 64507. State institution. Established as St. Joseph Junior College 1915. Became: Missouri Western Junior College 1966. Adopted present name 1968.

Missouri Western Junior College 1966. See Missouri Western College, St. Joseph, Mo.

Mitchell Home School 1903. See Pfeiffer College, Misenheimer, N. C.

Mitchell Junior College 1928. See Pfeiffer College, Misenheimer, N. C.

Molloy Catholic College for Women 1955. See Molloy College, Rockville Centre, N. Y.

MOLLOY COLLEGE. Rockville Centre, N. Y. 11570. Non-public institution. Affiliated with the Dominican Sisters of Amityville, N. Y. Roman Catholic Church. Established as Malloy Catholic College for Women 1955. Adopted present name 1971.

MONMOUTH COLLEGE. West Long Branch, N. J. 07764. Non-public institution. Established as Monmouth Junior College 1933. Adopted present name 1956.

Monmouth Junior College 1933. See Monmouth College, West Long Branch, N. J.

Monmouth University 1856. See Oregon College of Education, Monmouth, Ore.

Monogalia Academy 1814. See West Virginia University, Morgantown, W. Va.

Monroe College of Oratory 1881. See Emerson College, Boston, Mass.

Monroe Female College 1867. See Tift College, Forsyth, Ga.

MONTANA COLLEGE OF MINERAL SCIENCE AND TECHNOLOGY. Butte, Mont. 59701. State institution. Established as Montana School of Mines 1895. Adopted present name 1965.

Montana School of Mines 1895. See Montana College of Mineral Science and Technology, Butte, Mont.

Montana State College 1935. See Montana State University, Bozeman, Mont.

MONTANA STATE UNIVERSITY. Bozeman, Mont. 59715. State institution. Established as Agricultural College of the State of Montana at Bozeman 1893. Became: College of Agriculture and Mechanical Arts 1913; Montana State College 1935. Adopted present name 1965.

Montana State University 1935. See University of Montana, Missoula, Mont.

Montana Wesleyan University 1923. See Rocky Mountain College, Billings, Mont.

MONTCLAIR STATE COLLEGE. Upper Montclair, N. J. 07043. State institution. Established as New Jersey Normal School at Montclair 1908. Became: Montclair State Teachers College 1927. Adopted present name 1958.

Montclair State Teachers College 1927. See Montclair State College, Upper Montclair, N. J.

Montgomery Masonic College 1848. See Southwestern at Memphis, Memphis, Tenn.

Montgomery Preparatory Branch of West Virginia University 1895. See West Virginia Institute of Technology, Montgomery, W. Va.

Monticello College, Godfrey, Ill. Closed June 1971.

Montpelier Seminary 1895. See Vermont College, Montpelier, Vt.

MOORE COLLEGE OF ART. Philadelphia, Pa. 19103. Non-public institution. Established as Moore Institute of Art, Industry and Science 1844. Merged with Philadelphia School of Design 1932. Adopted present name 1963.

Moore Institute of Art, Industry and Science 1844. See Moore College of Art, Philadelphia, Pa.

Moores Hill College 1887. See University of Evansville, Evansville, Ind.

Moores Hill Male and Female Collegiate Institute 1845. See University of Evansville, Evansville, Ind.

Moorhead State College 1957. See Moorhead State University, Moorhead, Minn.

Moorhead State Normal School 1885. See Moorhead State University, Moorhead, Minn.

Moorhead State Teachers College 1921. See Moorhead State University, Moorhead, Minn.

MOORHEAD STATE UNIVERSITY. Moorhead, Minn. 56560. State institution. Established as Moorhead State Normal School 1885. Became: Moorhead State Teachers College 1921; Moorhead State College 1957. Adopted present name 1975.

MORAVIAN COLLEGE. Bethlehem, Pa. 18018. Non-public institution. Affiliated with the Moravian Church in America. Established through merger of Moravian Seminary and College for Women 1954 and Moravian College and Theological Seminary 1954. Adopted present name 1954.

Moravian College and Theological Seminary 1954. See Moravian College, Bethlehem, Pa.

Moravian Seminary and College for Women 1954. See Moravian College, Bethlehem, Pa.

Morehead State College 1948. See Morehead State University, Morehead, Ky.

Morehead State Normal School 1922. See Morehead State University, Morehead, Ky.

Morehead State Normal School and Teachers College 1926. See Morehead State University, Morehead, Ky.

Morehead State Teachers College 1930. See Morehead State University, Morehead, Ky.

MOREHEAD STATE UNIVERSITY. Morehead, Ky. 40351. State institution. Established as Morehead State Normal School 1922. Became: Morehead State Normal School and Teachers College 1926; Morehead State Teachers College 1930; Morehead State College 1948. Adopted present name 1966.

MOREHOUSE COLLEGE. Atlanta, Ga. 30314. Non-public institution. Established as Augusta Institute 1867. Became: Augusta Baptist Seminary 1879; Atlanta Baptist College 1897. Adopted present name 1913.

Morgan Business College 1894. See Thomas College, Waterville, Me.

Morgan College 1890. See Morgan State University, Baltimore, Md.

Morgan State College 1939. See Morgan State University, Baltimore, Md.

MORGAN STATE UNIVERSITY. Baltimore, Md. 21239. State institution. Established as Centenary Biblical Institute 1867. Became: Morgan College 1890; Morgan State College 1939. Adopted present name 1975.

MORNINGSIDE COLLEGE. Sioux City, Ia. 51106. Non-public institution. Affiliated with The United Methodist Church. Established as the University of the Northwest 1889. Adopted present name 1894. Absorbed Charles City College 1914.

MORRIS BROWN COLLEGE. Atlanta, Ga. 30314. Non-public institution. Affiliated with the African Methodist Episcopal Church. Established as Morris Brown College 1881. Became: Morris Brown University 1913. Adopted present name 1929.

Morris Brown University 1913. See Morris Brown College, Atlanta, Ga.

MORRIS HARVEY COLLEGE. Charleston, W. Va. 25304. Non-public institution. Established as Barboursville Seminary 1888. Became: Barboursville College 1889 under control of the Methodist Church, South. Adopted present name 1901. Became independent institution 1941.

Mossy Creek Baptist College 1856. See Carson-Newman College, Jefferson City, Tenn.

Mossy Creek Baptist Seminary 1851. See Carson-Newman College, Jefferson City, Tenn.

Mount Alvernia College, Newton, Mass. Closed June 1973.

Mount Angel College 1887. See Mount Angel Seminary, St. Benedict, Ore.

Mount Angel College, Mount Angel, Ore. Closed June 1973.

MOUNT ANGEL SEMINARY. St. Benedict, Ore. 97373. Non-public institution. Owned by the Mount Angel Abbey, Roman Catholic Church. Established as Mount Angel College 1887. Adopted present name 1947.

Mount Carroll Seminary 1853. See Shimer College, Mt. Carroll, Ill.

MOUNT HOLYOKE COLLEGE. South Hadley, Mass. 01075. Non-public institution. Established as Mount Holyoke Female Seminary 1836. Became: Mount Holyoke Seminary and College 1888. Adopted present name 1893.

Mount Holyoke Female Seminary 1836. See Mount Holyoke College, South Hadley, Mass.

Mount Holyoke Seminary and College 1888. See Mount Holyoke College, South Hadley, Mass.

MOUNT MARTY COLLEGE. Yankton, S. D. 57078. Non-public institution. Affiliated with the Sisters of St. Benedict of Sacred Heart, Roman Catholic Church. Established as Mount Marty Junior College 1936. Adopted present name 1948.

Mount Marty Junior College 1936. See Mount Marty College, Yankton, S. D.

MOUNT MARY COLLEGE. Milwaukee, Wisc. 53222. Non-public institution. Owned by the School Sisters of Notre Dame, Roman Catholic Church. Established as St. Mary's College and Academy 1913 at Prairie du Chien, Wisc. Moved to present location and adopted present name 1929.

Mount Mercy College 1929. See Carlow College, Pittsburgh, Pa.

Mount Morris College 1932. See Manchester College, North Manchester, Ind.

Mount St. Agnes College for Women 1971. See Loyola College, Baltimore, Md.

Mount St. Bernard 1850. See Loras College, Dubuque, Ia.

Mount St. Charles College 1909. See Carroll College, Helena, Mont.

Mount St. Joseph Academy 1858. See Chestnut Hill College, Philadelphia, Pa.

Mount St. Joseph Academy 1878. See Brescia College, Owensboro, Ky.

Mount St. Joseph Academy 1879. See Clarke College, Dubuque, Ia.

Mount St. Joseph College 1901. See Clarke College, Dubuque, Ia.

Mount St. Joseph College 1925. See Saint Joseph College, West Hartford, Conn.

Mount St. Joseph College 1964. See Medaille College, Buffalo, N.Y.

Mount St. Joseph College, Wakefield, R.I. Closed Dec. 1975.

Mount St. Joseph Junior College 1925. See Brescia College, Owensboro, Ky.

Mount St. Joseph Normal School 1927. See Medaille College, Buffalo, N.Y.

Mount St. Joseph Teachers College 1937. See Medaille College, Buffalo, N.Y.

MOUNT ST. MARY COLLEGE. Newburgh, N.Y. 12550. Non-public institution. Controlled by the Sisters of St. Dominic, Roman Catholic Church. Established as Mount St. Mary Normal and Training School 1930. Adopted present name 1954.

Mount St. Mary College 1905. See Georgian Court College, Lakewood, N.J.

Mount St. Mary Normal and Training School 1930. See Mount St. Mary College, Newburgh, N.Y.

Mount St. Mary's of the West 1851.   See   The Athenaeum of Ohio, Norwood, Cincinnati, Oh.

Mount St. Paul College, Waukesha, Wisc.   Closed June 1970.

Mount St. Scholastica College 1924.   See   Benedictine College, Atchison, Kan.

MOUNT UNION COLLEGE.   Alliance, Oh. 44601.   Non-public institution.   Affiliated with the East Ohio, West Ohio, Western Pennsylvania Conference of the United Methodist Church.   Established as Mount Union Seminary 1849.   Adopted present name 1858.   Merged with Scio College 1911.

Mount Union Seminary 1849.   See   Mount Union College, Alliance, Oh.

Mount Vernon College 1885.   See   Peru State College, Peru, Neb.

MUHLENBERG COLLEGE.   Allentown, Pa. 18104.   Non-public institution.   Affiliated with the Lutheran Church in America.   Established as Allentown Seminary 1848.   Became: Allentown Collegiate Institute and Military Academy 1864.   Sponsorship assumed by the Lutheran Church 1867.   Adopted present name 1867.

Muncie Normal Institute 1912.   See   Ball State University, Muncie, Ind.

Municipal University of Akron 1913.   See   University of Akron, Akron, Oh.

Municipal University of Omaha 1931.   See   University of Nebraska at Omaha, Omaha, Neb.

Municipal University of Wichita 1926.   See   Wichita State University, Wichita, Kan.

Murphy Collegiate Institute 1938.   See   Lee College, Cleveland, Tenn.

Murray State College 1948.   See   Murray State University, Murray, Ky.

Murray State Normal School 1922.   See   Murray State University, Murray, Ky.

Murray State Normal School and Teachers College 1926.   See   Murray State University, Murray, Ky.

Murray State Teachers College 1930.   See   Murray State University, Murray, Ky.

MURRAY STATE UNIVERSITY.   Murray, Ky. 42071.   State institution.   Established as Murray State Normal School 1922.   Became: Murray State Normal School and Teachers College 1926; Murray

State Teachers College 1930; Murray State College 1948.   Adopted
present name 1966.

- N -

Nashville Bible School 1891.   See   David Lipscomb College, Nashville, Tenn.

Nassau-Hofstra Memorial 1935.   See   Hofstra University, Hempstead,
N. Y.

NASSON COLLEGE.   Springvale, Me.   04083.   Non-public institution.
Established as Nasson Institute 1912.   Adopted present name 1935.

Nasson Institute 1912.   See   Nasson College, Springvale, Me.

Natchez Seminary 1877.   See   Jackson State University, Jackson,
Miss.

National Agricultural College 1948.   See   Delaware Valley College
of Science and Agriculture, Doylestown, Pa.

National Bible Institute 1895.   See   Philadelphia College of Bible,
Philadelphia, Pa.

National College, Kansas City, Mo.   Closed June 1965.

NATIONAL COLLEGE OF BUSINESS.   Rapid City, S.D. 57701.   Non-
public institution.   Established as National School of Business 1941.
Adopted present name 1963.

NATIONAL COLLEGE OF CHIROPRACTIC.   Lombard, Ill. 60148.
Non-public institution.   Established as National School of Chiroprac-
tic 1906 by Dr. John F. Allen Howard.   Adopted present name 1921.
Merged with: University of Natural Healing Arts 1965; Chiropractic
Institute of New York 1968; Eastern College of Chiropractic 1968;
New York Carver College of Chiropractic 1968; New York College
of Chiropractic 1968; Detroit Chiropractic College 1969; O'Neil Ross
Chiropractic College 1970; International College of Chiropractic 1971;
Lincoln Chiropractic College 1971; Universal Chiropractic College
1971; Metropolitan College of Chiropractic and Mechanotherapy 1973;
Kansas State Chiropractic College 1974; Central States College of
Physiatrics 1976.

NATIONAL COLLEGE OF EDUCATION.   Evanston, Ill. 60201.   Non-
public institution.   Established as Chicago Kindergarten Training
School 1886.   Became: Chicago Kindergarten College 1893; National
Kindergarten College 1912.   Adopted present name 1930.

National Deaf Mute College 1864.   See   Gallaudet College, Washington, D.C.

The National Farm School 1896. See Delaware Valley College of Science and Agriculture, Doylestown, Pa.

The National Farm School and Junior College 1946. See Delaware Valley College of Science and Agriculture, Doylestown, Pa.

National Kindergarten College 1912. See National College of Education, Evanston, Ill.

National Religious Training School and Chatauqua 1919. See North Carolina Central University, Durham, N. C.

National School of Business 1941. See National College of Business, Rapid City, S. D.

National School of Chiropractic 1906. See National College of Chiropractic, Lombard, Ill.

National Teachers Normal and Business College 1907. See Freed-Hardeman College, Henderson, Tenn.

National Training School 1915. See North Carolina Central University, Durham, N. C.

NAVAL POSTGRADUATE SCHOOL. Monterey, Calif. 93940. U. S. federal government institution. Established as School of Marine Engineering, U. S. Naval Academy, Annapolis, Md. 1909. Became: Postgraduate Department of the Naval Academy 1912; U. S. Naval Postgraduate School 1921; all facilities transferred to present location 1951. Adopted present name 1968.

The Naval School 1845. See United States Naval Academy, Annapolis, Md.

Nazareth Academy 1889. See Nazareth College, Kalamazoo, Mich.

NAZARETH COLLEGE. Kalamazoo, Mich. 49074. Non-public institution. Conducted by the Sisters of St. Joseph, Roman Catholic Church. Established as Nazareth Academy 1889. Adopted present name 1924.

Nazareth College 1920. See Spalding College, Louisville, Ky.

Nazareth College in Louisville 1961. See Spalding College, Louisville, Ky.

Nazareth Junior College 1938. See Spalding College, Louisville, Ky.

Nebraska State Normal College 1910. See Chadron State College, Chadron, Neb.

Nebraska State Normal School 1905. See Kearney State College, Kearney, Neb.

Nebraska State Normal School 1910. See Wayne State College, Wayne, Neb.

Nebraska State Normal School and Teachers College 1921. See Wayne State College, Wayne, Neb.

Nebraska State Teachers College 1921. See Kearney State College, Kearney, Neb.

Nebraska State Teachers College 1937. See Chadron State College, Chadron, Neb.

Nebraska State Teachers College 1949. See Wayne State College, Wayne, Neb.

Nebraska State Teachers College at Peru 1949. See Peru State College, Peru, Neb.

Nebraska University, Pontenelle 1858. See Doane College, Crete, Neb.

Needles Institute of Optometry 1926. See Illinois College of Optometry, Chicago, Ill.

Nevada Southern University 1965. See University of Nevada, Las Vegas, Las Vegas, Nev.

Nevada State University 1874. See University of Nevada, Reno, Reno, Nev.

New Bedford Institute of Technology. See Southeastern Massachusetts University, North Dartmouth, Mass.

New Britain Normal School 1849. See Central Connecticut State College, New Britain, Conn.

New College, Sarasota, Fla. See University of South Florida, Tampa, Fla.

NEW ENGLAND COLLEGE OF OPTOMETRY. Boston, Mass. 02115. Non-public institution. Established as Klein School of Optics 1894 by Augustus A. Klein, M.D. Became: Massachusetts School of Optometry 1909; Massachusetts College of Optometry 1950. Adopted present name 1976.

NEW ENGLAND INSTITUTE. Ridgefield, Conn. 06877. Non-public institution. Established as New England Institute for Medical Research 1954. Adopted present name 1966.

New England Institute for Medical Research 1954. See New England Institute, Ridgefield, Conn.

NEW ENGLAND SCHOOL OF LAW. Boston, Mass. 02116. Non-public institution. Established as Portia School of Law 1918 by A. W. Maclean and A. C. York. Adopted present name 1969.

New Garden Boarding School 1837. See Guilford College, Greensboro, N.C.

NEW HAMPSHIRE COLLEGE. Manchester, N.H. 03104. Non-public institution. Established as the New Hampshire School of Accounting and Secretarial Science 1932. Became: New Hampshire School of Accounting and Finance 1945; New Hampshire School of Accounting and Commerce 1947; New Hampshire College of Accounting and Commerce, Inc. 1961; New Hampshire College of Accounting and Commerce 1968. Adopted present name 1969.

New Hampshire College of Accounting and Commerce, Inc. 1961. See New Hampshire College, Manchester, N.H.

New Hampshire College of Agriculture and the Mechanic Arts 1866. See University of New Hampshire, Durham, N.H.

New Hampshire School of Accounting and Finance 1945. See New Hampshire College, Manchester, N.H.

New Hampshire School of Accounting and Secretarial Science 1932. See New Hampshire College, Manchester, N.H.

New Haven College 1920. See University of New Haven, New Haven, Conn.

New Haven Normal School 1893. See Southern Connecticut State College, New Haven, Conn.

New Haven State Teachers College 1937. See Southern Connecticut State College, New Haven, Conn.

New Haven YMCA Junior College 1926. See University of New Haven, New Haven, Conn.

NEW JERSEY INSTITUTE OF TECHNOLOGY. Newark, N.J. 07102. Professional school receiving state and municipal support. Established as Newark Technical School 1881. Became: Newark College of Engineering 1929. Adopted present name 1974.

New Jersey Normal School at Montclair 1908. See Montclair State College, Upper Montclair, N.J.

New Jersey State Normal and Model Schools 1855. See Trenton State College, Trenton, N.J.

New Jersey State Normal School 1927. See Jersey City State College, Jersey City, N.J.

New Jersey State Normal School at Newark 1913. See Kean College of New Jersey, Union, N.J.

New Jersey State Teachers College 1937. See The William Paterson College of New Jersey, Wayne, N. J.

New Jersey State Teachers College 1937. See Trenton State College, Trenton, N. J.

New Jersey State Teachers College 1955. See Jersey City State College, Jersey City, N. J.

New London Academy 1743. See University of Delaware, Newark, Del.

New Mexico Baptist College 1958. See College of the Southwest, Hobbs, N. M.

New Mexico College of Agriculture and Mechanic Arts 1889. See New Mexico State University, Las Cruces, N. M.

NEW MEXICO HIGHLANDS UNIVERSITY. Las Vegas, N. M. 87701. State institution. Established as New Mexico Normal College 1893. Became: New Mexico Normal University 1898. Adopted present name 1941.

NEW MEXICO INSTITUTE OF MINING AND TECHNOLOGY. Socorro, N. M. 87801. State institution. Established as New Mexico School of Mines 1889. Adopted present name 1951.

New Mexico Normal College 1893. See New Mexico Highlands University, Las Vegas, N. M.

New Mexico Normal School 1912. See Western New Mexico University, Silver City, N. M.

New Mexico Normal University 1898. See New Mexico Highlands University, Las Vegas, N. M.

New Mexico School of Mines 1889. See New Mexico Institute of Mining and Technology, Socorro, N. M.

New Mexico State Teachers College 1923. See Western New Mexico University, Silver City, N. M.

NEW MEXICO STATE UNIVERSITY. Las Cruces, N. M. 88001. State institution. Established as Las Cruces College 1888. Became: New Mexico College of Agriculture and Mechanic Arts 1889; New Mexico State University of Agriculture Engineering and Science 1958. Adopted present name 1960.

New Mexico State University of Agriculture Engineering and Science 1958. See New Mexico State University, Las Cruces, N. M.

New Mexico Western College 1949. See Western New Mexico University, Silver City, N. M.

NEW ORLEANS BAPTIST THEOLOGICAL SEMINARY. New Orleans, La. 70126. Non-public institution. Owned by the Southern Baptist Convention. Established as Baptist Bible Institute 1917. Adopted present name 1946.

New Orleans University 1930. See Dillard University, New Orleans, La.

New River State College 1931. See West Virginia Institute of Technology, Montgomery, W. Va.

New River State School 1921. See West Virginia Institute of Technology, Montgomery, W. Va.

New York Carver College of Chiropractic 1968. See National College of Chiropractic, Lombard, Ill.

New York College for Teachers 1914. See State University at New York at Albany, Albany, N. Y.

New York College of Chiropractic 1968. See National College of Chiropractic, Lombard, Ill.

New York College of Music, New York, N. Y. Closed June 1968.

NEW YORK COLLEGE OF PODIATRIC MEDICINE. New York, N. Y. 10035. Non-public institution. Established as New York School of Chiropody 1911 by the Chiropodists of America. Became: The First Institute of Podiatry 1919; Long Island University College of Podiatry 1939, on affiliation with that University; New York College of Podiatry 1955, after becoming independent; M. J. Lewi College of Podiatry 1957. Adopted present name 1972.

New York College of Podiatry 1955. See New York College of Podiatric Medicine, New York, N. Y.

The New York Homeopathic Medical College 1869. See New York Medical College, New York, N. Y.

The New York Homeopathic Medical College and Flower Hospital 1908. See New York Medical College, New York, N. Y.

The New York Homeopathic Medical College and Hospital 1887. See New York Medical College, New York, N. Y.

NEW YORK MEDICAL COLLEGE. New York, N. Y. 10029. State institution. Established as The Homeopathic Medical College of the State of New York in New York City 1860. Became: The New York Homeopathic Medical College 1869; The New York Homeopathic Medical College and Hospital 1887; The New York Homeopathic Medical College and Flower Hospital 1908; New York Medical College and Flower Hospital 1936; New York Medical College, Flower and Fifth Avenue Hospitals 1938. Adopted present name 1974.

New York Medical College and Flower Hospital 1936. See New York
Medical College, New York, N. Y.

New York Medical College, Flower and Fifth Avenue Hospitals 1938.
See New York Medical College, New York, N. Y.

New York Nautical School 1874. See State University of New York
Maritime College, New York, N. Y.

The New York School of Art 1902. See Parsons School of Design,
New York, N. Y.

New York School of Chiropody 1911. See New York College of
Podiatric Medicine, New York, N. Y.

The New York School of Fine and Applied Art. See Parsons School
of Design, New York, N. Y.

New York State College for Teachers Buffalo, N. Y. 1928. See
State University of New York College at Buffalo, Buffalo, N. Y.

New York State Maritime Academy 1942. See State University of
New York Maritime College, New York, N. Y.

New York State Merchant Marine Academy 1929. See State University of New York Maritime College, New York, N. Y.

New York State Normal College 1890. See State University of New
York at Albany, Albany, N. Y.

New York State Normal School 1844. See State University of New
York at Albany, Albany, N. Y.

New York Theological Seminary 1836. See Union Theological Seminary, New York, N. Y.

NEW YORK UNIVERSITY. New York, N. Y. 10003. Non-public institution. Established as the University of the City of New York
1831. Adopted present name 1896.

Newark Academy 1769. See University of Delaware, Newark, Del.

Newark College 1833. See University of Delaware, Newark, Del.

Newark College of Engineering 1929. See New Jersey Institute of
Technology, Newark, N. J.

Newark Normal School 1855. See Kean College of New Jersey,
Union, N. J.

Newark State College 1958. See Kean College of New Jersey,
Union, N. J.

Newark State Teachers College 1935. See Kean College of New Jersey, Union, N. J.

Newark Technical School 1881. See New Jersey Institute of Technology, Newark, N. J.

Newbury Seminary 1834. See Vermont College, Montpelier, Vt.

Newton College, Newton, Mass. Closed June 1975.

Newton College of the Sacred Heart. See Boston College, Chestnut Hill, Mass.

NIAGARA UNIVERSITY. Niagara University, N. Y. 14109. Non-public institution. Owned by the Congregation of the Mission, Roman Catholic Church. Established as College and Seminary of Our Lady of the Angels 1856. Became: Seminary of Our Lady of Angels 1863. Adopted present name 1883.

NICHOLLS STATE UNIVERSITY. Thibodaux, La. 70301. State institution. Established as Francis T. Nicholls Junior College of La. State University 1948. Became: Francis T. Nicholls State College 1956, after becoming independent. Adopted present name 1970.

Nichols Academy 1815. See Nichols College, Dudley, Mass.

NICHOLS COLLEGE. Dudley, Mass. 01570. Non-public institution. Established as Nichols Academy 1815. Closed 1911. Reorganized as Nichols Junior College 1931. Became: Nichols College of Business Administration 1958. Adopted present name 1971.

Nichols College of Business Administration 1958. See Nichols College, Dudley, Mass.

Nichols Junior College 1931. See Nichols College, Dudley, Mass.

Norfolk College of William and Mary of the Colleges of William and Mary 1960. See Old Dominion University, Norfolk, Va.

Norfolk Division of the College of William and Mary 1930. See Old Dominion University, Norfolk, Va.

Norfolk Division of Virginia State College 1944. See Norfolk State College, Norfolk, Va.

Norfolk Polytechnic College 1942. See Norfolk State College, Norfolk, Va.

NORFOLK STATE COLLEGE. Norfolk, Va. 23504. State institution. Established as Norfolk Unit of Virginia Union University 1935. Became: Norfolk Polytechnic College 1942; Norfolk Division of Virginia State College 1944. Adopted present name 1969.

Norfolk Unit of Virginia Union University 1935. See Norfolk State College, Norfolk, Va.

Normal and Industrial School for Women 1908. See Madison College, Harrisonburg, Va.

Normal College 1851. See Duke University, Durham, N. C.

Normal School, Fajardo, P. R. 1900. See University of Puerto Rico, Rio Piedras, P. R.

Normal School of Arizona 1896. See Arizona State University, Tempe, Ariz.

The Normal School of the Territory of Oklahoma 1890. See Central State University, Edmond, Okla.

Normandy Residence Center of the University of Missouri 1960. See University of Missouri-St. Louis, St. Louis, Mo.

NORTH ADAMS STATE COLLEGE. North Adams, Mass. 02147. State institution. Established as State Normal School at North Adams 1894. Became: State Teachers College at North Adams 1932. Adopted present name 1968.

North Campus of Chicago Teachers College 1957. See Northeastern Illinois University, Chicago, Ill.

NORTH CAROLINA AGRICULTURAL AND TECHNICAL STATE UNIVERSITY. Greensboro, N. C. 17411. State institution. Established as A. and T. College for the Colored Race 1891, in Raleigh, N. C. Moved to Greensboro, N. C. 1893. Became: Agricultural and Technical College of North Carolina 1915. Adopted present name 1967.

NORTH CAROLINA CENTRAL UNIVERSITY. Durham, N. C. 27707. State institution. Established as National Religious Training School and Chatauqua 1919 by private group. Sold and reorganized as National Training School 1915. Became: Durham State Normal School 1923, after control was assumed by state; North Carolina College for Negroes 1925; North Carolina College at Durham 1947. Adopted present name 1969.

NORTH CAROLINA STATE UNIVERSITY AT RALEIGH. Raleigh, N. C. 27607. State institution. Established as North Carolina College of Agriculture and Mechanic Arts 1889, although created by state general assembly 1887. Adopted present name 1965.

NORTH CENTRAL BIBLE COLLEGE. Minneapolis, Minn. 55404. Non-public institution. Established as North Central Bible Institute 1930. Adopted present name 1957.

North Central Bible Institute 1930. See North Central Bible College, Minneapolis, Minn.

NORTH CENTRAL COLLEGE. Chicago, Ill. 60625. Non-public institution. Affiliated with The United Methodist Church. Established as Plainfield College 1861. Became: Northwestern College 1864; North Park College 1926. Adopted present name 1974.

NORTH CENTRAL COLLEGE. Naperville, Ill. 60540. Non-public institution. Affiliated with The United Methodist Church. Established as Plainfield College 1861. Became: Northwestern College 1864. Adopted present name 1926.

North Carolina College at Durham 1947. See North Carolina Central University, Durham, N. C.

North Carolina College for Negroes 1925. See North Carolina Central University, Durham, N. C.

North Carolina College for Women 1919. See University of North Carolina at Greensboro, Greensboro, N. C.

North Carolina College of Agriculture and Mechanic Arts 1889. See North Carolina State University at Raleigh, Raleigh, N. C.

North Dakota Agricultural College 1890. See North Dakota State University, Fargo, N. D.

NORTH DAKOTA STATE UNIVERSITY. Fargo, N. D. 58102. State institution. Established as North Dakota Agricultural College 1890. Adopted present name 1960.

North Missouri Normal School and Commercial College 1867. See Northeast Missouri State University, Kirksville, Mo.

NORTH PARK COLLEGE. Chicago, Ill. 60625. Non-public institution. Owned by the Evangelical Covenant Church of America. Established as North Park College and Theological Seminary 1958.

North Park College 1926. See North Central College, Chicago, Ill.

North Park College and Theological Seminary 1958. See North Park College, Chicago, Ill.

North Texas Junior Agricultural, Mechanical and Industrial College 1923. See University of Texas at Arlington, Arlington, Tex.

North Texas State College 1949. See North Texas State University, Denton, Tex.

North Texas State Normal College 1899. See North Texas State University, Denton, Tex.

North Texas State Teachers College 1923. See North Texas State University, Denton, Tex.

NORTH TEXAS STATE UNIVERSITY. Denton, Tex. 76203. State
institution. Established as Texas Normal College 1890. Became:
North Texas State Normal College 1899; North Texas State Teachers
College 1923; North Texas State College 1949. Adopted present name
1961.

North Western Christian University 1850. See Butler University,
Indianapolis, Ind.

North Western University 1851. See Northwestern University,
Evanston, Ill.

North Wisconsin Academy 1892. See Northland College, Ashland,
Wisc.

Northeast Bible College 1938. See Valley Forge Christian College,
Green Lane, Pa.

Northeast Center of La. State University 1934. See Northeast
Louisiana University, Monroe, La.

Northeast Junior College of Louisiana State University 1939. See
Northeast Louisiana University, Monroe, La.

Northeast Louisiana State College 1950. See Northeast Louisiana
University, Monroe, La.

NORTHEAST LOUISIANA UNIVERSITY. Monroe, La. 71201. State
institution. Established as Ouachita Parish Junior College 1931.
Became: Northeast Center of La. State University 1934; Northeast
Junior College of Louisiana State University 1939; Northeast Louisiana State College 1950. Adopted present name 1970.

Northeast Missouri State College 1968. See Northeast Missouri
State University, Kirksville, Mo.

Northeast Missouri State Teachers College 1919. See Northeast
Missouri State University, Kirksville, Mo.

NORTHEAST MISSOURI STATE UNIVERSITY. Kirksville, Mo.
63501. State institution. Established as North Missouri Normal
School and Commercial College 1867. Became: First District Normal School 1870; Northeast Missouri State Teachers College 1919;
Northeast Missouri State College 1968. Adopted present name 1972.

NORTHEASTERN BIBLE COLLEGE. Essex Falls, N.J. 07021.
Non-public institution. Established as Northeastern Collegiate Bible
Institute 1950. Adopted present name 1973.

Northeastern Collegiate Bible Institute 1950. See Northeastern
Bible College, Essex Falls, N.J.

Northeastern Illinois State College 1967. See Northeastern Illinois
University, Chicago, Ill.

NORTHEASTERN ILLINOIS UNIVERSITY. Chicago, Ill. 60625. State institution. Established as the North Campus of Chicago Teachers College 1957. Became: Illinois Teachers College Chicago-North 1965 after purchase by the state; Northeastern Illinois State College 1967. Adopted present name 1971.

NORTHEASTERN OKLAHOMA UNIVERSITY. Tahlequah, Okla. 74464. State institution. Established as Cherokee Female Seminary 1846. Became: Northeastern State Normal School 1909; Northeastern State Teachers College 1919; Northeastern State College 1939. Adopted present name 1974.

Northeastern State College 1939. See Northeastern Oklahoma University, Tahlequah, Okla.

Northeastern State Normal School 1909. See Northeastern Oklahoma University, Tahlequah, Okla.

Northeastern State Teachers College 1919. See Northeastern Oklahoma University, Tahlequah, Okla.

NORTHEASTERN UNIVERSITY. Boston, Mass. 02115. Non-public institution. Established under present name 1898. Merged with Boston-Bouvé College 1964.

Northern Arizona Normal School 1899. See Northern Arizona University, Flagstaff, Ariz.

Northern Arizona State Teachers College 1925. See Northern Arizona University, Flagstaff, Ariz.

NORTHERN ARIZONA UNIVERSITY. Flagstaff, Ariz. 86001. State institution. Established as Northern Arizona Normal School 1899. Became: Northern Arizona State Teachers College 1925; Arizona State Teachers College at Flagstaff 1929; Arizona State College at Flagstaff 1945. Adopted present name 1966.

Northern Conservatory of Music, Bangor, Me. Closed June 1972.

Northern Idaho College of Education 1947. See Lewis-Clark State College, Lewiston, Id.

Northern Illinois College of Ophthalmology and Otology 1872. See Illinois College of Optometry, Chicago, Ill.

Northern Illinois College of Optometry 1926. See Illinois College of Optometry, Chicago, Ill.

Northern Illinois State College 1955. See Northern Illinois University, DeKalb, Ill.

Northern Illinois State Normal School 1895. See Northern Illinois University, DeKalb, Ill.

Northern Illinois State Teachers College 1921. See Northern Illinois University, DeKalb, Ill.

NORTHERN ILLINOIS UNIVERSITY. DeKalb, Ill. 60115. State institution. Established as Northern Illinois State Normal School 1895. Became: Northern Illinois State Teachers College 1921; Northern Illinois State College 1955. Adopted present name 1957.

Northern Indiana Normal School and Business Institute 1873. See Valparaiso University, Valparaiso, Ind.

Northern Kentucky State College 1968. See Northern Kentucky University, Covington, Ky.

NORTHERN KENTUCKY UNIVERSITY. Covington, Ky. 41011. State institution. Established as Northern Kentucky State College 1968. Merged with Salmon P. Chase College of Law (Cincinnati, Oh.) 1972. Adopted present name 1976.

Northern Michigan College 1955. See Northern Michigan University, Marquette, Mich.

Northern Michigan College of Education 1941. See Northern Michigan University, Marquette, Mich.

Northern Michigan Normal School 1899. See Northern Michigan University, Marquette, Mich.

NORTHERN MICHIGAN UNIVERSITY. Marquette, Mich. 49855. State institution. Established as Northern Michigan Normal School 1899. Became: Northern State Teachers College 1928; Northern Michigan College of Education 1941; Northern Michigan College 1955. Adopted present name 1963.

Northern Montana Agricultural and Manual Training School 1913. See Northern Montana College, Havre, Mont.

NORTHERN MONTANA COLLEGE. Havre, Mont. 59501. State institution. Established as Northern Montana Agricultural and Manual Training School 1913. Became: Northern Montana School 1929. Adopted present name 1931.

Northern Montana School 1929. See Northern Montana College, Havre, Mont.

Northern Normal and Industrial College 1901. See Northern State College, Aberdeen, S.D.

NORTHERN STATE COLLEGE. Aberdeen, S.D. 57401. State institution. Established as Northern Normal and Industrial College 1901. Became: Northern State Teachers College 1939. Adopted present name 1964.

Northern State Teachers College 1928. See Northern Michigan University, Marquette, Mich.

Northern State Teachers College 1939. See Northern State College, Aberdeen, S.D.

Northfield College 1866. See Carleton College, Northfield, Minn.

NORTHLAND COLLEGE. Ashland, Wisc. 54806. Non-public institution. Affiliated with The United Church of Christ. Established as North Wisconsin Academy 1892. Adopted present name 1906.

Northrup Aeronautical Institute 1942. See Northrup University of Technology, Inglewood, Calif.

Northrup Institute of Technology 1958. See Northrup University of Technology, Inglewood, Calif.

NORTHRUP UNIVERSITY OF TECHNOLOGY. Inglewood, Calif. 90306. Non-public institution. Established as Northrup Aeronautical Institute 1942, by Northrup Aircraft Company, but became independent 1953. Became: Northrup Institute of Technology 1958. Adopted present name 1974.

Northwest Bible College 1949. See Northwest College of the Assemblies of God, Kirkland, Wash.

Northwest Bible Institute 1934. See Northwest College of the Assemblies of God, Kirkland, Wash.

NORTHWEST CHRISTIAN COLLEGE. Eugene, Ore. 97401. Non-public institution. Affiliated with The Christian Church (Disciples of Christ). Established as Eugene Divinity School 1895. Became: Eugene Bible University 1908; Eugene Bible College 1930. Merged with Spokane University 1933. Adopted present name 1934.

Northwest Classical Academy 1882. See Northwestern College, Orange City, Ia.

Northwest College, Kirkland 1962. See Northwest College of the Assemblies of God, Kirkland, Wash.

NORTHWEST COLLEGE OF THE ASSEMBLIES OF GOD. Kirkland, Wash. 98033. Non-public institution. Controlled by the Assembly of God Church. Established as Northwest Bible Institute 1934. Became: Northwest Bible College 1949; Northwest College, Kirkland 1962. Adopted present name 1976.

Northwest Missouri State College 1949. See Northwest Missouri State University, Maryville, Mo.

Northwest Missouri State Teachers College 1919. See Northwest Missouri State University, Maryville, Mo.

NORTHWEST MISSOURI STATE UNIVERSITY. Maryville, Mo.
64468. State institution. Established as Fifth Normal School District 1905. Became: Northwest Missouri State Teachers College
1919; Northwest Missouri State College 1949. Adopted present name
1972.

Northwestern Bible and Missionary Training School 1902. See
Northwestern College, Roseville, Minn.

NORTHWESTERN COLLEGE. Orange City, Ia. 51401. Non-public
institution. Affiliated with the Reformed Church in America. Established as Northwest Classical Academy 1882. Adopted present
name 1957.

NORTHWESTERN COLLEGE. Roseville, Minn. 55113. Non-public
institution. Established as Northwestern Bible and Missionary Training School 1902 by William B. Riley. Became: Northwestern Schools
1951. Adopted present name 1966.

Northwestern College 1864. See North Central College, Chicago,
Ill.

Northwestern College 1864. See North Central College, Naperville,
Ill.

Northwestern Normal School 1913. See Minot State College, Minot,
S. D.

Northwestern Ohio Normal School 1871. See Ohio Northern University, Ada, Oh.

NORTHWESTERN OKLAHOMA STATE UNIVERSITY. Alva, Okla.
73717. State institution. Established as Northwestern Territorial
Normal School 1897. Became: Northwestern State Normal School
1907; Northwestern State Teachers College 1919; Northwestern State
College 1939. Adopted present name 1975.

Northwestern Schools 1951. See Northwestern College, Roseville,
Minn.

Northwestern State College 1939. See Northwestern Oklahoma State
University, Alva, Okla.

Northwestern State College of Louisiana 1944. See Northwestern
State University of Louisiana, Natchitoches, La.

Northwestern State Normal School 1907. See Northwestern Oklahoma State University, Alva, Okla.

Northwestern State Teachers College 1919. See Northwestern Oklahoma State University, Alva, Okla.

NORTHWESTERN STATE UNIVERSITY OF LOUISIANA. Natchitoches,

La. 71457. State institution. Established as Louisiana Normal School
1884. Became: Louisiana State Normal College 1918; Northwestern
State College of Louisiana 1944. Adopted present name 1970.

Northwestern Territorial Normal School 1897. See Northwestern
Oklahoma State University, Alva, Okla.

NORTHWESTERN UNIVERSITY. Evanston, Ill. 60201. Non-public
institution. Established as North Western University 1851. Adopted
present name 1867.

NORWICH UNIVERSITY. Northfield, Vt. 05663. Non-public insti-
tution. Established as American Literary, Scientific and Military
Academy 1819. Adopted present name 1834. Merged with Vermont
College 1972.

Notre Dame College, St. Louis, Mo. Closed May 1977.

Notre Dame College of Staten Island 1971. See St. John's University, Jamaica, N.Y.

Notre Dame of Maryland Collegiate Institute for Young Ladies 1873.
See College of Notre Dame of Maryland, Baltimore, Md.

Notre Dame Seminary 1923. See Notre Dame Seminary--Graduate
School of Theology, New Orleans, La.

NOTRE DAME SEMINARY-GRADUATE SCHOOL OF THEOLOGY.
New Orleans, La. 70122. Non-public institution. Owned by the
Archdiocese of New Orleans, Roman Catholic Church. Established
as Notre Dame Seminary 1923. Adopted present name 1968.

Novitiate Normal School 1886. See Aquinas College, Grand Rapids,
Mich.

NYACK COLLEGE. Nyack, N.Y. 10960. Non-public institution.
Affiliated with The Christian and Missionary Alliance. Established
as the Missionary Training Institute 1882. Became: Nyack Missionary College 1956. Adopted present name 1972.

Nyack Missionary College 1956. See Nyack College, Nyack, N.Y.

- O -

OAKLAND UNIVERSITY. Rochester, Mich. 48063. State institution.
Established as Michigan State University at Oakland 1957. Adopted
present name 1963. Became independent of Michigan State University
1970.

OAKWOOD COLLEGE. Huntsville, Ala. 35806. Non-public institution. Owned by the General Converence, Seventh-Day Adventists.

Established as Oakwood Industrial School 1896. Became: Oakwood
Manual Training School 1904; Oakwood Junior College 1917. Adopted
present name 1943.

Oakwood Industrial School 1896. See Oakwood College, Huntsville,
Ala.

Oakwood Junior College 1917. See Oakwood College, Huntsville, Ala.

Oakwood Manual Training School 1904. See Oakwood College, Huntsville, Ala.

Oberlin Home and School 1885. See Pfeiffer College, Misenheimer,
N. C.

Oblate College and Seminary, Bar Harbor, Me. Closed June 1969.

Oblate College and Seminary, Natwick, Mass. Closed Oct. 1974.

OBLATE COLLEGE OF THE SOUTHWEST. San Antonio, Tex.
78216. Non-public institution. Owned by Oblates of Mary Immaculate, Roman Catholic Church. Established as The San Antonio Philosophical and Theological Seminary 1903. Became: The Sacred
Heart Scholasticate 1920; De Mazenod Scholasticate 1927. Adopted
present name 1962.

OCCIDENTAL COLLEGE. Los Angeles, Calif. 90041. Non-public
institution, historically related to the United Presbyterian Church
in the U.S. Established as The Occidental University of Los Angeles
1887. Adopted present name 1892.

The Occidental University of Los Angeles 1887. See Occidental
College, Los Angeles, Calif.

OGLETHORPE COLLEGE. Atlanta, Ga. 30319. Non-public institution. Established as Oglethorpe University 1835, by Presbyterian
group. Became: Oglethorpe College 1964; Oglethorpe University
1971. Readopted present name 1974.

Oglethorpe College 1964. See Oglethorpe College, Atlanta, Ga.

Oglethorpe University 1835. See Oglethorpe College, Atlanta, Ga.

Ohio Agricultural and Mechanical College 1870. See Ohio State
University, Columbus, Oh.

Ohio College of Applied Science 1969. See University of Cincinnati,
Cincinnati, Oh.

Ohio College of Chiropody 1916. See Ohio College of Podiatric
Medicine, Cleveland, Oh.

OHIO COLLEGE OF PODIATRIC MEDICINE. Cleveland, Oh. 44106.

Non-public institution. Established as Ohio College of Chiropody 1916 by Dr. C. P. Beach and others. Became: Ohio College of Podiatry 1964. Adopted present name 1969.

Ohio College of Podiatry 1964. See Ohio College of Podiatric Medicine, Cleveland, Oh.

OHIO DOMINICAN COLLEGE. Columbus, Oh. 43219. Non-public institution. Affiliated with the Dominican Sisters of St. Mary of the Springs, Roman Catholic Church. Established as College of St. Mary of the Springs 1911. Adopted present name 1968.

Ohio Mechanics Institute 1969. See University of Cincinnati, Cincinnati, Oh.

Ohio Normal University 1885. See Ohio Northern University, Ada, Oh.

OHIO NORTHERN UNIVERSITY. Ada, Oh. 45810. Non-public institution. Related to the United Methodist Church. Established as Northwestern Ohio Normal School 1871. Became: Ohio Normal University 1885. Adopted present name 1903.

OHIO STATE UNIVERSITY. Columbus, Oh. 43210. State university. Established as Ohio Agricultural and Mechanical College 1870. Adopted present name 1878.

Ohio Wesleyan Female College 1877. See Ohio Wesleyan University, Delaware, Oh.

OHIO WESLEYAN UNIVERSITY. Delaware, Oh. 43015. Non-public institution. Affiliated with The United Methodist Church. Established 1841 under present name. Merged with Ohio Wesleyan Female College 1877.

Oklahoma Agricultural and Mechanical College 1890. See Oklahoma State University, Stillwater, Okla.

OKLAHOMA CHRISTIAN COLLEGE. Oklahoma City, Okla. 73111. Non-public institution. Affiliated with the Church of Christ. Established as Central Christian College 1950. Adopted present name 1959.

Oklahoma Christian University 1906. See Phillips University, Enid, Okla.

Oklahoma City College 1919. See Oklahoma City University, Oklahoma City, Okla.

OKLAHOMA CITY UNIVERSITY. Oklahoma City, Okla. Non-public institution. Owned by The United Methodist Church. Established as Epworth University 1904. Became: Methodist University of Oklahoma 1911; Oklahoma City College 1919. Adopted present name 1924.

Oklahoma College for Women 1916. See University of Arts and Sciences of Oklahoma, Chickasha, Okla.

Oklahoma College of Liberal Arts 1965. See University of Sciences and Arts of Oklahoma, Chickasha, Okla.

Oklahoma Holiness College 1909. See Bethany Nazarene College, Bethany, Okla.

Oklahoma Panhandle State College of Agriculture and Applied Science 1967. See Oklahoma Panhandle State University, Goodwell, Okla.

OKLAHOMA PANHANDLE STATE UNIVERSITY. Goodwell, Okla. 73939. State institution. Established as Pan-Handle Agricultural Institute 1909. Became: Panhandle Agricultural and Mechanical College 1921. Oklahoma Panhandle State College of Agriculture and Applied Science 1967, but known as Oklahoma Panhandle State College. Adopted present name 1974.

OKLAHOMA STATE UNIVERSITY. Stillwater, Okla. 74074. State institution. Established as Oklahoma Agricultural and Mechanical College 1890. Adopted present official name Oklahoma State University of Agriculture and Applied Sciences 1957.

Oklahoma State University of Agriculture and Applied Sciences 1957. See Oklahoma State University, Stillwater, Okla.

Okolona College, Okolona, Miss. Closed 1966/67 School Year.

Old Dominion College 1962. See Old Dominion University, Norfolk, Va.

OLD DOMINION UNIVERSITY. Norfolk, Va. 23508. State institution. Established as The Extension Center of the College of William and Mary 1919. Became: Norfolk Division of the College of William and Mary 1930; College of William and Mary in Norfolk 1956; Norfolk College of William and Mary of the Colleges of William and Mary 1960; Old Dominion College 1962, after becoming independent. Adopted present name 1969.

OLIVET COLLEGE. Olivet, Mich. 49076. Non-public institution. Affiliated with the Congregational Church and the United Church of Christ. Established as Olivet College 1844. Became: Olivet Institute 1847; readopted present name 1859.

Olivet College 1921. See Olivet Nazarene College, Kankakee, Ill.

Olivet Institute 1847. See Olivet College, Olivet, Mich.

OLIVET NAZARENE COLLEGE. Kankakee, Ill. 60901. Non-public institution. Owned by the Church of the Nazarene. Established as Illinois Holiness University 1909. Became: Olivet University 1915; Olivet College 1921. Adopted present name 1940.

Olivet University 1915. See Olivet Nazarene College, Kankakee, Ill.

Omaha Baptist Bible College 1960. See Faith Baptist Bible College, Ankeny, Ia.

Omaha Baptist Bible Institute 1952. See Faith Baptist Bible College, Ankeny, Ia.

Omaha Bible Institute 1921. See Faith Baptist Bible College, Ankeny, Ia.

O'Neil Ross Chiropractic College 1970. See National College of Chiropractic, Lombard, Ill.

Oneonta State Normal School 1889. See State University of New York College at Oneonta, Oneonta, N.Y.

Orange County State College 1957. See California State University, Fullerton; Fullerton, Calif.

Orange State College 1962. See California State University, Fullerton, Fullerton, Calif.

Oregon City College 1849. See Linfield College, McMinnville, Ore.

OREGON COLLEGE OF EDUCATION. Monmouth, Ore. 97361. State institution. Established as Monmouth University 1856. Became: Christian College 1965; Oregon State Normal School 1882; Oregon Normal School 1911. Adopted present name 1939.

Oregon Institute 1842. See Willamette University, Salem, Ore.

OREGON INSTITUTE OF TECHNOLOGY. Kalmath Falls, Ore. 97601. State institution. Established as Oregon Vocational School 1947. Became: Oregon Technical Institute 1943. Adopted present name 1973.

Oregon Normal School 1911. See Oregon College of Education, Monmouth, Ore.

Oregon State Agricultural College 1868. See Oregon State University, Corvallis, Ore.

Oregon State College 1920. See Oregon State University, Corvallis, Ore.

Oregon State Normal School 1882. See Oregon College of Education, Monmouth, Ore.

OREGON STATE UNIVERSITY. Corvallis, Ore. 97331. State institution. Established as Corvallis College 1858. Became: Oregon State Agricultural College 1868; Oregon State College 1920. Adopted present name 1961.

Oregon Technical Institute 1943. See Oregon Institute of Technology, Klamath Falls, Ore.

Oregon Vocational School 1947. See Oregon Institute of Technology, Klamath Falls, Ore.

Oshkosh Normal School 1871. See University of Wisconsin-Oshkosh, Oshkosh, Wisc.

Oshkosh Teachers College 1925. See University of Wisconsin-Oshkosh, Oshkosh, Wisc.

Oswego Normal School 1861. See State University of New York College at Oswego, Oswego, N. Y.

Oswego State Teachers College 1942. See State University of New York College at Oswego, Oswego, N. Y.

Otis Art Institute 1918. See Otis Art Institute of Los Angeles County, Los Angeles, Calif.

OTIS ART INSTITUTE OF LOS ANGELES COUNTY. Los Angeles, Calif. 90057. Public institution. Operated by Los Angeles County. Established as Otis Art Institute 1918. Became: Los Angeles County Art Institute 1947. Adopted present name 1960.

Ouachita Baptist College 1885. See Ouachita Baptist University, Arkadelphia, Ark.

OUACHITA BAPTIST UNIVERSITY. Arkadelphia, Ark. 71923. Non-public institution. Owned by the Arkansas Baptist State Convention (Southern Baptist). Established as Ouachita Baptist College 1885. Adopted present name 1966.

Ouachita Parish Junior College 1931. See Northeast Louisiana University, Monroe, La.

Our Lady of Cincinnati College 1935. See Edgecliff College, Cincinnati, Oh.

OUR LADY OF HOLY CROSS COLLEGE. New Orleans, La. 70114. Non-public institution. Owned and operated by the Marianites of Holy Cross, Roman Catholic Church. Established as Academy of the Holy Angels Normal School 1916 by Mother Mary of St. James Dooley and Marianites of Holy Cross. Became: Holy Cross Normal College 1931; Academy of the Holy Angels College Department 1941. Adopted present name 1960.

Our Lady of Hope Mission Seminary, Newburgh, N. Y. Closed June 1971.

Our Lady of Snows Scholasticate, Pass Christian, Miss. Closed 1971/72 School Year.

Our Lady of the Lake Academy 1896. See Our Lady of the Lake University of San Antonio, San Antonio, Tex.

Our Lady of the Lake College 1912. See Our Lady of the Lake University of San Antonio, San Antonio, Tex.

OUR LADY OF THE LAKE UNIVERSITY OF SAN ANTONIO. San Antonio, Tex. 78285. Non-public institution. Sponsored by the Sisters of Divine Providence, Roman Catholic Church. Established as Our Lady of the Lake Academy 1896. Became: Our Lady of the Lake College 1912. Adopted present name 1976.

Owen College 1968. See LeMoyne-Owen College, Memphis, Tenn.

Owosso College 1909. See John Wesley College, Owosso, Mich.

- P -

PMC Colleges (Pennsylvania Military College and Penn Morton College) 1966. See Widener College, Chester, Pa.

Pace and Pace 1906. See Pace University, New York, N.Y.

Pace College 1948. See Pace University, New York, N.Y.

Pace Institute 1935. See Pace University, New York N.Y.

PACE UNIVERSITY. New York, N.Y. 10038. Non-public institution. Established as Pace and Pace 1906. Became: Pace Institute 1935; Pace College 1948. Adopted present name 1973. Merged with College of White Plains to form Pace University White Plains Campus 1974.

Pacific Bible College 1937. See Warner Pacific College, Portland, Ore.

Pacific Bible College, Los Angeles 1902. See Point Loma College, San Diego, Calif.

Pacific Bible Institute 1944. See Pacific College, Fresno, Calif.

Pacific Bible Seminary 1928. See Pacific Christian College, Long Beach, Calif.

PACIFIC CHRISTIAN COLLEGE. Long Beach, Calif. 90804. Non-public institution. Affiliated with the Churches of Christ and Christian Churches. Established as Pacific Bible Seminary 1928. Adopted present name 1962.

PACIFIC COLLEGE. Fresno, Calif. 93702. Non-public institution. Controlled by the Mennonite Brethren Conference of the U.S. Established as Pacific Bible Institute 1944. Adopted present name 1960.

Pacific College 1891. See George Fox College, Newberg, Ore.

Pacific Lutheran Academy 1894. See Pacific Lutheran University, Tacoma, Wash.

Pacific Lutheran College 1920. See Pacific Lutheran University, Tacoma, Wash.

PACIFIC LUTHERAN UNIVERSITY. Tacoma, Wash. 98447. Non-public institution. Controlled by The American Lutheran Church. Established as Pacific Lutheran University 1890. Became: Pacific Lutheran Academy 1894; Pacific Lutheran College 1920. Readopted present name 1960.

PACIFIC OAKS COLLEGE. Pasadena, Calif. 91105. Non-public institution. Affiliated with the Society of Friends. Established as Pacific Oaks Friends School 1945. Adopted present name 1961.

Pacific Oaks Friends School 1945. See Pacific Oaks College, Pasadena, Calif.

PACIFIC SCHOOL OF RELIGION. Berkeley, Calif. 94709. Non-public institution. Established as Pacific Theological Seminary by Congregationalists 1866. Became interdenominational and adopted present name 1916.

Pacific Theological Seminary 1866. See Pacific School of Religion, Berkeley, Calif.

PACIFIC UNION COLLEGE. Angwin, Calif. 94508. Non-public institution. Owned by the Seventh-day Adventists Church. Established as Healdsburg College, Healdsburg, Calif. 1882. Adopted present name 1906. Moved to present location 1909.

PACIFIC UNIVERSITY. Forest Grove, Ore. 97116. Non-public institution. Affiliated with the United Church of Christ. Established as Tualitin Academy 1849. Became: Tualitin Academy and Pacific University 1854. Adopted present name 1914.

Packer Collegiate Institute, Brooklyn, N.Y. Closed June 1972.

PAINE COLLEGE. Augusta, Ga. 30901. Non-public institution. Affiliated with the Christian Methodist Episcopal Church and the United Methodist Church. Established as Paine Institute 1882. Adopted present name 1903.

Paine Institute 1882. See Paine College, Augusta, Ga.

PALMER COLLEGE OF CHIROPRACTIC. Davenport, Ia. 52803. Non-profit institution. Established as The Palmer School of Chiropractic 1895 by David D. Palmer. Adopted present name 1961.

The Palmer School of Chiropractic 1895. See Palmer College of Chiropractic, Davenport, Ia.

Palmer University 1902. See Ball State University, Muncie, Ind.

Pan American College 1951. See Pan American University, Edinburg, Tex.

PAN AMERICAN UNIVERSITY. Edinburg, Tex. 78501. State institution. Established as Edinburg Junior College 1927. Became: Edinburg Regional College 1948; Pan American College 1951. State assumed control 1965. Adopted present name 1971.

Panhandle Agricultural and Mechanical College 1921. See Oklahoma Panhandle State University, Goodwell, Okla.

Pan-Handle Agricultural Institute 1909. See Oklahoma Panhandle State University, Goodwell, Okla.

Park Region College of Fergus Falls 1912. See Concordia College, Moorhead, Minn.

Parks Air College 1927. See Parks College of Aeronautical Technology, Cahokia, Ill.

PARKS COLLEGE OF AERONAUTICAL TECHNOLOGY. Cahokia, Ill. 62206. Non-public institution. Established as Parks Air College 1927. Became part of St. Louis University and adopted present name 1946.

Parsons College, Fairfield, Ia. Closed June 1973.

PARSONS SCHOOL OF DESIGN. New York, N.Y. 10011. Non-public institution. An affiliate of The New School for Social Research. Established as The Chase School 1896 by William M. Chase. Became: The New York School of Art 1902; The New York School of Fine and Applied Art 1907. Adopted present name 1941. Merged with The New School for Social Research 1970.

Parsons Seminary 1866. See Coe College, Cedar Rapids, Ia.

Pasadena College 1915. See Point Loma College, San Diego, Calif.

Pasadena Playhouse College of the Theater Arts, Pasadena, Calif. Closed Feb. 1971.

Pasadena University 1910. See Point Loma College, San Diego, Calif.

Passionist Monastic Seminary, Jamaica, N.Y. Closed June 1974.

Paterson Normal School 1855. See The William Paterson College of New Jersey, Wayne, N.J.

Paterson State College 1958. See The William Paterson College of New Jersey, Wayne, N.J.

Paterson State Normal School 1923. See The William Paterson
College of New Jersey, Wayne, N. J.

Payne Institute 1889. See Daniel Payne College, Inc. Birmingham,
Ala.

Payne University 1903. See Daniel Payne College, Inc. Birmingham,
Ala.

Peabody Academy of Music 1857. See Peabody Conservatory of
Music, Baltimore, Md.

PEABODY CONSERVATORY OF MUSIC. Baltimore, Md. 21202.
Non-public institution. Established as Peabody Academy of Music
1857. Adopted present official name Peabody Institute of the City
of Baltimore 1874.

Peabody Institute of the City of Baltimore 1874. See Peabody Conservatory of Music, Baltimore, Md.

Peabody Normal College 1889. See George Peabody College for
Teachers, Nashville, Tenn.

Pembroke State College 1949. See Pembroke State University,
Pembroke, N. C.

PEMBROKE STATE UNIVERSITY. Pembroke, N. C. 28372. State
institution. Established as Croatan Normal School 1887. Became:
Indian Normal School of Robeson County 1911; Pembroke State University for Indians 1941; Pembroke State College 1949. Adopted
present name 1969.

Pembroke State University for Indians 1941. See Pembroke State
University, Pembroke, N. C.

Peniel University 1920. See Bethany Nazarene College, Bethany,
Okla.

Penn College 1873. See William Penn College, Oskaloosa, Ia.

Penn Wesleyan College 1970. See United Wesleyan College, Allentown, Pa.

Pennsylvania College for Women 1890. See Chatham College,
Pittsburgh, Pa.

PENNSYLVANIA COLLEGE OF OPTOMETRY. Philadelphia, Pa.
19141. Non-public institution, receiving state aid. Established as
Pennsylvania State College of Optometry 1919. Adopted present
name 1964.

Pennsylvania Female College 1869. See Chatham College, Pittsburgh, Pa.

Pennsylvania Military Academy 1862. See Widener College, Chester, Pa.

Pennsylvania Military College 1892. See Widener College, Chester, Pa.

Pennsylvania Museum and School of Industrial Art 1876. See Philadelphia College of Art, Philadelphia, Pa.

Pennsylvania State College 1874. See The Pennsylvania State University, University Park, Pa.

Pennsylvania State College of Optometry 1919. See Pennsylvania College of Optometry, Philadelphia, Pa.

THE PENNSYLVANIA STATE UNIVERSITY. University Park, Pa. 16802. State institution. Established as Farmer's High School 1855. Became: Agriculture College of Pennsylvania 1862; Pennsylvania State College 1874. Adopted present name 1953.

Pentecostal Collegiate Institute, Saratoga Springs, N.Y. 1900. See Eastern Nazarene College, Quincy, Mass.

Pepperdine College 1962. See Pepperdine University, Los Angeles, Calif.

PEPPERDINE UNIVERSITY. Los Angeles, Calif. 90044. Non-public institution. Affiliated with the Church of Christ. Established as George Pepperdine College 1937. Became: Pepperdine College 1962. Adopted present name 1971.

Peru Normal College 1867. See Peru State College, Peru, Neb.

PERU STATE COLLEGE. Peru, Neb. 68421. State institution. Established as Mount Vernon College 1855. Became: Peru Normal College 1867; Peru State Teachers College 1921; Nebraska State Teachers College at Peru 1949. Adopted present name 1963.

Peru State Teachers College 1921. See Peru State College, Peru, Neb.

Pestalozzi Froebel Teachers College, Chicago, Ill. Closed Mar. 1971.

PFEIFFER COLLEGE. Misenheimer, N.C. 28109. Non-public institution. Affiliated with the Western North Carolina United Methodist Conference. Established as Oberlin Home and School 1885, near Lenoir, N.C. by private group. Became: Mitchell Home School 1903, after control was assumed by Methodist Episcopal Church. Moved to present site 1910; Mitchell Junior College 1928; Pfeiffer Junior College 1935. Adopted present name 1954.

Pfeiffer Junior College 1935. See Pfeiffer College, Misenheimer, N.C.

Philadelphia Bible Institute 1951. See Philadelphia College of
Bible, Philadelphia, Pa.

Philadelphia College of Apothecaries 1821. See Philadelphia College
of Pharmacy and Science, Philadelphia, Pa.

PHILADELPHIA COLLEGE OF ART. Philadelphia, Pa. 19102. Non-
public institution receiving state aid. Established as Pennsylvania
Museum and School of Industrial Art 1876. Became: Philadelphia
Museum and School of Industrial Art 1939; Philadelphia Museum College of Art 1959. Adopted present name 1964.

PHILADELPHIA COLLEGE OF BIBLE. Philadelphia, Pa. 19103.
Non-public institution. Established as National Bible Institute 1895.
Became: Bible Institute of Pennsylvania 1913; Philadelphia Bible
Institute 1951, after merging with Philadelphia School of Bible 1951.
Adopted present name 1958.

Philadelphia College of Pharmacy 1822. See Philadelphia College
of Pharmacy and Science, Philadelphia, Pa.

PHILADELPHIA COLLEGE OF PHARMACY AND SCIENCE. Philadelphia, Pa. 19104. Non-public institution. Established as Philadelphia College of Apothecaries 1821. Became: Philadelphia College of Pharmacy 1822. Adopted present name 1921.

PHILADELPHIA COLLEGE OF TEXTILES AND SCIENCE. Philadelphia, Pa. 19144. Non-public institution, receiving state aid. Established as Philadelphia Manufacturers Association. Became: Philadelphia Textile Institute of the Philadelphia Museum of Art 1941.
Adopted present name 1960, after becoming independent in 1949.

PHILADELPHIA COLLEGE OF THE PERFORMING ARTS. Philadelphia, Pa. 19107. Non-public institution. Receives state aid. Established as Philadelphia Musical Academy 1870. Merged with the
Philadelphia Conservatory of Music 1962. Adopted present name
1976.

Philadelphia Conservatory of Music 1962. See Philadelphia College
of the Performing Arts, Philadelphia, Pa.

Philadelphia Museum and School of Industrial Art 1939. See Philadelphia College of Art, Philadelphia, Pa.

Philadelphia Museum College of Art 1959. See Philadelphia College
of Art, Philadelphia, Pa.

Philadelphia School of Bible 1951. See Philadelphia College of
Bible, Philadelphia, Pa.

Philadelphia School of Design 1932. See Moore College of Art,
Philadelphia, Pa.

The Philadelphia Seminary of St. Charles Borromeo 1838. See
St. Charles Seminary, Philadelphia, Pa.

Philadelphia Textile Institute of the Philadelphia Museum of Art 1941.
See Philadelphia College of Textiles and Science, Philadelphia, Pa.

Philadelphia Textile School of the Pennsylvania Museum of Art 1884.
See Philadelphia College of Textiles and Science, Philadelphia, Pa.

PHILANDER SMITH COLLEGE. Little Rock, Ark. 72202. Non-
public institution. Affiliated with The United Methodist Church. Established as Walden Seminary 1877. Adopted present name 1883.

PHILLIPS UNIVERSITY. Enid, Okla. 73701. Non-public institution.
Affiliated with the Christian Churches (Disciples of Christ). Established as Oklahoma Christian University 1906. Adopted present
name 1913.

Phillips University 1909. See Texas College, Tyler, Tex.

PIEDMONT COLLEGE. Demerest, Ga. 30535. Non-public institu-
tion. Affiliated with the Congregational Churches. Established as
J. and S. Green Collegiate Institute 1897. Became: J. S. Green
College 1899. Adopted present name 1903.

Pierce College for Women, Concord, N. H. Closed June 1972.

Pierre University 1883. See Huron College, Huron, S. D.

PIKEVILLE COLLEGE. Pikeville, Ky. 41501. Non-public institution. Affiliated with The United Presbyterian Church in the U. S.
Established as Pikeville Collegiate Institute 1889. Adopted present
name 1909.

Pikeville Collegiate Institute 1889. See Pikeville College, Pikeville,
Ky.

Pine Grove Normal Academy 1879. See Grove City College, Grove
City, Pa.

PINE MANOR COLLEGE. Chestnut Hill, Mass. 02167. Non-public
institution. Established as Pine Manor Junior College 1911. Adopted present name 1977.

Pine Manor Junior College 1911. See Pine Manor College, Chestnut Hill, Mass.

Pioneer School 1851. See Hope College, Holland, Mich.

Pittsburgh Academy 1878. See University of Pittsburgh, Pittsburgh,
Pa.

Pittsburgh Catholic College of the Holy Ghost 1878. See Duquesne
University of the Holy Ghost, Pittsburgh, Pa.

Pittsburgh School of Accountancy 1921. See Robert Morris College, Corapolis, Pa.

Pittsburgh Seminary 1930. See Pittsburgh Theological Seminary, Pittsburgh, Pa.

PITTSBURGH THEOLOGICAL SEMINARY. Pittsburgh, Pa. 15206. Non-public institution. Controlled by The United Presbyterian Church in the U.S.A. Established as Service Seminary 1794. Became: Xenia Theological Seminary 1858; Pittsburgh-Xenia Seminary 1930, after merging with Pittsburgh Seminary 1930. Merged with Western Theological Seminary 1958, and adopted present name 1958.

Pittsburgh-Xenia Seminary 1930. See Pittsburgh Theological Seminary, Pittsburgh, Pa.

Plainfield College 1861. See North Central College, Chicago, Ill.

Plainfield College 1861. See North Central College, Naperville, Ill.

Platteville Normal School 1866. See University of Wisconsin-Platteville, Platteville, Wisc.

Platteville State Teachers College 1927. See University of Wisconsin-Platteville, Platteville, Wisc.

Plattsburgh State Normal School 1889. See State University of New York College at Plattsburgh, N.Y.

Plymouth Normal School 1870. See Plymouth State College, Plymouth, N.H.

PLYMOUTH STATE COLLEGE. Plymouth, N.H. 03264. State institution. Established as Plymouth Normal School 1870. Became: Plymouth Teachers College 1928. Adopted present name 1963.

Plymouth Teachers College 1928. See Plymouth State College, Plymouth, N.H. '

POINT LOMA COLLEGE. San Diego, Calif. 92106. Non-public institution. Controlled by the Church of the Nazarene. Established as Pacific Bible College, Los Angeles 1902. Became: Pasadena University 1910, after moving to Pasadena; Pasadena College 1915. Adopted present name 1973, after moving to present location.

POINT PARK COLLEGE. Pittsburgh, Pa. 13222. Non-public institution. Established as Point Park Junior College 1960. Adopted present name 1966.

Point Park Junior College 1960. See Point Park College, Pittsburgh, Pa.

Polish National Alliance College 1912. See Alliance College, Cambridge Springs, Pa.

Polytechnic College 1891. See Texas Wesleyan College, Fort Worth, Tex.

Polytechnic Institute of Brooklyn 1889. See Polytechnic Institute of New York, Brooklyn, N.Y.

POLYTECHNIC INSTITUTE OF NEW YORK. Brooklyn, N.Y. 11201. Non-public institution. Established as Brooklyn Collegiate and Polytechnic Institute 1854. Became: Polytechnic Institute of Brooklyn 1889. Adopted present name 1973.

Polytechnic Institute of Puerto Rico 1912. See Inter-American University of Puerto Rico, San Germain, P.R.

Portia School of Law 1918. See New England School of Law, Boston, Mass.

Portland Campus of the University of Maine at Orono 1970. See University of Maine at Portland-Gorham, Gorham, Me.

PORTLAND SCHOOL OF ART. Portland, Me. 04101. Non-public institution. Established as the School of Fine and Applied Art 1811. Adopted present name 1971.

Portland State College 1955. See Portland State University, Portland, Ore.

Portland State Extension Center 1952. See Portland State University, Portland, Ore.

PORTLAND STATE UNIVERSITY. Portland, Ore. 97207. State institution. Established as Vanport Extension Center 1946. Became: Portland State Extension Center 1952; Portland State College 1955. Adopted present name 1969.

Postgraduate Department of the Naval Academy 1912. See Naval Postgraduate School, Monterey, Calif.

Potsdam Normal School 1866. See State University of New York College at Potsdam, Potsdam, N.Y.

Prairie College 1836. See Knox College, Galesburg, Ill.

Prairie View Agricultural and Mechanical College 1947. See Prairie View Agricultural and Mechanical University, Prairie View, Tex.

PRAIRIE VIEW AGRICULTURAL AND MECHANICAL UNIVERSITY. Prairie View, Tex. 77445. State institution. Established as Alta Vista Agricultural College 1876. Became: Prairie View Normal School 1879; Prairie View University 1945; Prairie View Agricultural and Mechanical College 1947. Adopted present name 1973.

Prairie View Normal School 1879. See Prairie View Agricultural and Mechanical University, Prairie View, Tex.

Prairie View University 1945. See Prairie View Agricultural and Mechanical University, Prairie View, Tex.

Prairieville Academy 1840. See Carroll College, Waukesha, Wisc.

Preparatory College of Immaculate Conception 1847. See Loyola University in New Orleans, New Orleans, La.

PRESBYTERIAN COLLEGE. Clinton, S.C. 29325. Non-public institution. Affiliated with the Georgia and South Carolina Synods of the Presbyterian Church in the U.S. Established as Clinton College 1880. Became: Presbyterian College of South Carolina 1890. Adopted present name 1928.

Presbyterian College 1958. See St. Andrews Presbyterian College, Laurinburg, N.C.

Presbyterian College of South Carolina 1890. See Presbyterian College, Clinton, S.C.

Presbyterian Female College 1896. See Queens College, Charlotte, N.C.

Presbyterian University of Southern Dakota 1883. See Huron College, Huron, S.D.

Prescott College, Prescott, Ariz. Closed Dec. 1974. (Reactivated as Prescott Center College, Jan. 1975)

Presentation Junior College 1937. See Madonna College, Livonia, Mich.

President and Trustees of the University of Louisville 1846. See University of Louisville, Louisville, Ky.

Princess Anne Academy 1886. See University of Maryland, Eastern Shore, Princess Anne, Md.

Princess Anne College 1936. See University of Maryland, Eastern Shore, Princess Anne, Md.

PRINCETON UNIVERSITY. Princeton, N.J. 08540. Non-public institution. Established as College of New Jersey 1746. Adopted present name 1896.

Providence Bible Institute 1929. See Barrington College, Barrington, R.I.

Providence Branch of Northeastern University 1919. See Roger Williams College, Main Campus, Bristol, R.I.

Providence Institute of Engineering and Finance 1939. See Roger Williams College Main Campus, Bristol, R.I.

Pueblo Junior College 1937.   See   University of Southern Colorado, Pueblo, Colo.

PURDUE UNIVERSITY-CALUMET CAMPUS.   Hammond, Ind. 46323. State institution.   Established as Purdue University Center, Hammond 1946.   Became: Purdue University, Calumet Center 1959.   Adopted present name 1962.

Purdue University, Calumet Center 1959.   See   Purdue University-Calumet Campus, Hammond, Ind.

Purdue University Center, Hammond 1946.   See   Purdue University-Calumet Campus, Hammond, Ind.

Purdue University Fort Wayne Campus.   See   Indiana University-Purdue University at Fort Wayne, Fort Wayne, Ind.

- Q -

Queen of Peace College, Jaffrey Center, N. H.   Closed June 1969.

QUEENS COLLEGE.   Charlotte, N. C. 28207.   Non-public institution. Affiliated with the Presbyterian Church in the U. S.   Established as Charlotte Female Institute 1857.   Became: Seminary for Girls 1891; Presbyterian Female College 1896.   Adopted present name 1912.

QUEENS COLLEGE.   Flushing, N. Y. 11367.   Municipal institution. Established as Queens College of the City of New York 1937.   Adopted present official name Queens College of The City University of New York 1961.

Queens College of the City of New York 1937.   See   Queens College, Flushing, N. Y.

Queens College of The City University of New York 1961.   See Queens College, Flushing, N. Y.

Queen's College 1766.   See   Rutgers-The State University, New Brunswick, N. J.

QUINCY COLLEGE.   Quincy, Ill. 62301.   Non-public institution. Affiliated with the Roman Catholic Church.   Established as College of St. Francis Solano 1860.   Became: Quincy College and Seminary 1917.   Adopted present name 1970.

Quincy College and Seminary 1917.   See   Quincy College, Quincy, Ill.

QUINNIPIAC COLLEGE.   Hamden, Conn. 06518.   Non-public institution.   Established as Connecticut College of Commerce 1929 in New Haven.   Became: Junior College of Commerce 1935.   Adopted present name 1951.   Moved to present location 1966.

- R -

RADCLIFFE COLLEGE.   Cambridge, Mass. 02138. Non-public institution.   Established as The Society for the Collegiate Instruction of Women 1882. Adopted present name 1894.

RADFORD COLLEGE. Radford, Va. 24141. State institution. Established as State Normal and Industrial School for Women at Radford 1910. Became: State Teachers College 1924; Women's Division, Virginia Polytechnic Institute 1944. Adopted present name 1944. Became independent institution 1964.

Raleigh Institute 1865. See Shaw University, Raleigh, N.C.

The Regency of West Virginia Normal School at Fairmont 1865. See Fairmont State College, Fairmont, W.Va.

REGIS COLLEGE. Denver, Colo. 80221. Non-public institution. Conducted under the auspices of the Society of Jesus, Roman Catholic Church. Established as Las Vegas College in New Mexico Territory 1877. Became: College of the Sacred Heart, after moving to Morrison, Colo. 1884; Sacred Heart College, 1888, after moving to Denver. Adopted present name 1921.

REGIS COLLEGE. Weston, Mass. 02193. Non-public institution. Conducted by the Congregation of the Sisters of St. Joseph, Roman Catholic Church. Established as Regis College for Women 1927. Adopted present name 1971.

Regis College for Women 1927. See Regis College, Weston, Mass.

Rensselaer Institute 1837. See Rensselaer Polytechnic Institute, Troy, N.Y.

RENSSELAER POLYTECHNIC INSTITUTE. Troy, N.Y. 12181. Non-public institution. Established as Rensselaer School 1824. Became: Rensselaer Institute 1837. Adopted present name 1861.

Rensselaer Polytechnic Institute of Connecticut 1961. See Hartford Graduate Center, Hartford, Conn.

Rensselaer School 1824. See Rensselaer Polytechnic Institute, Troy, N.Y.

Residence Division, Capitol Radio Engineering Institute 1932. See Capitol Institute of Technology, Kensington, Md.

Revenue Cutter Academy 1914. See United States Coast Guard Academy, New London, Conn.

RHODE ISLAND COLLEGE. Providence, R.I. 02908. State institution. Established as Rhode Island State Normal School 1854.

Became: Rhode Island College of Education 1920.   Adopted present name 1960.

Rhode Island College 1764. See Brown University, Providence, R. I.

Rhode Island College of Agriculture and Mechanic Arts 1892. See University of Rhode Island, Kingston, R. I.

Rhode Island College of Education 1920. See Rhode Island College, Providence, R. I.

Rhode Island State College 1909. See University of Rhode Island, Kingston, R. I.

Rhode Island State Normal School 1854. See Rhode Island College, Providence, R. I.

RICE UNIVERSITY. Houston, Tex. 77001. Non-public institution. Established as William M. Rice Institute 1891. Adopted present official name William Marsh Rice University 1960.

Richland County Teachers College, Richland Center, Wisc. Closed June 1967.

Richmond College 1840. See University of Richmond, Richmond, Va.

Richmond Professional Institute 1968. See Virginia Commonwealth University, Richmond, Va.

Richmond Theological Seminary 1899. See Virginia Union University, Richmond, Va.

Ricker Classical Institute 1887. See Ricker College, Houlton, Me.

Ricker Classical Institute and Ricker Junior College 1926. See Ricker College, Houlton, Me.

Ricker Classical Institute, Ricker Junior College, Ricker College 1949. See Ricker College, Houlton, Me.

RICKER COLLEGE. Houlton, Me. 04730. Non-public institution. Established as Houlton Academy 1848. Became: Ricker Classical Institute 1887; Ricker Classical Institute and Ricker Junior College 1926; Ricker Classical Institute, Ricker Junior College, Ricker College 1949. Adopted present name 1966.

The Rider Business College 1897. See Rider College, Trenton, N. J.

RIDER COLLEGE. Trenton, N. J. 08602. Non-public institution. Established as The Rider Business College 1897. Became: Rider-Moore Business College 1898. Merged with Stewart School of Busi-

ness and became Rider-Moore and Stewart School of Business 1901.
Adopted present name 1921.

Rider-Moore and Stewart School of Business 1901. See Rider College, Trenton, N. J.

Rider-Moore Business College 1898. See Rider College, Trenton,
N. J.

RIPON COLLEGE. Ripon, Wisc. 54971. Non-public institution.
Established as Lyceum of Ripon 1850. Became: Brockway College
1851. Adopted present name 1864.

River Falls State Teachers College 1926. See University of Wisconsin-River Falls, River Falls, Wisc.

Roanoke Classical Seminary 1860. See Manchester College, North
Manchester, Ind.

ROANOKE COLLEGE. Salem, Va. 24153. Non-public institution.
Affiliated with the Lutheran Church in America. Established as
The Virginia Institute 1842. Became: The Virginia Collegiate In-
stitute 1845. Adopted present name 1853.

Roanoke College 1904. See Averett College, Danville, Va.

Roanoke Female College 1893. See Averett College, Danville, Va.

Roanoke Institute 1910. See Averett College, Danville, Va.

ROBERT MORRIS COLLEGE. Corapolis, Pa. 15108. Non-public
institution. Established as Pittsburgh School of Accountancy 1921.
Became: The Robert Morris School 1935; Robert Morris Junior
College 1962. Adopted present name 1969.

Robert Morris Junior College 1962. See Robert Morris College,
Corapolis, Pa.

The Robert Morris School 1935. See Robert Morris College,
Corapolis, Pa.

Roberts Junior College 1945. See Roberts Wesleyan College,
Rochester, N. Y.

ROBERTS WESLEYAN COLLEGE. Rochester, N. Y. 14624. Non-
public institution. Affiliated with the Free Methodist Church of
North America. Established as Chili Seminary 1866. Became:
Chesborough Seminary 1885; Roberts Junior College 1945. Adopted
present name 1949.

Rochester Athenaeum 1829. See Rochester Institute of Technology,
Rochester, N. Y.

ROCHESTER INSTITUTE OF TECHNOLOGY. Rochester, N.Y. 14623.
Non-public institution. Established as Rochester Athenaeum 1829.
Merged with Mechanics Institute 1891. Adopted present name 1944.

ROCKFORD COLLEGE. Rockford, Ill. 61101. Non-public institution. Established as Rockford Female Seminary 1847. Adopted
present name 1892.

Rockford Female Seminary 1847. See Rockford College, Rockford,
Ill.

ROCKY MOUNTAIN COLLEGE. Billings, Mont. 59102. Non-public
institution. Affiliated with The United Presbyterian Church in the
U.S., The United Methodist Church and United Church of Christ.
Established as College of Montana 1878. Merged with Montana Wesleyan University 1923 and became Intermountain Union College 1923.
Merged with Billings Polytechnic Institute 1946 and adopted present
name 1946.

ROGER WILLIAMS COLLEGE MAIN CAMPUS. Bristol, R.I. 02809.
Non-public institution. Established as Providence Branch of Northeastern University 1919. Became: Providence Institute of Engineering and Finance 1939; YMCA Institute 1942; Roger Williams Junior
College 1956; Roger Williams College 1968. Adopted present name
1974.

Roger Williams College 1968. See Roger Williams College Main
Campus, Bristol, R.I.

Roger Williams Junior College 1956. See Roger Williams College
Main Campus, Bristol, R.I.

Rogers College, Maryknoll, N.Y. Closed June 1973.

Roosevelt College of Chicago 1945. See Roosevelt University,
Chicago, Ill.

ROOSEVELT UNIVERSITY. Chicago, Ill. 60605. Non-public institution. Established as Roosevelt College of Chicago 1945. Adopted
present name 1954.

ROSARY COLLEGE. River Forest, Ill. 60305. Non-public institution. Affiliated with the Sisters of St. Dominic of Sinsinawa, Wisc.,
Roman Catholic Church. Established as Sinsinawa Academy 1848,
at Sinsinawa, Wisc. Became: St. Clara College 1901. Adopted
present name after moving to present location 1918.

Rosary Hill College 1947. See Daemen College, Buffalo, N.Y.

ROSE-HULMAN INSTITUTE OF TECHNOLOGY. Terre Haute, Ind.
47803. Non-public institution. Established as Terre Haute School
of Industrial Science 1874. Became: Rose Polytechnic Institute
1875. Adopted present name 1970.

Rose Polytechnic Institute 1875. See Rose-Hulman Institute of Technology, Terre Haute, Ind.

Russell College, Burlingame, Calif. Closed Oct. 1974.

Russell Creek Academy 1906. See Campbellsville College, Campbellsville, Ky.

RUST COLLEGE. Holly Springs, Miss. 38635. Non-public institution. Related to The United Methodist Church. Established as Shaw School 1866. Became: Shaw University 1870; Rust University 1892. Adopted present name 1915.

Rust University 1892. See Rust College, Holly Springs, Miss.

Rutersville College 1838. See Southwestern University, Georgetown, Tex.

Rutgers College 1825. See Rutgers-The State University, New Brunswick, N.J.

Rutgers College, The State University of New Jersey 1917. See Rutgers-The State University, New Brunswick, N.J.

RUTGERS-THE STATE UNIVERSITY. New Brunswick, N.J. 08903. State institution. Established as Queen's College 1766. Became: Rutgers College 1825; Rutgers College, The State University of New Jersey 1917; Rutgers University, The State University of New Jersey 1946. Adopted present name 1956.

Rutgers University, The State University of New Jersey 1946. See Rutgers-The State University, New Brunswick, N.J.

Rutland County Grammar School 1787. See Castleton State College, Castleton, Vt.

- S -

Sacred Heart Academy 1892. See Sacred Heart College, Belmont, N.C.

Sacred Heart Academy Menlo Park 1898. See Lone Mountain College, San Francisco, Calif.

SACRED HEART COLLEGE. Belmont, N.C. 28012. Non-public institution. Sponsored by the Sisters of Mercy, Roman Catholic Church. Established as Sacred Heart Academy 1892. Adopted present name 1935.

Sacred Heart College 1888. See Regis College, Denver, Colo.

Sacred Heart College 1923. See Aquinas College, Grand Rapids, Mich.

Sacred Heart College 1933. See Kansas Newman College, Wichita, Kan.

SACRED HEART COLLEGE. Wichita, Kan. 67213. Non-public institution. Owned by the Sisters Adorers of the Blood of Christ, Roman Catholic Church. Established as Sacred Heart Junior College 1933. Adopted present name 1952.

Sacred Heart High School and College 1921. See Sacred Heart Seminary, Detroit, Mich.

Sacred Heart Junior College 1933. See Sacred Heart College, Wichita, Kan.

The Sacred Heart Scholasticate 1920. See Oblate College of the Southwest, San Antonio, Tex.

SACRED HEART SEMINARY. Detroit, Mich. 48206. Non-public institution. Owned by the Archdiocese of Detroit, Roman Catholic Church. Established as Sacred Heart High School and College 1921. Became: Sacred Heart Seminary, High School and College 1959. Adopted present official name Sacred Heart Seminary College 1970.

Sacred Heart Seminary College 1970. See Sacred Heart Seminary, Detroit, Mich.

Sacred Heart Seminary, High School and College 1959. See Sacred Heart Seminary, Detroit, Mich.

Saginaw Valley College 1963. See Saginaw Valley State College, University Center, Mich.

SAGINAW VALLEY STATE COLLEGE. University Center, Mich. State institution. Established as Saginaw Valley College 1963. Became: Saginaw Valley State College 1966; Saginaw Valley College 1966. Readopted present name 1975.

St. Aloysius Academy 1857. See Marquette University, Milwaukee, Wisc.

ST. AMBROSE COLLEGE. Davenport, Ia. 52803. Non-public institution. Affiliated with the Diocese of Davenport, Roman Catholic Church. Established as St. Ambrose Seminary 1882. Women's division, Marycrest College established 1939. Adopted present name 1908.

St. Ambrose College 1939. See Marycrest College, Davenport, Ia.

St. Ambrose Seminary 1882. See St. Ambrose College, Davenport, Ia.

ST. ANDREWS PRESBYTERIAN COLLEGE. Laurinburg, N.C. 28352.
Non-public institution. Established through merger of Flora Macdonald College and Presbyterian College 1958. Adopted present name
1958.

St. Ansgar's Academy 1863. See Gustavus Adolphus College, St.
Peter, Minn.

St. Augustine's Academy 1811. See Villanova University, Villanova, Pa.

ST. AUGUSTINE'S COLLEGE. Raleigh, N.C. 27602. Non-public
institution. Affiliated with The Episcopal Church. Established as
St. Augustine's Normal School and Collegiate Institute 1867. Became: St. Augustine's School 1893; St. Augustine's Junior College
1919. Adopted present name 1928.

St. Augustine's Junior College 1919. See St. Augustine's College,
Raleigh, N.C.

St. Augustine's Normal School and Collegiate Institute 1867. See
St. Augustine's College, Raleigh, N.C.

St. Augustine's School 1893. See St. Augustine's College, Raleigh,
N.C.

St. Benedict College, Ferdinand, Ind. Closed Aug. 1970.

St. Benedict's Academy 1887. See College of St. Benedict, St.
Joseph, Minn.

St. Benedict's College 1859. See Benedictine College, Atchison,
Kan.

St. Benedict's College and Academy 1913. See College of St. Benedict, St. Joseph, Minn.

St. Bernadine of Siena College 1937. See Siena College, Loudonville, N.Y.

St. Bernard College 1932. See Southern Benedictine College, St.
Bernard, Ala.

St. Bonaventure College and Seminary 1855. See St. Bonaventure
University, St. Bonaventure, N.Y.

ST. BONAVENTURE UNIVERSITY. St. Bonaventure, N.Y. 14778.
Non-public institution. Conducted by the Franciscan Fathers of the
Order of Friars Minor, Roman Catholic Church. Established as
St. Bonaventure College and Seminary 1855. Adopted present name
1950.

ST. CHARLES SEMINARY. Philadelphia, Pa. 1915. Non-public

institution. Owned by the Archdiocese of Philadelphia, Roman Catholic Church. Established under present official name The Philadelphia Seminary of St. Charles Borromeo 1838.

St. Clara College 1901. See Rosary College, River Forest, Ill.

St. Clare College 1934. See Cardinal Stritch College, Milwaukee, Wisc.

St. Clare College, Williamsville, N.Y. Closed June 1971.

St. Cloud State College 1957. See St. Cloud State University, St. Cloud, Minn.

St. Cloud State Teachers College 1921. See St. Cloud State University, St. Cloud, Minn.

ST. CLOUD STATE UNIVERSITY. St. Cloud, Minn. 56301. State institution. Established as Third State Normal School at St. Cloud 1869. Became: St. Cloud State Teachers College 1921; St. Cloud State College 1957. Adopted present name 1975.

St. Dominic College, St. Charles, Ill. Closed May 1970.

St. Edward's College 1885. See St. Edward's University, Austin, Tex.

ST. EDWARD'S UNIVERSITY. Austin, Tex. 78704. Non-public institution. Established as St. Edward's College 1885. Adopted present name 1925.

ST. FIDELIS COLLEGE. Herman, Pa. 16039. Non-public institution. Owned by the Province of St. Augustine of the Capuchin Order, Inc., Roman Catholic Church. Established as St. Fidelis College and Seminary 1877. Adopted present name 1970.

St. Fidelis College and Seminary 1877. See St. Fidelis College, Herman, Pa.

St. Francis Academy 1847. See Saint Francis College, Loretto, Pa.

St. Francis Academy 1858. See St. Francis College, Brooklyn, N.Y.

ST. FRANCIS COLLEGE. Biddeford, Me. 04005. Non-public institution. Owned by the Franciscan Fathers of Maine, Roman Catholic Church. Established as St. Francis High School 1939. Adopted present name 1943.

ST. FRANCIS COLLEGE. Brooklyn, N.Y. 11201. Non-public institution. Controlled by Franciscan Fathers, Roman Catholic Church. Established as St. Francis Academy 1858. Became: The St. Francis Monastery of the City of Brooklyn 1868. Adopted present name 1884.

ST. FRANCIS COLLEGE. Loretto, Pa. 15940. Non-public institution. Conducted by the Third Order Regular of Saint Francis, Roman Catholic Church. Established as St. Francis Academy 1847. Adopted present name 1920.

ST. FRANCIS de SALES COLLEGE. Milwaukee, Wisc. 53207. Non-public institution. Controlled by the Archdiocese of Milwaukee, Roman Catholic Church. Established as St. Francis Seminary 1856, as secondary and junior departments. Became: St. Francis Minor Department 1941; De Sales Preparatory Seminary 1963. Adopted present name 1970, after merger with Senior Department of St. Francis Seminary.

St. Francis High School 1939. See Saint Francis College, Biddeford, Me.

St. Francis Minor Department 1941. See Saint Francis de Sales College, Milwaukee, Wisc.

St. Francis Monastery of the City of Brooklyn 1868. See St. Francis College, Brooklyn, N. Y.

St. Francis Normal School for Women 1851. See Marian College, Indianapolis, Ind.

St. Francis Seminary 1856. See Saint Francis de Sales College, Milwaukee, Wisc.

St. Francis Summer College 1920. See University of Albuquerque, Albuquerque, N. M.

Saint Francis Xavier Academy for Females 1847. See Saint Xavier College, Chicago, Ill.

ST. HYACINTH COLLEGE AND SEMINARY. Granby, Mass. 01033. Non-public institution. Owned by the St. Anthony Province of the Order of Friars Minor Conventual, Roman Catholic Church. Established as St. Hyacinth Seminary 1926. Adopted present name 1958.

St. Hyacinth Seminary 1926. See St. Hyacinth College and Seminary, Granby, Mass.

St. Ignatius College 1855. See University of San Francisco, San Francisco, Calif.

St. Ignatius College 1870. See Loyola University of Chicago, Chicago, Ill.

St. Ignatius College 1886. See John Carroll University, Cleveland, Oh.

St. John College of Cleveland, Cleveland, Oh. Closed July 1974.

St. John Vianney Seminary, East Aurora, N. Y. Closed June 1974.

St. John Vianney Seminary, Elkhorn, Neb. Closed June 1969.

ST. JOHN'S COLLEGE. Annapolis, Md. 21404. Non-public institution. Established as King William's School 1696. Adopted present name 1784. Established St. John's College, Santa Fe (New Mexico) Campus 1964.

St. John's College 1841. See Fordham University, Bronx, N. Y.

St. John's College 1870. See St. John's University, Jamaica, N. Y.

St. John's College, Santa Fe (New Mexico) Campus 1964. See St. John's College, Annapolis, Md.

ST. JOHN'S SEMINARY. Brighton, Mass. 02135. Non-public institution. Owned by the Archdiocese of Boston, Roman Catholic Church. Established as Boston Ecclesiastical Seminary 1883. Adopted present name 1941. Merged with Cardinal O'Connell Seminary 1968.

St. John's Seminary 1856. See Saint John's University, Collegeville, Minn.

St. John's University, Brooklyn 1933. See St. John's University, Jamaica, N. Y.

ST. JOHN'S UNIVERSITY. Collegeville, Minn. 56321. Non-public institution. Owned by the Order of St. Benedict, Roman Catholic Church. Established as St. John's Seminary 1856. Adopted present name 1883.

ST. JOHN'S UNIVERSITY. Jamaica, N. Y. 11432. Non-public institution. Sponsored by the Congregation of the Mission (Vincentian Fathers) Roman Catholic Church. Established as St. John's College 1870. Became: St. John's University, Brooklyn 1933. Adopted present name 1954. Merged with Notre Dame College of Staten Island 1971.

St. Joseph Academy 1846. See Clarke College, Dubuque, Ia.

St. Joseph Academy 1893. See Siena Heights College, Adrian, Mich.

St. Joseph Business School 1926. See Southern Vermont College, Bennington, Vt.

St. Joseph College, Emmitsburg, Md. Closed June 1973.

ST. JOSEPH COLLEGE. North Windham, Me. 04062. Non-public institution. Owned and operated by the Sisters of Mercy of Portland, Me. Established as St. Joseph College 1915. Became: College of Our Lady of Mercy 1948. Adopted present name 1956.

ST. JOSEPH COLLEGE. West Hartford, Conn. 06117. Non-public institution. Conducted by the Sisters of Mercy, Roman Catholic Church. Established as Mount St. Joseph College 1925. Adopted present name 1935.

St. Joseph College 1873. See Loras College, Dubuque, Ia.

Saint Joseph College 1898. See Saint Joseph Seminary College, St. Benedict, La.

St. Joseph College 1919. See Siena Heights College, Adrian, Mich.

St. Joseph College 1973. See Southern Vermont College, Bennington, Vt.

St. Joseph College of Florida, Jensen Beach, Fla. Closed 1972/73 School Year.

St. Joseph House of Studies 1928. See Don Bosco College, Newton, N.J.

St. Joseph Junior College 1915. See Missouri Western College, St. Joseph, Mo.

St. Joseph Junior College 1962. See Southern Vermont College, Bennington, Vt.

St. Joseph Normal School 1887. See Alverno College, Milwaukee, Wisc.

St. Joseph Preparatory Seminary 1891. See Saint Joseph Seminary College, St. Benedict, La.

St. Joseph Seminary 1911. See Saint Joseph Seminary College, St. Benedict, La.

ST. JOSEPH SEMINARY COLLEGE. St. Benedict, La. 70457. Non-public institution. Conducted by the Benedictine Monks of St. Joseph Abbey and the Ecclesiastical Province of New Orleans, Roman Catholic Church. Established as Saint Joseph Preparatory Seminary in Ponchatoula, La. 1891. Became: Saint Joseph College 1898; Saint Joseph Seminary 1911, after moving to present location. Adopted present name 1969.

St. Joseph Seraphic Seminary, Callicoon, N.Y. Closed June 1968.

St. Joseph's Calumet College 1971. See Calumet College, East Chicago, Ind.

ST. JOSEPH'S COLLEGE. Brooklyn, N.Y. 11205. Non-public institution. Conducted by the Congregation of Sisters of St. Joseph of Brentwood, Roman Catholic Church. Established as St. Joseph's College for Women 1916. Adopted present name 1970.

ST. JOSEPH'S COLLEGE. Philadelphia, Pa. 19131. Non-public institution. Affiliated with the Society of Jesus, Roman Catholic Church. Established under present official name The St. Joseph's College in the City of Philadelphia 1851.

St. Joseph's College 1924. See St. Patrick's College, Mountain View, Calif.

St. Joseph's College Calumet Campus 1960. See Calumet College, East Chicago, Ind.

St. Joseph's College Calumet Center 1951. See Calumet College, East Chicago, Ind.

St. Joseph's College for Women 1916. See St. Joseph's College, Brooklyn, N.Y.

St. Joseph's College in the City of Philadelphia 1851. See St. Joseph's College, Philadelphia, Pa.

St. Joseph's Normal College 1899. See College of Our Lady of the Elms, Chicopee, Mass.

ST. JOSEPH'S SEMINARY. Yonkers, N.Y. 10704. Non-public institution. Owned by the Archbishopric of New York. Established as St. Joseph's Seminary 1896. Adopted present official name St. Joseph's Seminary and College 1898.

St. Joseph's Seminary and College 1898. See St. Joseph's Seminary, Yonkers, N.Y.

St. Joseph's Seminary College, Washington, D.C. Closed 1971/72 School Year.

St. Joseph's Teacher College 1954. See The College of St. Joseph the Provider, Rutland, Vt.

St. Lawrence Academy 1816. See State University of New York College at Potsdam, Potsdam, N.Y.

ST. LEO COLLEGE. St. Leo, Fla. 33574. Non-public institution. Affiliated with the Order of St. Benedict, Roman Catholic Church. Established as St. Leo Military Academy 1889. Became: St. Leo Preparatory School 1921. Adopted present name 1959.

St. Leo Military Academy 1889. See St. Leo College, St. Leo, Fla.

St. Leo Preparatory School 1921. See St. Leo College, St. Leo, Fla.

St. Louis Academy 1818. See St. Louis University, St. Louis, Mo.

St. Louis Baptist College 1957. See Missouri Baptist College, St.
Louis, Mo.

St. Louis College 1820. See Saint Louis University, St. Louis, Mo.

St. Louis College 1894. See St. Mary's University of San Antonio,
San Antonio, Tex.

ST. LOUIS COLLEGE OF PHARMACY. St. Louis, Mo. 63110. Non-
public institution. Established as St. Louis College of Pharmacy
1864. Became: St. Louis College of Pharmacy and Allied Sciences
1946. Re-adopted present name 1962.

St. Louis College of Pharmacy and Allied Sciences 1946. See St.
Louis College of Pharmacy, St. Louis, Mo.

ST. LOUIS CONSERVATORY OF MUSIC. St. Louis, Mo. 63141.
Non-public institution. Established as St. Louis Institute of Music
1924. Adopted present name 1974.

St. Louis Institute of Music 1924. See St. Louis Conservatory of
Music, St. Louis, Mo.

St. Louis Junior College 1955. See Chaminade College of Honolulu,
Honolulu, Haw.

St. Louis Normal School 1857. See Harris Teachers College, St.
Louis, Mo.

ST. LOUIS UNIVERSITY. St. Louis, Mo. 63103. Non-public insti-
tution. Affiliated with the Society of Jesus, Roman Catholic Church.
Established as Saint Louis Academy 1818. Became: Saint Louis
College 1820. Adopted present name 1832.

ST. MARY COLLEGE. Leavenworth, Kan. 66048. Non-public institution. Owned by the Sisters of Charity of Leavenworth, Roman
Catholic Church. Established as St. Mary's Academy 1860. Became: Saint Mary Junior College 1923. Adopted present name 1930.

St. Mary Junior College 1923. See Saint Mary College, Leavenworth, Kan.

ST. MARY-OF-THE-WOODS COLLEGE. St. Mary-of-the-Woods,
Ind. 47876. Non-public institution. Conducted by the Sisters of
Providence of St. Mary-of-the-Woods, Roman Catholic Church. Established as St. Mary's Female Institute, 1841. Adopted present
name 1909.

St. Mary's Academy 1843. See Clarke College, Dubuque, Ia.

St. Mary's Academy 1844. See Saint Mary's College, Notre Dame,
Ind.

St. Mary's Academy 1859.   See   Marylhurst Education Center, Marylhurst, Ore.

St. Mary's Academy 1860.   See   Saint Mary College, Leavenworth, Kan.

St. Mary's Academy and College 1893.   See   Marylhurst Education Center, Marylhurst, Ore.

ST. MARY'S COLLEGE.   Notre Dame, Ind.   46566.   Non-public institution.   Owned by the Sisters of the Holy Cross, Roman Catholic Church.   Established as St. Mary's Academy 1844.   Adopted present name 1903.

St. Mary's College 1876.   See   Belmont Abbey, Belmont, N.C.

St. Mary's College, 1905.   See   Marygrove College, Detroit, Mich.

St. Mary's College 1914.   See   University of Dayton, Dayton, Oh.

St. Mary's College, St. Mary's, Ky.   Closed July 1976.

St. Mary's College and Academy at Prairie du Chien, Wisc. 1913.
See   Mount Mary College, Milwaukee, Wisc.

ST. MARY'S COLLEGE OF MARYLAND.   St. Mary's City, Md.
20686.   State institution.   Established as St. Mary's Female Seminary 1839.   Became: St. Mary's Seminary Junior College 1949.
Adopted present name 1964.

St. Mary's Dominican Academy 1860.   See   St. Mary's Dominican College, New Orleans, La.

ST. MARY'S DOMINICAN COLLEGE.   New Orleans, La.   70118.
Non-public institution.   Owned by the Dominican Sisters of the Congregation of St. Mary's, Roman Catholic Church.   Established as St. Mary's Dominican Academy 1860.   Adopted present name 1910.

St. Mary's Female Institute, 1841.   See   Saint Mary-of-the-Woods College, St. Mary-of-the-Woods, Ind.

St. Mary's Female Seminary 1839.   See   St. Mary's College of Maryland, St. Mary's City, Md.

St. Mary's Institute 1850.   See   University of Dayton, Dayton, Oh.

St. Mary's Institute 1852.   See   St. Mary's University of San Antonio, San Antonio, Tex.

St. Mary's Seminary 1791.   See   St. Mary's Seminary and University, Baltimore, Md.

St. Mary's Seminary 1818.   See   Cardinal Glennon College, St. Louis, Mo.

ST. MARY'S SEMINARY AND UNIVERSITY. Baltimore, Md. 21210.
Non-public institution. Owned by the Society of St. Sulpice, Roman
Catholic Church. Established as St. Mary's Seminary 1791. Adop-
ted present name 1969.

St. Mary's Seminary Junior College 1949. <u>See</u> St. Mary's College
of Maryland, St. Mary's City, Md.

St. Mary's University 1927. <u>See</u> St. Mary's University of San Antonio, San Antonio, Tex.

ST. MARY'S UNIVERSITY OF SAN ANTONIO. San Antonio, Tex.
78228. Non-public institution. Owned by the Society of Mary, Roman Catholic Church. Established as St. Mary's Institute 1852.
Became: St. Louis College 1894; St. Mary's University 1927. Adopted present name 1976.

ST. MEINRAD COLLEGE. St. Meinrad, Ind. 47577. Non-public
institution. Conducted by the Benedictine Monks of St. Meinrad Arch-
abbey, Roman Catholic Church. Established as St. Meinrad Seminary, a secondary school 1857. Incorporated as St. Meinrad's Abbey
1890. Adopted present name after becoming separate liberal arts
college 1959.

St. Meinrad Seminary, 1857. <u>See</u> Saint Meinrad College, St. Meinrad, Ind.

St. Meinrad's Abbey 1890. <u>See</u> Saint Meinrad College, St. Meinrad,
Ind.

St. Michael's College 1874. <u>See</u> College of Sante Fe, Sante Fe,
N. M.

ST. OLAF COLLEGE. Northfield, Minn. 55057. Non-public institution. Affiliated with The American Lutheran Church. Established
as St. Olaf's School 1874. Adopted present name 1889.

St. Olaf's School 1874. <u>See</u> St. Olaf College, Northfield, Minn.

ST. PATRICK'S COLLEGE. Mountain View, Calif. 94040. Non-
public institution. Owned by the Roman Catholic Archdiocese of
San Francisco. Established as St. Joseph's College 1924. Adopted
present name 1968.

ST. PATRICK'S SEMINARY. Menlo Park, Calif. 94025. Non-public
institution. Owned by the Roman Catholic Archdiocese of San Francisco. Established as St. Patrick's Seminary 1891. Became: St.
Patrick's Seminary-Theologate 1924. Adopted present name 1969.

St. Patrick's Seminary 1891. <u>See</u> St. Patrick's Seminary, Menlo
Park, Calif.

St. Patrick's Seminary-Theologate 1924. <u>See</u> St. Patrick's Seminary, Menlo Park, Calif.

ST. PAUL COLLEGE. Lawrenceville, Va. 23868. Non-public in-
stitution. Affiliated with The Episcopal Church. Established as
Saint Paul's Normal and Industrial School 1888. Became: St. Paul's
Polytechnic Institute 1942. Adopted present name 1957.

St. Paul College of Law 1900. See William Mitchell College of
Law, St. Paul, Minn.

St. Paul's College, Washington, D.C. Closed 1973/74 School Year.

St. Paul's Normal and Industrial School 1888. See Saint Paul College, Lawrenceville, Va.

St. Paul's Polytechnic Institute 1942. See Saint Paul College, Lawrenceville, Va.

St. Peters College, Baltimore, Md. Closed June 1968.

St. Procopius College 1887. See Illinois Benedictine College,
Lisle, Ill.

St. Raphael's Seminary 1839. See Loras College, Dubuque, Ia.

St. Regina Academy 1881. See Edgewood College, Madison, Wisc.

St. Rose Junior College 1931. See Viterbo College, La Crosse,
Wisc.

St. Scholastica's Academy 1863. See Benedictine College, Atchison,
Kan.

St. Stephens College 1860. See Bard College, Annandale-on-Hudson,
N.Y.

St. Thomas Aquinas Seminary 1885. See College of St. Thomas,
St. Paul, Minn.

St. Thomas College 1888. See University of Scranton, Scranton,
Pa.

St. Vincent's College 1865. See Loyola Marymount College, Los
Angeles, Calif.

St. Vincent's College 1898. See DePaul University, Chicago, Ill.

St. Vincent's Seminary 1862. See Mary Immaculate Seminary and
College, Northampton, Pa.

ST. XAVIER COLLEGE. Chicago, Ill. 60655. Non-public institu-
tion. Owned by the Sisters of Mercy-Chicago Province, Roman
Catholic Church. Established as Saint Francis Xavier Academy for
Females 1847. Adopted present name 1956.

St. Xavier College 1840. See Xavier University, Cincinnati, Oh.

Salem Academy and College 1907. See Salem College, Winston-Salem, N. C.

SALEM COLLEGE. Winston-Salem, N. C. 27108. Non-public institution. Affiliated with the Southern Province of the Moravian Church. Established as Salem Female Academy 1772. Became: Salem Female Academy and College 1886. Present official name Salem Academy and College adopted 1907.

Salem Female Academy 1772. See Salem College, Winston-Salem, N. C.

Salem Female Academy and College 1886. See Salem College, Winston-Salem, N. C.

Salem Normal School 1854. See Salem State College, Salem, Mass.

SALEM STATE COLLEGE. Salem, Mass. 01970. State institution. Established as Salem Normal School 1854. Became: State Teachers College at Salem 1932; State College at Salem 1960. Adopted present name 1968.

SALISBURY STATE COLLEGE. Salisbury, Md. 21801. State institution. Established as Maryland State Normal School 1925. Became: State Teachers College at Salisbury 1935. Adopted present name 1963.

Salmon P. Chase College of Law 1972. See Northern Kentucky University, Covington, Ky.

Salt Lake Collegiate Institute 1875. See Westminister College, Salt Lake City, Ut.

Salve Regina College 1934. See Salve Regina-The Newport College, Newport, R. I.

SALVE REGINA-THE NEWPORT COLLEGE. Newport, R. I. 02840. Non-public institution. Conducted by Religious Sisters of Mercy of the Union, Roman Catholic Church. Established as Salve Regina College 1934. Adopted present name 1976.

Sam Houston Normal Institute 1879. See Sam Houston State University, Huntsville, Tex.

Sam Houston State College 1965. See Sam Houston State University, Huntsville, Tex.

Sam Houston State Teachers College 1923. See Sam Houston State University, Huntsville, Tex.

SAM HOUSTON STATE UNIVERSITY. Huntsville, Tex. 77340. State

institution. Established as Sam Houston Normal Institute 1879. Became: Sam Houston State Teachers College 1923; Sam Houston State College 1965. Adopted present name 1969.

SAMFORD UNIVERSITY. Birmingham, Ala. 35209. Non-public institution. Owned by the Alabama Baptist State Convention (Southern Baptist). Established as Howard College 1841. Adopted present name 1965.

Samuel Houston College 1952. See Houston-Tillotson College, Austin, Tex.

San Angelo Junior College 1928. See Angelo State University, San Angelo, Tex.

The San Antonio Philosophical and Theological Seminary 1903. See Oblate College of the Southwest, San Antonio, Tex.

San Diego College for Women, 1967. See University of San Diego, San Diego, Calif.

San Diego State College 1935. See San Diego State University, San Diego, Calif.

San Diego State Normal School 1897. See San Diego State University, San Diego, Calif.

San Diego State Teachers College 1921. See San Diego State University, San Diego, Calif.

SAN DIEGO STATE UNIVERSITY. San Diego, Calif. 92115. State institution. Established as San Diego State Normal School 1897. Became: San Diego State Teachers College 1921; San Diego State College 1935; California State University, San Diego 1972. Adopted present name 1974.

San Fernando Valley Campus of Los Angeles State College of Applied Arts and Sciences 1956. See California State University, Northridge, Northridge, Calif.

San Fernando Valley State College 1958. See California State University, Northridge, Northridge, Calif.

San Francisco Art Association 1871. See San Francisco Art Institute, San Francisco, Calif.

SAN FRANCISCO ART INSTITUTE. San Francisco, Calif. 94133. Non-public institution. Affiliated with the University of California. Established as San Francisco Art Association 1871. Became: Mark Hopkins Institute 1893; California School of Fine Arts 1916; San Francisco Art Institute College 1961. Adopted present name 1976.

San Francisco Art Institute College 1961. See San Francisco Art Institute, San Francisco, Calif.

San Francisco College for Women 1930. See Lone Mountain College, San Francisco, Calif.

San Francisco State College 1935. See California State University, San Francisco, San Francisco, Calif.

San Francisco State Normal School 1899. See California State University, San Francisco, San Francisco, Calif.

San Francisco State Teachers' College 1921. See California State University, San Francisco, San Francisco, Calif.

San Isabel Junior College 1933. See University of Southern Colorado, Pueblo, Colo.

San Jose State College 1935. See San Jose State University, San Jose, Calif.

San Jose State Normal School 1887. See San Jose State University, San Jose, Calif.

San Jose State Teachers College 1921. See San Jose State University, San Jose, Calif.

SAN JOSE STATE UNIVERSITY. San Jose, Calif. 95114. State institution. Established as Minn's Evening Normal School, department of San Francisco school system 1857. Control passed to state and became California State Normal School 1862. Moved to present location 1871. Became: San Jose State Normal School 1887; San Jose State Teachers College 1921; San Jose State College 1935; California State University, San Jose 1972. Adopted present name 1974.

San Luis Rey College, San Luis Rey, Calif. Closed Sept. 1969.

Santa Barbara Art Institute, Santa Barbara, Calif. Closed Oct. 1975.

Santa Barbara Normal School 1919. See University of California Santa Barbara, Santa Barbara, Calif.

Santa Barbara Normal School of Manual Arts and Home Economics 1909. See University of California, Santa Barbara, Santa Barbara, Calif.

Santa Barbara State College 1935. See University of California, Santa Barbara, Santa Barbara, Calif.

Santa Barbara State Teachers College 1921. See University of California, Santa Barbara, Santa Barbara, Calif.

Santa Clara College 1851. See University of Santa Clara, Santa Clara, Calif.

SARAH LAWRENCE COLLEGE. Bronxville, N.Y. 10708. Non-public institution. Established as Sarah Lawrence College for Women 1928. Adopted present name 1947.

Sarah Lawrence College for Women 1928. See Sarah Lawrence College, Bronxville, N.Y.

Sault Sainte Marie Branch of Michigan Technological University 1946. See Lake Superior State College, Sault Sainte Marie, Mich.

SAVANNAH STATE COLLEGE. Savannah, Ga. 31404. State institution. Established as Georgia State Industrial College for Colored Youth 1890. Became: Georgia State College 1931. Adopted present name 1950.

Scandinavian Department of Baptist Union Theological Seminary of the University of Chicago 1871. See Bethel College, St. Paul, Minn.

Scarritt Bible and Training School for Women 1892. See Scarritt College for Christian Workers, Nashville, Tenn.

SCARRITT COLLEGE FOR CHRISTIAN WORKERS. Nashville, Tenn. 37203. Non-public institution. Owned by The United Methodist Church. Established as Scarritt Bible and Training School for Women 1892, in Kansas City. Adopted present name 1924, after moving to present location.

Scarritt-Morrisville College. See Central Methodist College, Fayette, Mo.

Schenectady Academy 1795. See Union College, Schenectady, N.Y.

School for Christian Workers 1885. See Springfield College, Springfield, Mass.

School of Automotive Trades 1920. See General Motors Institute, Flint, Mich.

School of Business and Civic Administration of The City College 1919. See Bernard M. Baruch College, New York, N.Y.

School of Engineering of Milwaukee 1903. See Milwaukee School of Engineering, Milwaukee, Wisc.

School of Expression 1879. See Curry College, Milton, Mass.

School of Fine and Applied Art 1811. See Portland School of Art, Portland, Me.

School of Household Economics of the Cincinnati General Hospital 1916. See University of Cincinnati, Cincinnati, Oh.

School of Insurance 1947. See The College of Insurance, New York, N.Y.

School of Law of the Youngstown Association School 1908. See Youngstown State University, Youngstown, Oh.

School of Marine Engineering, U.S. Naval Academy, Annapolis, Md. 1909. See Naval Postgraduate School, Monterey, Calif.

School of Medicine, Marquette University 1913. See The Medical College of Wisconsin, Milwaukee, Wisc.

School of the California Guild of Arts and Crafts in Berkeley 1907. See California College of Arts and Crafts, Oakland, Calif.

School of the Immaculate Conception 1891. See Seattle University, Seattle, Wash.

SCHOOL OF THEOLOGY AT CLAREMONT. Claremont, Calif. 91711. Non-public institution. Affiliated with The United Methodist Church, The Episcopal Church and the Christian Church (Disciples of Christ). Established as Maclay College of Theology, San Fernando 1885. Became affiliated with the University of Southern California 1922. Adopted present official name Southern California School of Theology 1956, after becoming independent and moving to present location.

SCHOOL OF VISUAL ARTS. New York, N.Y. 10010. Non-public institution. Established as Cartoonist and Illustrator's School 1947 by Silas H. Rhodes and Burne Hogarth. Adopted present name 1956.

Schools of the Art Institute of Chicago 1882. See Art Institute of Chicago, Chicago, Ill.

Schuylkill Seminary 1928. See Albright College, Reading, Pa.

Scio College 1911. See Mount Union College, Alliance, Oh.

Scotia Seminary 1867. See Barber-Scotia College, Concord, N.C.

Scotia Women's College 1916. See Barber-Scotia College, Concord, N.C.

SCRIPPS COLLEGE. Claremont, Calif. 91711. Non-public institution. Established as Scripps College for Women 1926. Adopted present name 1927. Member of the Claremont Colleges system.

Scripps College for Women 1926. See Scripps College, Claremont, Calif.

Scripps Institution of Biological Research 1912. See University of California, San Diego, La Jolla, Calif.

Seattle College 1898. See Seattle University, Seattle, Wash.

SEATTLE PACIFIC COLLEGE. Seattle, Wash. 98119. Non-public institution. Affiliated with the Free Methodist Church of North

America. Established as Seattle Seminary 1891. Adopted present name 1915.

Seattle Seminary 1891. See Seattle Pacific College, Seattle, Wash.

SEATTLE UNIVERSITY. Seattle, Wash. 98122. Non-public institution. Sponsored by the Society of Jesus, Roman Catholic Church. Established as School of the Immaculate Conception 1891. Became: Seattle College 1898. Adopted present name 1948.

Second District Agricultural School 1909. See Arkansas Tech University, Russellville, Ark.

Secretarial Institute and Training School 1896. See George Williams College, Downers Grove, Ill.

Select School at Pine Grove 1858. See Grove City College, Grove City, Pa.

Seminary for Girls 1891. See Queens College, Charlotte, N. C.

Seminary of Our Lady of Angels 1863. See Niagara University, Niagara University, N. Y.

Seminary of Our Lady of Providence, Providence, R. I. Closed June 1975.

Seminary of St. Francis Xavier 1829. See The Athenaeum of Ohio, Norwood, Cincinnati, Oh.

Seminary of St. Mary of the Barrens, Perryville, Mo. 1818. See Mary Immaculate Seminary and College, Northampton, Pa.

Seminary West of the Suwannee 1851. See Florida State University, Tallahassee, Fla.

Service Seminary 1794. See Pittsburgh Theological Seminary, Pittsburgh, Pa.

Seton Hall College 1856. See Seton Hall University, South Orange, N. J.

Seton Hall College of Medicine and Dentistry 1954. See College of Medicine and Dentistry of New Jersey at Newark, Newark, N. J.

SETON HALL UNIVERSITY. South Orange, N. J. 07079. Non-public institution. Affiliated with the Archdiocese of Newark, Roman Catholic Church. Established as Seton Hall College 1856. Adopted present name 1950.

Seventh-day Adventist Theological Seminary 1934. See Andrews University, Berrien Springs, Mich.

Shaw Business School 1898. See Husson College, Bangor, Me.

Shaw Collegiate Institute 1870. See Shaw University, Raleigh, N. C.

Shaw School 1866. See Rust College, Holly Springs, Miss.

SHAW UNIVERSITY. Raleigh, N. C. 27602. Non-public institution.
Affiliated with the American Baptist Convention. Established as
Raleigh Institute 1865. Became: Shaw Collegiate Institute 1870.
Adopted present name 1875.

Shaw University 1870. See Rust College, Holly Springs, Miss.

Sheldon Jackson College 1902. See Westminister College, Salt Lake
City, Ut.

Shelton College, Cape May, N. J. Closed June, 1971.

Shenandoah College 1937. See Shenandoah College and Conservatory
of Music, Winchester, Va.

SHENANDOAH COLLEGE AND CONSERVATORY OF MUSIC. Winchester, Va. 22601. Non-public institution. Affiliated with the
United Methodist Church. Established as Shenandoah Seminary 1875,
Dayton, Va., by A. P. Funkhauser. Became: Shenandoah Institute
1884; Shenandoah Collegiate Institute and School of Music 1902; Shenandoah College and Conservatory of Music 1924; Shenandoah College
1937; Shenandoah Conservatory of Music 1937. Adopted present name
1974.

Shenandoah Collegiate Institute and School of Music 1902. See Shenandoah College and Conservatory of Music, Winchester, Va.

Shenandoah Conservatory of Music 1937. See Shenandoah College
and Conservatory of Music, Winchester, Va.

Shenandoah Institute 1884. See Shenandoah College and Conservatory of Music, Winchester, Va.

Shenandoah Seminary, Dayton, Va. 1875. See Shenandoah College
and Conservatory of Music, Winchester, Va.

Shepardson College 1897. See Denison University, Granville, Oh.

SHEPHERD COLLEGE. Shepherdstown, W. Va. 25443. State insti-
tution. Established under present name 1871. Became: Shepherd
State Normal School 1872; Shepherd State Teachers College 1931.
Readopted present name 1943.

Shepherd State Normal School 1872. See Shepherd College, Shepherdstown, W. Va.

Shepherd State Teachers College 1931. See Shepherd College,
Shepherdstown, W. Va.

SHIMER COLLEGE. Mt. Carroll, Ill. 61053. Non-public institution. Affiliated with the Episcopal Church. Established as Mt. Carroll Seminary 1853. Became: Frances Shimer Academy of the University of Chicago 1896; Frances Shimer Academy and Junior College 1908; Frances Shimer School 1910; Frances Shimer Junior College 1932; Frances Shimer College 1942. Adopted present name 1950.

SHIPPENSBURG STATE COLLEGE. Shippensburg, Pa. 17257. State institution. Established as Cumberland Valley State Normal School 1871. Became: State Teachers College at Shippenburg 1927. Adopted present name 1960.

SHORTER COLLEGE. Rome, Ga. 30161. Non-public institution. Affiliated with the Georgia Baptist Convention (Southern Baptist). Established as Cherokee Baptist Female College 1873. Became: Shorter Female College 1877. Adopted present name 1923.

Shorter Female College 1877. See Shorter College, Rome, Ga.

SIENA COLLEGE. Loudonville, N. Y. 12211. Established as St. Bernadine of Siena College 1937. Adopted present name 1968.

Siena College, Memphis, Tenn. Closed Dec. 1970.

SIENA HEIGHTS COLLEGE. Adrian, Mich. 49221. Non-public institution. Owned by the Sisters of St. Dominic, Roman Catholic Church. Established as St. Joseph Academy 1893. Became: St. Joseph College 1919. Adopted present name 1938.

Siloam School of the Bible. See John Brown University, Siloam Springs, Ark.

SILVER LAKE COLLEGE. Manitowoc, Wisc. 54220. Non-public institution. Owned by the Franciscan Sisters of Christian Charity, Roman Catholic Church. Established as Holy Family Normal School 1869. Became: Holy Family College 1935; Silver Lake College of the Holy Family 1972. Adopted present name 1975.

Silver Lake College of the Holy Family 1972. See Silver Lake College, Manitowoc, Wisc.

Silvermine College of Art, New Canaan, Conn. Closed June 1971.

SIMMONS COLLEGE. Boston, Mass. 02155. Non-public institution. Established as Simmons Female College 1899. Adopted present name 1915. Absorbed Garland Junior College 1976.

Simmons College 1891. See Hardin-Simmons University, Abilene, Tex.

Simmons Female College 1899. See Simmons College, Boston, Mass.

Simmons University 1925. See Hardin-Simmons University, Abilene, Tex.

Simon's Rock 1964. See Simon's Rock Early College, Great Barrington, Mass.

SIMON'S ROCK EARLY COLLEGE. Great Barrington, Mass. 01230. Non-public institution. Established as Simon's Rock 1964. Adopted present name 1976.

Simpson Bible College 1955. See Simpson College, San Francisco, Calif.

Simpson Bible Institute, Seattle, Wash. 1921. See Simpson College, San Francisco, Calif.

Simpson Centenary College 1866. See Simpson College, Indianola, Ia.

SIMPSON COLLEGE. Indianola, Ia. 50125. Non-public institution. Established as Indianola Seminary 1860. Became: Simpson Centenary College 1866. Adopted present name 1885.

SIMPSON COLLEGE. San Francisco, Calif. 94134. Non-public institution. Owned by the Christian and Missionary Alliance. Established as Simpson Bible Institute, Seattle, Wash. 1921. Became: Simpson Bible College 1955 after moving to present location. Adopted present name 1971.

Sinsinawa Academy 1848, at Sinsinawa, Wisc. See Rosary College, River Forest, Ill.

SIOUX FALLS COLLEGE. Sioux Falls, S.D. 57101. Non-public institution. Affiliated with the American Baptist Convention. Established as Dakota Collegiate Institute 1883. Became: Sioux Falls University 1885. Adopted present name after merger with Grand Island College of Nebraska 1931.

Sioux Falls University 1885. See Sioux Falls College, Sioux Falls, S.D.

SKIDMORE COLLEGE. Saratoga Springs, N.Y. 12866. Non-public institution. Established as Skidmore School of Arts of Saratoga Springs 1911. Adopted present name 1922.

Skidmore School of Arts of Saratoga Springs 1911. See Skidmore College, Saratoga Springs, N.Y.

Slater Industrial Academy 1892. See University of North Carolina at Winston-Salem, N.C.

SLIPPERY ROCK STATE COLLEGE. Slippery Rock, Pa. 16057. State institution. Established as State Normal School at Slippery

Rock 1889.   Became: State Teachers College at Slippery Rock 1926. Adopted present name 1960.

Society for the Collegiate Instruction of Women 1882.   See Radcliffe College, Cambridge, Mass.

Sonoma State College 1960.   See California State College, Sonoma, Rohnert Park, Calif.

Soule University, 1873.   See Southwestern University, Georgetown, Tex.

South Bend-Mishawaka Center of Indiana University 1933.   See Indiana University at South Bend, South Bend, Ind.

South Carolina College 1801.   See University of South Carolina, Columbia, S. C.

South Carolina Industrial and Winthrop Normal College 1891.   See Winthrop College, Rock Hill, S. C.

South Carolina Military Academy 1887.   See The Citadel, Charleston, S. C.

SOUTH CAROLINA STATE COLLEGE.   Orangeburg, S. C. 29115. State institution.   Established as Colored Normal, Industrial, Agricultural and Mechanical College of South Carolina 1895.   Adopted present name 1954.

South Dakota School of Mines 1889.   See South Dakota School of Mines and Technology, Rapid City, S. D.

SOUTH DAKOTA SCHOOL OF MINES AND TECHNOLOGY.   Rapid City, S. C. 57701.   State institution.   Established as Dakota School of Mines 1885.   Became: South Dakota School of Mines 1889. Adopted present name 1943.

SOUTH DAKOTA STATE UNIVERSITY.   Brookings, S. D. 57006. State institution.   Established as Agricultural College of South Dakota 1881.   Became: State College of Agriculture and Mechanic Arts 1907.   Adopted present name 1964.

South Georgia State Normal College 1906.   See Valdosta State College, Valdosta, Ga.

South Georgia Teachers College 1929.   See Georgia Southern College, Statesboro, Ga.

South Lancaster Academy 1883.   See Atlantic Union College, South Lancaster, Mass.

South Mississippi College 1906.   See William Carey College, Hattiesburg, Miss.

South Park Junior College 1923. See Lamar University, Beaumont,
Tex.

South Texas State Teachers College 1925. See Texas Agricultural
and Industrial University, Kingsville, Tex.

Southeastern Louisiana College 1928. See Southeastern Louisiana
University, Hammond, La.

SOUTHEASTERN LOUISIANA UNIVERSITY. Hammond, La. 70401.
State institution. Established as Hammond Junior College 1925. Became: Southeastern Louisiana College 1928. Adopted present name
1970.

Southeastern Massachusetts Technological Institute 1964. See Southeastern Massachusetts University, North Dartmouth, Mass.

SOUTHEASTERN MASSACHUSETTS UNIVERSITY. North Dartmouth,
Mass. 02747. State institution. Established as Southeastern Massa-
chusetts Technological Institute 1964, as the result of a merger of
New Bedford Institute of Technology and Bradford Durfee College of
Technology. Adopted present name 1969.

Southeastern Normal School 1909. See Southeastern Oklahoma State
University, Durant, Okla.

SOUTHEASTERN OKLAHOMA STATE UNIVERSITY. Durant, Okla.
74701. State institution. Established as Southeastern Normal School
1909. Became: Southeastern State Teachers College 1919; Southeastern State College 1939. Adopted present name 1975.

Southeastern State College 1939. See Southeastern Oklahoma State
University, Durant, Okla.

Southeastern State Teachers College 1919. See Southeastern Oklahoma State University, Durant, Okla.

Southern and Western Theological Seminary 1819. See Maryville
College, Maryville, Tenn.

SOUTHERN ARKANSAS UNIVERSITY MAIN CAMPUS. Magnolia,
Ark. 71753. State institution. Established as Third District Agricultural School 1909. Became: State Agricultural and Mechanical
College, Third District 1925; Southern State College 1951. Adopted
present name 1976.

SOUTHERN BENEDICTINE COLLEGE. St. Bernard, Ala. 35138.
Non-public institution. Owned by the Benedictine Society of Alabama,
Roman Catholic Church. Established as Benedictine Society of Alabama 1893. Became: St. Bernard College 1932. Merged with Cullman College 1976. Adopted present name 1976.

SOUTHERN BIBLE COLLEGE. Houston, Tex. 77028. Non-public

institution.   Affiliated with the Pentecostal Church of God.   Established as Southern Pentecostal Bible Institute 1958 by Dr. Worden McDonald.   Adopted present name 1959.

Southern Branch of the University of Idaho 1927.   See Idaho State University, Pocatello, Ida.

Southern Branch, University of California 1919.   See University of California, Los Angeles, Los Angeles, Calif.

Southern California Bible College 1939.   See Southern California College, Costa Mesa, Calif.

Southern California Bible School 1920.   See Southern California College, Costa Mesa, Calif.

SOUTHERN CALIFORNIA COLLEGE.   Costa Mesa, Calif. 92626. Non-public institution.   Owned by the Southern California District Council, Assemblies of God.   Established as Southern California Bible School 1920.   Became: Southern California Bible College 1939. Adopted present name 1959.

SOUTHERN CALIFORNIA COLLEGE OF OPTOMETRY.   Fullerton, Calif. 92631.   Non-public institution.   Established as Los Angeles Medical School of Ophthalmology and Optometry 1904.   Became: Los Angeles School of Optometry 1922; Los Angeles College of Optometry 1950.   Adopted present name 1974, after moving to present location.

Southern California School of Theology 1956.   See School of Theology at Claremont, Claremont, Calif.

Southern Christian Institute 1954.   See Tougaloo College, Tougaloo, Miss.

Southern College 1906.   See Florida Southern College, Lakeland, Fla.

Southern Colorado Junior College 1934.   See University of Southern Colorado, Pueblo, Colo.

Southern Colorado State College 1963.   See University of Southern Colorado, Pueblo, Colo.

SOUTHERN CONNECTICUT STATE COLLEGE.   New Haven, Conn. 06515.   State institution.   Established as New Haven Normal School 1893.   Became: New Haven State Teachers College 1937.   Adopted present name 1959.

Southern Illinois Normal University 1869.   See Southern Illinois University at Carbondale, Carbondale, Ill.

SOUTHERN ILLINOIS UNIVERSITY AT CARBONDALE.   Carbondale,

Ill. 62901. State institution. Established as Southern Illinois Normal University 1869. Adopted present name 1947.

Southern Industrial School 1896. See Southern Missionary College, Collegedale, Tenn.

Southern Junior College 1916. See Southern Missionary College, Collegedale, Tenn.

SOUTHERN MISSIONARY COLLEGE. Collegedale, Tenn. 37315. Nonpublic institution. Owned by the Southern Union Conference of Seventh-day Adventists. Established as Graysville Academy 1892. Became: Southern Industrial School 1896; Southern Training School 1901; Southern Junior College 1916. Adopted present name 1944.

Southern Oregon College 1956. See Southern Oregon State College, Ashland, Ore.

Southern Oregon College of Education 1939. See Southern Oregon State College, Ashland, Ore.

Southern Oregon Normal School 1926. See Southern Oregon State College, Ashland, Ore.

SOUTHERN OREGON STATE COLLEGE. Ashland, Ore. 97520. State institution. Established as Southern Oregon Normal School 1926. Became: Southern Oregon College of Education 1939; Southern Oregon College 1956. Adopted present name 1975.

Southern Pentecostal Bible Institute 1958. See Southern Bible College, Houston, Tex.

Southern Regional Branch of the University of Nevada 1951. See University of Nevada, Las Vegas; Las Vegas, Nev.

Southern State College 1951. See Southern Arkansas University Main Campus, Magnolia, Ark.

Southern State College 1964. See University of South Dakota at Springfield, Springfield, S.D.

Southern State Normal School 1881. See University of South Dakota at Springfield, Springfield, S.D.

Southern State Teachers College 1947. See University of South Dakota at Springfield, Springfield, S.D.

SOUTHERN TECHNICAL INSTITUTE. Marietta, Ga. 30060. State institution. Established as The Technical Institute 1947. Adopted present name 1949.

Southern Training School 1901. See Southern Missionary College, Collegedale, Tenn.

Southern University 1856. See Birmingham-Southern College, Birmingham, Ala.

SOUTHERN UNIVERSITY AND AGRICULTURAL AND MECHANICAL COLLEGE. Baton Rouge, La. 70813. State institution. Established as Southern University of New Orleans 1879. Adopted present name 1914, after moving to present location.

Southern University of New Orleans 1879. See Southern University and Agricultural and Mechanical College, Baton Rouge, La.

SOUTHERN UTAH STATE COLLEGE. Cedar City, Ut. 84720. State institution. Established as Branch Normal School 1897. Became: Branch Agricultural College 1913; College of Southern Utah 1953. Adopted present name 1969.

SOUTHERN VERMONT COLLEGE. Bennington, Vt. 05201. Non-public institution. Established as St. Joseph Business School 1926 by Sisters of St. Joseph, Rutland, Vt. Became: St. Joseph Junior College 1962; St. Joseph College 1973. Ownership transferred to secular Board of Trustees 1974, adopted present name 1974.

The Southwest Kansas Conference College 1885. See Southwestern College, Winfield, Kan.

Southwest Missouri State Teachers College 1919. See Southwest Missouri State University, Springfield, Mo.

SOUTHWEST MISSOURI STATE UNIVERSITY. Springfield, Mo. 65802. State institution. Established as Missouri State Normal School 1906. Became: Southwest Missouri State Teachers College 1919; Southwest Missouri State College 1945. Adopted present name 1972.

Southwest State Teachers College 1923. See Southwest Texas State University, San Marcos, Tex.

Southwest Texas State College 1959. See Southwest Texas State University, San Marcos, Tex.

Southwest Texas State Normal School 1899. See Southwest Texas State University, San Marcos, Tex.

SOUTHWEST TEXAS STATE UNIVERSITY. San Marcos, Tex. 78666. State institution. Established as Southwest Texas State Normal School 1899. Became: Southwest State Teachers College 1923; Southwest Texas State College 1959. Adopted present name 1969.

Southwest Virginia Institute 1888. See Virginia Intermont College, Bristol, Va.

SOUTHWESTERN AT MEMPHIS. Memphis, Tenn. 38112. Non-public institution. Affiliated with the Presbyterian Church in the U. S.

Established as Montgomery Masonic College 1848, Clarksville, Tenn. Became: Stewart College 1855; Southwestern Presbyterian University 1875. Moved to present location 1925. Adopted present name 1945.

SOUTHWESTERN BAPTIST THEOLOGICAL SEMINARY. Fort Worth, Tex. 76122. Non-public institution. Controlled by the Southern Baptist Convention. Established as Baylor Theological Seminary, Waco 1901, a part of Baylor University. Became independent, adopted present name 1907. Moved to present location 1910.

Southwestern Baptist University 1875. See Union University, Jackson, Tenn.

SOUTHWESTERN COLLEGE. Winfield, Kan. 67156. Non-public institution. Owned by the Kansas West Annual Conference of The United Methodist Church. Established as The Southwest Kansas Conference College 1885. Adopted present name 1908. Merged with Winfield College of Music 1926.

Southwestern Collegiate Institute 1919. See John Brown University, Siloam Springs, Ark.

Southwestern Institute of Technology 1941. See Southwestern Oklahoma State University, Weatherford, Okla.

Southwestern Junior College 1916. See Southwestern Union College, Keene, Tex.

Southwestern Louisiana Industrial Institute 1898. See The University of Southwestern Louisiana, Lafayette, La.

Southwestern Louisiana Institute of Liberal and Technical Learning 1921. See The University of Southwestern Louisiana, Lafayette, La.

Southwestern Normal School 1901. See Southwestern State College, Weatherford, Okla. Southwestern Oklahoma State University, Weatherford, Okla.

SOUTHWESTERN OKLAHOMA STATE UNIVERSITY. Weatherford, Okla. 73096. State institution. Established as Southwestern Normal School 1901. Became: Southwestern State Teachers College 1920; Southwestern State College of Diversified Occupations 1939; Southwestern Institute of Technology 1941; Southwestern State College 1949. Adopted present name 1975.

Southwestern Presbyterian University 1875. See Southwestern at Memphis, Memphis, Tenn.

Southwestern State College 1949. See Southwestern Oklahoma State University, Weatherford, Okla.

195   Southwestern State

Southwestern State College of Diversified Occupations 1939. See
Southwestern Oklahoma State University, Weatherford, Okla.

Southwestern State Normal School 1874. See California State College, California, Pa.

Southwestern State Teachers College 1920. See Southwestern Oklahoma State University, Weatherford, Okla.

SOUTHWESTERN UNION COLLEGE. Keene, Tex. 70659. Non-public institution. Owned by the Seventh-day Adventists. Established
as Keene Academy 1893. Became: Southwestern Junior College 1916.
Adopted present name 1963.

SOUTHWESTERN UNIVERSITY. Georgetown, Tex. 78626. Non-public institution. Affiliated with The United Methodist Church. Established as Rutersville College 1838. Merged with Wesleyan College
1873, McKenzie College 1873, Soule University 1873. Became:
Texas University 1873, after moving to present location. Adopted
present name 1875.

SPALDING COLLEGE. Louisville, Ky. 40203. Non-public institution. Conducted by the Sisters of Charity of Nazareth, Roman Catholic Church. Established as Nazareth College 1920. Merged with
Nazareth Junior College 1938. Became: Nazareth College in Louisville when colleges separated 1961; Catherine Spalding College 1963.
Adopted present name 1968.

Spearfish Normal School 1898. See Black Hills State College,
Spearfish, S.D.

SPELMAN COLLEGE. Atlanta, Ga. 30314. Non-public institution.
Affiliated with the Atlanta University Center. Established as Atlanta
Baptist Female Seminary 1881. Adopted present name 1924.

Spencerian Business College 1877. See Dyke College, Cleveland,
Oh.

SPERTUS COLLEGE OF JUDAICA. Chicago, Ill. 60605. Non-public
institution. Established as College of Jewish Studies 1925. Adopted
present name 1970.

Spring Arbor Seminary 1835. See Albion College, Albion, Mich.

Spring Creek Normal School 1880. See Bridgewater College,
Bridgewater, Va.

SPRING GARDEN COLLEGE. Chestnut Hill, Pa. 19118. Non-public
institution. Established as Spring Garden Institute 1850. Adopted
present name 1969.

Spring Garden Institute 1850. See Spring Garden College, Chestnut
Hill, Pa.

SPRINGFIELD COLLEGE. Springfield, Mass. 01109. Non-public institution. Established as School for Christian Workers 1885. Became: International YMCA Training School 1890; International YMCA College 1912. Adopted present name 1953.

Springfield College 1873. See Drury College, Springfield, Mo.

Springfield Division, Northeastern University 1915. See Western New England College, Springfield, Mass.

Stanislaus State College 1957. See California State College, Stanislaus, Turlock, Calif.

State Agricultural and Mechanical College 1925. See Arkansas State University, State University, Ark.

State Agricultural and Mechanical College for Negroes 1890. See Alabama Agricultural and Mechanical University, Normal, Ala.

State Agricultural and Mechanical College, Third District 1925. See Southern Arkansas University Main Campus, Magnolia, Ark.

State Agricultural and Mechanical Institute for Negroes 1919. See Alabama Agricultural and Mechanical University, Normal, Ala.

State Agricultural College 1861. See Michigan State University, East Lansing, Mich.

State Agricultural School 1888. See University of Rhode Island, Kingston, R.I.

State College at Boston 1960. See Boston State College, Boston, Mass.

State College at Bridgewater 1960. See Bridgewater State College, Bridgewater, Mass.

State College at Fitchburg 1962. See Fitchburg State College, Fitchburg, Mass.

State College at Framingham 1960. See Framingham State College, Framingham, Mass.

State College at Salem 1960. See Salem State College, Salem, Mass.

State College at Westfield 1960. See Westfield State College, Westfield, Mass.

State College at Worcester 1960. See Worcester State College, Worcester, Mass.

State College for Alameda County 1957. See Hayward State University, Hayward, Calif.

State College for Colored Students 1891. See Delaware State College, Dover, Del.

State College of Agriculture and Mechanic Arts 1862. See University of Maine at Orono, Orono, Me.

State College of Agriculture and Mechanic Arts 1907. See South Dakota State University, Brookings, S.D.

State College of Arkansas 1967. See University of Central Arkansas, Conway, Ark.

State College of Iowa 1961. See University of Northern Iowa, Cedar Falls, Ia.

State College of Washington 1905. See Washington State University, Pullman, Wash.

State Colored Normal and Industrial School 1916. See Fayetteville State University, Fayetteville, N.C.

State Colored Normal School 1877. See Fayetteville State University, Fayetteville, N.C.

State Female Normal School 1884. See Longwood College, Farmville, Va.

State Normal and Industrial College 1897. See University of North Carolina at Greensboro, Greensboro, N.C.

State Normal and Industrial School 1891. See University of North Carolina at Greensboro, Greensboro, N.C.

State Normal and Industrial School at Huntsville 1878. See Alabama Agricultural and Mechanical University, Normal, Ala.

State Normal and Industrial School for Women at Radford 1910. See Radford College, Radford, Va.

State Normal College 1875. See George Peabody College for Teachers, Nashville, Tenn.

State Normal College 1903. See Western Montana College, Dillon, Mont.

State Normal College 1917. See Sul Ross State University, Alpine, Tex.

The State Normal College for Colored Students 1887. See Florida Agricultural and Mechanical University, Tallahassee, Fla.

State Normal School 1839. See Framingham State College, Framingham, Mass.

State Normal School 1862. See Mansfield State College, Mansfield, Pa.

State Normal School 1866. See State University of New York College at Fredonia, Fredonia, N. Y.

State Normal School 1874. See University of Wisconsin-River Falls, River Falls, Wisc.

State Normal School 1881. See University of California, Los Angeles, Los Angeles, Calif.

State Normal School 1883. See Jacksonville State University, Jacksonville, Ala.

State Normal School 1885. See State University of New York College at New Platz, New Platz, N. Y.

State Normal School 1889. See Mayville State College, Mayville, N. D.

State Normal School 1889. See University of Northern Colorado, Greeley, Colo.

State Normal School 1893. See Western Montana College, Dillon, Mont.

State Normal School 1894. See Fitchburg State College, Fitchburg, Mass.

State Normal School 1895. See University of Minnesota, Duluth, Duluth, Minn.

State Normal School 1909. See University of Wisconsin-La Crosse, LaCross, Wisc.

State Normal School 1920. See Cheyney State College, Cheyney, Pa.

State Normal School 1926. See Fayetteville State University, Fayetteville, N. C.

State Normal School and University for Colored Students and Teachers 1873. See Alabama State University, Montgomery, Ala.

State Normal School at Alamosa 1921. See Adams State College, Alamosa, Colo.

State Normal School at Cheney 1890. See Western Washington State College, Cheney, Wash.

State Normal School at Framingham 1853. See Framingham State College, Framingham, Mass.

State Normal School at Frostburg 1898. See Frostburg State College, Frostburg, Md.

State Normal School at North Adams 1894. See North Adams State College, North Adams, Mass.

State Normal School at Slippery Rock 1889. See Slippery Rock State College, Slippery Rock, Pa.

State Normal School for Colored Students 1889. See Alabama State University, Montgomery, Ala.

State Normal School for Second Normal District of Missouri 1871. See Central Missouri State University, Warrensburg, Mo.

State Normal School for the Negro Race 1921. See Fayetteville State University, Fayetteville, N.C.

State Normal School for Women 1914. See Longwood College, Farmville, Va.

State Normal School for Women at Harrisonburg 1914. See Madison College, Harrisonburg, Va.

State Teachers and Agricultural College at Forsyth 1939. See Fort Valley State College, Fort Valley, Ga.

State Teachers College at Boston 1952. See Boston State College, Boston, Mass.

State Teachers College at Brockport 1942. See State University of New York College at Brockport, Brockport, N.Y.

State Teachers College at Farmville 1924. See Longwood College, Farmville, Va.

State Teachers College at Fitchburg, Mass. 1933. See Fitchburg State College, Fitchburg, Mass.

State Teachers College at Frostburg 1935. See Frostburg State College, Frostburg, Md.

State Teachers College at Harrisonburg 1924. See Madison College, Harrisonburg, Va.

State Teachers College at North Adams 1932. See North Adams State College, North Adams, Mass.

State Teachers College at Plattsburgh, N.Y. 1942. See State University of New York College at Plattsburgh, Plattsburgh, N.Y.

State Teachers College at Salem 1932. See Salem State College, Salem, Mass.

State Teachers College at Salisbury 1935. See Salisbury State College, Salisbury, Md.

State Teachers College at Shippensburg 1927. See Shippensburg State College, Shippensburg, Pa.

State Teachers College at Slippery Rock 1926. See Slippery Rock State College, Slippery Rock, Pa.

State Teachers College at Towson 1934. See Towson State University, Baltimore, Md.

State Teachers College at Westfield 1932. See Westfield State College, Westfield, Mass.

State Teachers College at Worcester 1932. See Worcester State College, Worcester, Mass.

State Teachers College, Fredericksburg, Va. 1924. See Mary Washington College, Fredericksburg, Va.

State Teachers College, Fredonia, N.Y. 1942. See State University of New York College at Fredonia, Fredonia, N.Y.

State Teachers College, Hattiesburg, Miss. 1924. See University of Southern Mississippi, Hattiesburg, Miss.

State Teachers College, Jacksonville, Ala. 1929. See Jacksonville State University, Jacksonville, Ala.

State Teachers College, LaCrosse, Wisc. 1926. See University of Wisconsin-La Crosse, La Crosse, Wisc.

State Teachers College, Lock Haven, Pa. 1927. See Lock Haven State College, Lock Haven, Pa.

State Teachers College, Mayville, N.D. 1925. See Mayville State College, Mayville, N.D.

State Teachers College, Millersville, Pa. 1927. See Millersville State College, Millersville, Pa.

State Teachers College, Montgomery, Ala. 1929. See Alabama State University, Montgomery, Ala.

State Teachers College, Murfreesboro 1929. See Middle Tennessee State University, Murfreesboro, Tenn.

State Teachers College, New Platz, N.Y. 1942. See State University of New York College at New Platz, New Platz, N.Y.

State Teachers College, Oneonta, Oneonta, N.Y. 1942. See State University of New York College at Oneonta, Oneonta, N.Y.

State Teachers College, Potsdam, N.Y. 1942. See State University of New York College at Potsdam, Potsdam, N.Y.

State Teachers College, Radford, Va. 1924. See Radford College, Radford, Va.

State Teachers College-Superior 1925. See University of Wisconsin-Superior, Superior, Wisc.

State Teachers College and Normal School, Trenton, N.J. 1929. See Trenton State College, Trenton, N.J.

State University College at Albany 1961. See State University of New York at Albany, Albany, N.Y.

State University College of Education at Buffalo 1959. See State University of New York College at Buffalo, Buffalo, N.Y.

State University College of Education at Fredonia 1958. See State University of New York College at Fredonia, Fredonia, N.Y.

State University College of Education, Cortland, N.Y. 1959. See State University of New York College at Cortland, Cortland, N.Y.

State University College of Education, Geneseo, N.Y. 1959. See State University of New York College at Geneseo, Geneseo, N.Y.

State University College of Education, New Platz, N.Y. 1959. See State University of New York College at New Platz, New Platz, N.Y.

State University College of Education, Oneonta, N.Y. 1959. See State University of New York College at Oneonta, Oneonta, N.Y.

State University College of Education, Oswego 1959. See State University of New York College at Oswego, Oswego, N.Y.

State University College of Education, Potsdam, N.Y. 1959. See State University of New York College at Potsdam, Potsdam, N.Y.

State University College of Forestry at Syracuse University 1911. See State University of New York College of Environmental Science and Forestry, Syracuse, N.Y.

State University College of Science and Engineering on Long Island 1957. See State University of New York at Stony Brook, Stony Brook, N.Y.

State University College, Plattsburgh, N.Y. 1959. See State University of New York College at Plattsburgh, Plattsburgh, N.Y.

State University of Education, Albany, N.Y. 1959. See State University of New York at Albany, Albany, N.Y.

State University of Iowa 1855. See The University of Iowa, Iowa City, Ia.

State University of Kentucky 1908. See University of Kentucky, Lexington, Ky.

State University of Montana 1913. See University of Montana, Missoula, Mont.

STATE UNIVERSITY OF NEW YORK AT ALBANY. Albany, N.Y. 12222. State institution. Established as New York State Normal School 1844. Became: New York State Normal College 1890; New York College for Teachers 1914; State University of Education 1959; State University College at Albany 1961. Adopted present name 1962.

STATE UNIVERSITY OF NEW YORK AT BINGHAMTON. Binghamton, N.Y. 13901. State institution. Established as Triple Cities College of Syracuse University 1946. Became: Harpur College 1950. Adopted present name 1965.

STATE UNIVERSITY OF NEW YORK AT BUFFALO. Buffalo, N.Y. 14214. State university. Established as University of Buffalo 1846. Adopted present name 1962, after becoming part of state university system.

STATE UNIVERSITY OF NEW YORK AT STONY BROOK. Stony Brook, N.Y. 11790. State institution. Established as State University College of Science and Engineering on Long Island 1957. Became: State University's Long Island Center 1960. Adopted present name after moving to Stony Brook 1962.

STATE UNIVERSITY OF NEW YORK COLLEGE AT BROCKPORT. Brockport, N.Y. 14420. State institution. Established as Brockport Collegiate Institute 1836, by Baptist Church. Became: Brockport State Normal School 1866, after transfer to state control; State Teachers College at Brockport 1942; State University of New York College of Education at Brockport 1959, after becoming part of state university system in 1948. Adopted present name 1961.

STATE UNIVERSITY OF NEW YORK COLLEGE AT BUFFALO. Buffalo, N.Y. 14222. State institution. Established as Buffalo State Normal School 1867. Became: New York State College for Teachers, Buffalo, N.Y. 1928; State University of New York College for Teachers at Buffalo 1948, after becoming part of state university system; State university College of Education at Buffalo 1959. Adopted present name 1961.

STATE UNIVERSITY OF NEW YORK COLLEGE AT CORTLAND. Cortland, N.Y. 13045. State institution. Established as Cortland State Normal School 1868. Became: Cortland State Teachers College 1941, then part of the state university system 1948; State University College of Education Cortland, N.Y. 1959. Adopted present name 1961.

STATE UNIVERSITY OF NEW YORK COLLEGE AT FREDONIA. Fredonia, N. Y. 14063. State institution. Established as State Normal School 1866. Became: State Teachers College, Fredonia, N. Y. 1942; State University College of Education at Fredonia 1958, after becoming part of the state university system. Adopted present name 1961.

STATE UNIVERSITY OF NEW YORK COLLEGE AT GENESEO. Geneseo, N. Y. 14454. State institution. Established as Geneseo Normal and Training School 1867. Became: Geneseo Teachers College 1942; State University Teachers College Geneseo, N. Y. 1948, after becoming part of the state university system; State University College of Education Geneseo, N. Y. 1959. Adopted present name 1961.

STATE UNIVERSITY OF NEW YORK COLLEGE AT NEW PLATZ. New Platz, N. Y. 12561. State institution. Established as State Normal School 1885. Became: State Teachers College, New Platz, N. Y. 1942; State University College of Education, New Platz, N. Y. 1959, after becoming part of the state university system in 1948. Adopted present name 1961.

STATE UNIVERSITY OF NEW YORK COLLEGE AT ONEONTA. Oneonta, N. Y. 13820. State institution. Established as Oneonta State Normal School 1889. Became: State Teachers College, Oneonta, N. Y. 1942; State University Teachers College, Oneonta, N. Y. 1948, after becoming part of state university system; State University College of Education, Oneonta, N. Y. 1959. Adopted present name 1961.

STATE UNIVERSITY OF NEW YORK COLLEGE AT OSWEGO. Oswego, N. Y. 13126. State institution. Established as Oswego Normal School 1861. Became: Oswego State Teachers College 1942; State University College of Education, Oswego 1959, after becoming part of state system 1948. Adopted present name 1961.

STATE UNIVERSITY OF NEW YORK COLLEGE AT PLATTSBURGH. Plattsburgh, N. Y. 12901. State institution. Established as Plattsburgh State Normal School 1889. Became: State Teachers College at Plattsburgh, N. Y. 1942; State University College, Plattsburgh, N. Y. 1959, after becoming part of state university system 1948. Adopted present name 1962.

STATE UNIVERSITY OF NEW YORK COLLEGE AT POTSDAM. Potsdam, N. Y. 13676. State institution. Established as St. Lawrence Academy 1816. Became: Potsdam Normal School 1866. Merged with Crance Normal Institute of Music 1926. Became: State Teachers College, Potsdam, N. Y. 1942; State University Teachers College, Potsdam, N. Y. 1948, after becoming part of state university system; State University College of Education, Potsdam, N. Y. 1959. Adopted present name 1962.

State University of New York College for Teachers at Buffalo 1948. See State University of New York College at Buffalo, Buffalo, N. Y.

State University of New York College of Education at Brockport 1959.
See State University of New York College at Brockport, Brockport,
N. Y.

STATE UNIVERSITY OF NEW YORK COLLEGE OF ENVIRONMENTAL
SCIENCE AND FORESTRY. Syracuse, N. Y. 13210. State institution. Established as State University College of Forestry at Syracuse University 1911. Adopted present name 1972, after becoming
part of the state university system in 1949.

STATE UNIVERSITY OF NEW YORK DOWNSTATE MEDICAL CEN-
TER. Brooklyn, N. Y. 11203. State institution. Established as
The Long Island College Hospital Teaching Division 1860. Became:
Long Island College of Medicine 1930. Adopted present name 1950
after becoming part of state university system.

STATE UNIVERSITY OF NEW YORK MARITIME COLLEGE. New
York, N. Y. 10465. State institution. Established as New York
Nautical School 1874. Became: New York State Merchant Marine
Academy 1929; New York State Maritime Academy 1942. Adopted
present name 1948 after becoming part of the state university system.

STATE UNIVERSITY OF NEW YORK UPSTATE MEDICAL CENTER.
Syracuse, N. Y. 13210. State institution. Established as Geneva College Medical Division 1834. Became part of Syracuse University
system 1872. Adopted present name 1950 after becoming part of
state university system.

State University of South Dakota 1959. See The University of South
Dakota, Vermillion, S. D.

State University Teachers College, Geneseo, N. Y. 1948. See State
University of New York College at Geneseo, Geneseo, N. Y.

State University Teachers College, Oneonta, N. Y. 1948. See State
University of New York College at Oneonta, Oneonta, N. Y.

State University Teachers College, Potsdam, N. Y. 1948. See State
University of New York College at Potsdam, Potsdam, N. Y.

State University's Long Island Center 1960. See State University
of New York at Stony Brook, Stony Brook, N. Y.

STEED COLLEGE, INC. Johnson City, Tenn. 37601. Non-public
institution. Established as Steed College 1940 by C. C. and Mollie
Steed. Became: Steed College of Technology 1961. Readopted
present name 1976.

Steed College of Technology 1961. See Steed College, Inc. Johnson
City, Tenn.

Stephen F. Austin State College 1948. See Stephen F. Austin State
University, Nacogdoches, Tex.

STEPHEN F. AUSTIN STATE UNIVERSITY. Nacogdoches, Tex. 75961. State institution. Established as Stephen F. Austin Teachers College 1921. Became: Stephen F. Austin State College 1948. Adopted present name 1969.

Stephen F. Austin Teachers College 1921. See Stephen F. Austin State University, Nacogdoches, Tex.

STEPHENS COLLEGE. Columbia, Mo. 65201. Non-public institution. Established as Columbia Female Academy 1833. Became: Baptist Female College 1857; Stephens Female College 1870. Adopted present name 1917.

Stephens Female College 1870. See Stephens College, Columbia, Mo.

STERLING COLLEGE. Sterling, Kan. 67579. Non-public institution. Affiliated with The United Presbyterian Church in the U.S. Established as Cooper Memorial College 1886. Became: Cooper College 1909. Adopted present name 1920.

STETSON UNIVERSITY. DeLand, Fla. 32720. Non-public institution. Affiliated with the Florida Baptist Convention of the Southern Baptist Convention. Established as DeLand Academy 1883. Became: DeLand Academy and College 1885; DeLand University 1887. Adopted present official name John B. Stetson University 1889.

Stevens Henager College, Main Campus. Salt Lake City, Ut. Closed Dec. 1973.

Stevens Point State Normal School 1894. See University of Wisconsin-Stevens Point, Stevens Point, Wisc.

Stewart College 1855. See Southwestern at Memphis, Memphis, Tenn.

Stewart School of Business 1901. See Rider College, Trenton, N.J.

Still College of Osteopathy 1906. See College of Osteopathic Medicine and Surgery, Des Moines, Ia.

STILLMAN COLLEGE. Tuscaloosa, Ala. 35401. Non-public institution. Affiliated with the Presbyterian Church in the U.S. Established as Tuscaloosa Institute, a seminary, 1876. Adopted present name 1948.

Storrs Agricultural College 1893. See University of Connecticut, Storrs, Conn.

Storrs Agricultural School 1881. See University of Connecticut, Storrs, Conn.

Stout Institute 1908. See University of Wisconsin-Stout, Menomonie, Wisc.

Stout Manual Training and Domestic Science School 1891. See University of Wisconsin-Stout, Menomonie, Wisc.

Stout State College 1955. See University of Wisconsin-Stout, Menomonie, Wisc.

Stout State University 1964. See University of Wisconsin-Stout, Menomonie, Wisc.

Stowe Teachers College 1954. See Harris Teachers College, St. Louis, Mo.

Straight College 1930. See Dillard University, New Orleans, La.

Stratford College, Danville, Va. Closed June 1974.

Suffolk Law School 1906. See Suffolk University, Boston, Mass.

SUFFOLK UNIVERSITY. Boston, Mass. 02114. Non-public institution. Established as Suffolk Law School 1906. Adopted present name 1937.

Sul Ross State Teachers College 1924. See Sul Ross State University, Alpine, Tex.

SUL ROSS STATE UNIVERSITY. Alpine, Tex. 79830. State institution. Established as State Normal College 1917. Became: Sul Ross State Teachers College 1924. Adopted present name 1969.

Superior Normal School 1893. See University of Wisconsin-Superior, Superior, Wisc.

Susquehanna Female College 1873. See Susquehanna University, Selinsgrove, Pa.

SUSQUEHANNA UNIVERSITY. Selinsgrove, Pa. 17870. Non-public institution. Affiliated with the Central Pennsylvania Synod of the Lutheran Church in America. Established as Missionary Institute of the Evangelical Lutheran Church 1858. Merged with Susquehanna Female College 1873. Adopted present name 1895.

SWEET BRIAR COLLEGE. Sweet Briar, Va. 24595. Non-public institution. Established under present official name Sweet Briar Institute 1906.

Sweet Briar Institute 1906. See Sweet Briar College, Sweet Briar, Va.

- T -

Tahoe College, Tahoe Paradise, Calif. Closed Aug. 1971.

Tampa Junior College 1930. See University of Tampa, Tampa, Fla.

TARKIO COLLEGE. Tarkio, Mo. 64491. Affiliated with The United
Presbyterian Church in the USA. Established as Tarkio Valley and
Normal Institute 1883. Adopted present name 1884.

Tarkio Valley and Normal Institute 1883. See Tarkio College,
Tarkio, Mo.

Tarleton State College 1959. See Tarleton State University, Stephenville, Tex.

TARLETON STATE UNIVERSITY. Stephenville, Tex. 76401. State
institution. Established as John Tarleton College 1899. Became:
John Tarleton Agricultural College 1917; Tarleton State College 1959.
Adopted present name 1973.

TAYLOR UNIVERSITY. Upland, Ind. 46989. Non-public institution.
Established as Fort Wayne Female College 1846. Became: Fort
Wayne College 1855. Adopted present name 1890.

Teachers College 1904. See Harris Teachers College, St. Louis,
Mo.

Teachers College of Connecticut 1933. See Central Connecticut
State College, New Britain, Conn.

Teachers College of the City of Boston 1924. See Boston State College, Boston, Mass.

The Technical Institute 1947. See Southern Technical Institute,
Marietta, Ga.

Tempe Normal School of Arizona 1903. See Arizona State University, Tempe, Ariz.

Tempe State Teachers College 1925. See Arizona State University,
Tempe, Ariz.

Temple Buell College 1967. See Colorado Women's College, Denver, Col.

Temple College 1884. See Temple University, Philadelphia, Pa.

TEMPLE UNIVERSITY. Philadelphia, Pa. 19122. Non-public institution, state-related. Established as Temple College 1884. Became:
Temple University 1907. Adopted present official name Temple University of the Commonwealth System of Higher Education 1965, after
becoming state-related.

Temple University of the Commonwealth System of Higher Education
1965. See Temple University, Philadelphia, Pa.

Tennessee Agricultural and Industrial State University 1951. See
Tennessee State University, Nashville, Tenn.

Tennessee Polytechnic Institute 1915. See Tennessee Technological
University, Cookeville, Tenn.

TENNESSEE STATE UNIVERSITY. Nashville, Tenn. State institution. Established as Agricultural and Industrial State Normal School
1912. Became: Agricultural and Industrial State Normal College
1924; Agricultural and Industrial State College 1927; Tennessee Agricultural and Industrial State University 1951. Adopted present name
1969.

TENNESSEE TECHNOLOGICAL UNIVERSITY. Cookeville, Tenn.
38501. State institution. Established as Tennessee Polytechnic
Institute 1915. Adopted present name 1965.

TENNESSEE WESLEYAN COLLEGE. Athens, Tenn. 37303. Non-
public institution. Affiliated with the Holston Conference of The
United Methodist Church. Established as Athens Female College
1857. Became: East Tennessee Wesleyan College 1866; East Tennessee University 1867; Grant Memorial University 1886; U.S. Grant
University 1889; Athens School of the University of Chattanooga 1906.
Adopted present name 1925.

Terre Haute School of Industrial Science 1874. See Rose-Hulman
Institute of Technology, Terre Haute, Ind.

Territorial College of Guam 1952. See University of Guam, Agana,
Guam.

Territorial Normal School 1885. See Arizona State University,
Tempe, Ariz.

Territorial Normal School 1893. See Western New Mexico University, Silver City, N.M.

Territorial University of Washington 1861. See University of Washington, Seattle, Wash.

TEXAS AGRICULTURAL AND INDUSTRIAL UNIVERSITY. Kingsville,
Tex. 78363. State institution. Established as South Texas State
Teachers College 1925. Became: Texas College of Arts and Indus-
tries 1929. Adopted present name 1967.

TEXAS AGRICULTURAL AND INDUSTRIAL UNIVERSITY AT CORPUS
CHRISTI. Corpus Christi, Tex. 78411. State institution. Established as Arts and Technological College 1947, under auspices of the
Southern Baptist Convention. Became: University of Corpus Christi
1947, then became an upper division state university under the di-
rection of Texas A & I University 1973. Adopted present name 1973.

TEXAS AGRICULTURAL AND MECHANICAL UNIVERSITY. College

Station, Tex. 77843. State institution. Established as Agricultural and Mechanical College of Texas 1871. Adopted present name 1963.

TEXAS CHRISTIAN UNIVERSITY. Fort Worth, Tex. 76129. Non-public institution. Affiliated with the Christian Church, Disciples of Christ. Established as AddRan Male and Female College 1873. Became: AddRan Christian College 1889. Adopted present name 1902.

TEXAS COLLEGE. Tyler, Tex. 75701. Non-public institution. Sponsored by the Christian Methodist Episcopal Church. Established under present name 1894. Became: Phillips University 1909. Re-adopted present name 1912.

Texas College of Arts and Industries 1929. See Texas Agricultural and Industrial University, Kingsville, Tex.

Texas College of Mines and Metallurgy 1920. See University of Texas at El Paso, El Paso, Tex.

TEXAS LUTHERAN COLLEGE. Seguin, Tex. 78155. Non-public institution. Owned by the American Lutheran Church. Established as Evangelical Lutheran College 1891 in Brenham, Tex. Became: Lutheran College 1912, after moving to present location. Merged with Trinity College of Round Rock 1929. Adopted present name 1934. Merged with Clifton College 1954.

Texas Normal College 1890. See North Texas State University, Denton, Tex.

TEXAS SOUTHERN UNIVERSITY. Houston, Tex. 77004. State institution. Established as Texas State University for Negroes 1947. Adopted present name 1951.

Texas State College for Women 1935. See Texas Woman's University, Denton, Tex.

Texas State School of Mines and Metallurgy 1913. See University of Texas at El Paso, El Paso, Tex.

Texas State University for Negroes 1947. See Texas Southern University, Houston, Tex.

TEXAS TECH UNIVERSITY. Lubbock, Tex. 79409. State institution. Established as Texas Technological College 1923. Adopted present name 1969.

Texas Technological College 1923. See Texas Tech University, Lubbock, Tex.

Texas University 1873. See Southwestern University, Georgetown, Tex.

TEXAS WESLEYAN COLLEGE.   Fort Worth, Tex. 76105.   Non-public institution.   Affiliated with The United Methodist Church.   Established as Polytechnic College 1891.   Became: Texas Woman's College 1914.   Adopted present name 1934.

Texas Western College 1949. See University of Texas at El Paso, El Paso, Tex.

Texas Woman's College 1914. See Texas Wesleyan College, Fort Worth, Tex.

TEXAS WOMAN'S UNIVERSITY.   Denton, Tex. 76204.   State institution.   Established as Girls' Industrial College 1901.   Became: College of Industrial Arts 1905; Texas State College for Women 1935. Adopted present name 1957.

Thames College 1911. See Connecticut College, New London, Conn.

That New England School 1882. See Atlantic Union College, South Lancaster, Mass.

Theological Institute of Connecticut 1834. See The Hartford Seminary, Hartford, Conn.

Theological School 1876. See Calvin College, Grand Rapids, Mich.

The Theological Seminary of the Protestant Episcopal Church 1824. See Kenton College, Gambier, Oh.

Thiel Academy 1866, at Phillipsburg, Pa. See Thiel College, Greenville, Pa.

THIEL COLLEGE.   Greenville, Pa. 16125.   Non-public institution. Affiliated with the Lutheran Church in America.   Established as Thiel Academy 1866, at Phillipsburg, Pa.   Became: Thiel College of Evangelical Lutheran Church 1870, and moved to present location; Thiel College of Pittsburgh Synod of United Lutheran Church in America 1956.   Adopted present name 1964.

Thiel College of Evangelical Lutheran Church 1870. See Thiel College, Greenville, Pa.

Thiel College of Pittsburgh Synod of United Lutheran Church in America 1956. See Thiel College, Greenville, Pa.

Third District Agricultural and Mechanical College 1926. See Georgia Southwestern College, Americus, Ga.

Third District Agricultural and Mechanical School 1908. See Georgia Southwestern College, Americus, Ga.

Third District Agricultural School 1909. See Southern Arkansas University Main Campus, Magnolia, Ark.

Third State Normal School at St. Cloud 1869. See St. Cloud State University, St. Cloud, Minn.

Thomas Business College 1911. See Thomas College, Waterville, Me.

THOMAS COLLEGE. Waterville, Me. 04901. Non-public institution. Established as Morgan Business College 1894. Became: Thomas Business College 1911; Thomas Junior College 1956. Adopted present name 1963.

THOMAS JEFFERSON UNIVERSITY. Philadelphia, Pa. 19107. Non-public institution. Established as Jefferson Medical College of the Jefferson College of Canonsburg, Pa. 1824 by Dr. George McClellan and others. Became: Jefferson Medical College 1838. Adopted present name 1969.

Thomas Junior College 1956. See Thomas College, Waterville, Me.

THOMAS MORE COLLEGE. Ft. Mitchell, Ky. 41017. Non-public institution. Affiliated with the Roman Catholic Diocese of Covington, Ky. Established as Villa Madonna College 1921. Adopted present name 1968.

Thomas S. Clarkson Memorial College of Technology 1896. See Clarkson College of Technology, Potsdam, N. Y.

Throop College of Technology 1913. See California Institute of Technology, Pasadena, Calif.

Throop Polytechnic Institute 1891. See California Institute of Technology, Pasadena, Calif.

Thunderbird Graduate School of International Management 1968. See American Graduate School, Glendale, Ariz.

Tiffin Business University 1918. See Tiffin University, Tiffin, Oh.

TIFFIN UNIVERSITY. Tiffin, Oh. 44883. Non-public institution. Established as Tiffin Business University 1918 by Franklin J. Miller and Alfred M. Reichard. Adopted present name 1939.

TIFT COLLEGE. Forsyth, Ga. 31029. Non-public institution. Owned by the Georgia Convention of the Southern Baptist Convention. Established as Forsyth Female Collegiate Institute 1849. Became: Monroe Female College 1867; Bessie Tift College 1907. Adopted present name 1956.

Tillotson College 1894. See Huston-Tillotson College, Austin, Tex.

Tillotson Collegiate and Normal Institute 1875. See Huston-Tillotson College, Austin, Tex.

Toland Medical College 1864. See University of California, San Francisco, San Francisco, Calif.

Toledo University 1884. See University of Toledo, Toledo, Oh.

Toledo University of Arts and Trades 1872. See University of Toledo, Toledo, Oh.

Tolentine College, Olympia Fields, Ill. Closed Sept. 1973.

TOUGALOO COLLEGE. Tougaloo, Miss. 39174. Non-public institution. Affiliated with The United Church of Christ and the Disciples of Christ. Established as Tougaloo University 1871. Adopted present name 1916. Merged with Southern Christian Institute 1954 and became: Tougaloo Southern Christian College 1954. Readopted present name 1963.

Tougaloo Southern Christian College 1954. See Tougaloo College, Tougaloo, Miss.

Tougaloo University 1871. See Tougaloo College, Tougaloo, Miss.

Towson State College 1963. See Towson State University, Baltimore, Md.

TOWSON STATE UNIVERSITY. Baltimore, Md. 21204. State institution. Established as Maryland State Normal School 1865. Became: State Teachers College at Towson 1934; Towson State College 1963. Adopted present name 1976.

Transylvania College 1915. See Transylvania University, Lexington, Ky.

Transylvania Seminary 1780. See Transylvania University, Lexington, Ky.

TRANSYLVANIA UNIVERSITY. Lexington, Ky. Non-public institution. Affiliated with the Christian Church (Disciples of Christ). Established as Transylvania Seminary 1780. Became: Transylvania University 1799; Kentucky University 1865; Transylvania University 1908; Transylvania College 1915. Readopted present name 1969.

Transylvania University 1799. See Transylvania University, Lexington, Ky.

Transylvania University 1908. See Transylvania University, Lexington, Ky.

TRENTON STATE COLLEGE. Trenton, N.J. 08625. State institution. Established as New Jersey State Normal and Model Schools 1855. Became: State Teachers College and Normal School 1929; New Jersey State Teachers College 1937. Adopted present name 1958.

Trinitarian College, Baltimore, Md.   Closed June 1969.

TRINITY COLLEGE. Deerfield, Ill. 60015.   Non-public institution.
Owned by the Evangelical Free Church of America. Established as
Trinity Seminary and Bible College 1946, after merger of Evangelical Free Church Seminary 1946 and Bible Institute of Chicago 1946
and Trinity Seminary and Bible Institute of Minneapolis 1946. Divided
in 1960 to form Trinity College and Trinity Evangelical Divinity
School. Moved to present location 1965.

TRINITY COLLEGE. Hartford, Conn. 06106.   Non-public institution.
Established as Washington College 1823.   Adopted present name 1845.

Trinity College 1859. See Duke University, Durham, N.C.

Trinity College 1960. See Trinity College, Deerfield, Ill.

Trinity College of Round Rock 1929. See Texas Lutheran College,
Seguin, Tex.

Trinity Evangelical Divinity School 1960. See Trinity College,
Deerfield, Ill.

Trinity Seminary 1884. See Dana College, Blair, Neb.

Trinity Seminary and Bible College 1946. See Trinity College,
Deerfield, Ill.

Trinity Seminary and Bible Institute of Minneapolis 1946. See Trinity College, Deerfield, Ill.

Trinity Seminary and Blair College. See Dana College, Blair, Neb.

Triple Cities College of Syracuse University 1946. See State University of New York at Binghamton, Binghamton, N.Y.

Troy State College 1957. See Troy State University, Troy, Ala.

Troy State Normal School 1887. See Troy State University, Troy,
Ala.

Troy State Teachers College 1929. See Troy State University,
Troy, Ala.

TROY STATE UNIVERSITY. Troy, Ala. 36081.   State institution.
Established as Troy State Normal School 1887.   Became: Troy State
Teachers College 1929; Troy State College 1957.   Adopted present
name 1967.

Trustees of Assumption College 1904. See Assumption College,
Worcester, Mass.

Trustees of Clark University 1887. See Clark University, Worcester, Mass.

Trustees of Roanoke Female College 1863. See Averett College, Danville, Va.

Tualitin Academy 1849. See Pacific University, Forest Grove, Ore.

Tualitin Academy and Pacific University 1854. See Pacific University, Forest Grove, Ore.

Tufts College 1852. See Tufts University, Medford, Mass.

TUFTS UNIVERSITY. Medford, Mass. 02155. Non-public institution. Established as Tufts College 1852 under control of Universalist Church of America. Adopted present name 1855.

TULANE UNIVERSITY OF LOUISIANA. New Orleans, La. 70118. Non-public institution. Established as Medical College of University of Louisiana, a state institution, 1847. Adopted present name after reverting to private control 1884.

Tuscaloosa Institute 1876. See Stillman College, Tuscaloosa, Ala.

Tuskegee Female College 1854. See Huntingdon College, Montgomery, Ala.

TUSKEGEE INSTITUTE. Tuskegee Institute, Ala. 36088. Non-public institution. Established as Tuskegee Normal and Industrial Institute 1881. Adopted present name 1937.

Tuskegee Normal and Industrial Institute 1881. See Tuskegee Institute, Tuskegee Institute, Ala.

- U -

Union Business College 1874. See Dyke College, Cleveland, Oh.

UNION COLLEGE. Schenectady, N.Y. 12308. Non-public institution. Established as Schenectady Academy 1795. Adopted present name 1795.

Union Female College 1859. See Averett College, Danville, Va.

Union Institute 1839. See Duke University, Durham, N.C.

Union Seminary 1856. See Albright College, Reading, Pa.

UNION THEOLOGICAL SEMINARY. New York, N.Y. 10027. Non-public institution. Established as New York Theological Seminary 1836. Adopted present name 1839.

UNION UNIVERSITY. Jackson, Tenn. 38301. Non-public institution. Owned by the Tennessee Baptist Convention. Established as Jackson

Male Academy 1825.   Became: West Tennessee College 1844; Southwestern Baptist University 1875.   Adopted present name 1907.

U. S. COAST GUARD ACADEMY.   New London, Conn. 06320.   Federal government institution.   Established as U. S. Revenue Cutter Service School of Instruction 1876.   Became: Revenue Cutter Academy 1914.   Adopted present name 1915.

U. S. Grant University 1889.   See Tennessee Wesleyan College, Athens, Tenn.

U. S. INTERNATIONAL UNIVERSITY.   San Diego, Calif. 92101. Non-public institution.   Established as California Western University 1952, after assuming charter of Balboa University 1952.   Adopted present name 1966.   Merged with Mauna Olu College of Maui, Paia, Haw. 1972.

U. S. NAVAL ACADEMY.   Annapolis, Md. 21402.   Federal government institution.   Established as the Naval School 1845.   Adopted present name 1851.

U. S. Naval Postgraduate School 1921.   See Naval Postgraduate School, Monterey, Calif.

U. S. Revenue Cutter Service School of Instruction 1876. See U. S. Coast Guard Academy, New London, Conn.

UNITED WESLEYAN COLLEGE.   Allentown, Pa. 18103.   Non-public institution.   Affiliated with The Wesleyan Church.   Established as Beulah Park Bible School 1921 by the Pilgrim Holiness Church.   Became: Allentown Bible Institute 1934; Eastern Pilgrim College 1954; Penn Wesleyan College 1970.   Merged with Wesleyan College, Frankfort, Ind. 1972 and Wesleyan College, Kernersville, N. C. 1972. Adopted present name 1972.

UNITY COLLEGE.   Unity, Me. 04988.   Non-public institution.   Established as Unity Institute of Liberal Arts and Sciences 1966.   Adopted present name 1967.

Unity Institute of Liberal Arts and Sciences 1966.   See Unity College, Unity, Me.

Universal Chiropractic College 1971.   See National College of Chiropractic, Lombard, Ill.

University at Lewisburg 1846.   See Bucknell University, Lewisburg, Pa.

The University College 1957.   See George Mason University, Fairfax, Va.

University Farm 1906.   See University of California, Davis, Davis, Calif.

UNIVERSITY OF AKRON. Akron, Oh. 44325. State institution. Established as Buchel College 1870, by the Ohio Universalist Convention. Became: Municipal University of Akron 1913, after city assumed control. Adopted present name 1926. Became state-affiliated 1963, a state university 1967.

University of Alabama Birmingham Extension Center 1936. See University of Alabama in Birmingham, Birmingham, Ala.

UNIVERSITY OF ALABAMA IN BIRMINGHAM. Birmingham, Ala. 35233. State institution. Established as University of Alabama Birmingham Extension Center 1936. Became autonomous, adopted present name 1970.

UNIVERSITY OF ALABAMA IN HUNTSVILLE. Huntsville, Ala. 35807. State institution. Established as University of Alabama Resident Center 1936. Became autonomous, adopted present name 1969.

University of Alabama Resident Center 1936. See University of Alabama in Huntsville, Huntsville, Ala.

UNIVERSITY OF ALASKA. College, Alas. 99701. State institution. Established as The Alaska Agricultural College and School of Mines 1917. Adopted present name 1935.

UNIVERSITY OF ALBUQUERQUE. Albuquerque, N.M. 87120. Non-public institution. Founded by the Sisters of St. Francis, (Colorado Springs, Colo.) Roman Catholic Church. Established as St. Francis Summer College 1920. Became: Catholic Teachers College of New Mexico 1940; College of St. Joseph on the Rio Grande 1951. Adopted present name 1966.

UNIVERSITY OF ARKANSAS. Fayetteville, Ark. 72701. State institution. Established as Arkansas Industrial University 1871. Adopted present name 1899.

UNIVERSITY OF ARKANSAS AT LITTLE ROCK. Little Rock, Ark. 72204. State institution. Established as Little Rock Junior College 1927. Merged with University of Arkansas and adopted present name 1969.

UNIVERSITY OF ARKANSAS AT MONTICELLO. Monticello, Ark. 71655. State institution. Established as Fourth District Agricultural School 1909. Became: Agricultural and Mechanical College, Fourth District 1923; Arkansas Agricultural and Mechanical College 1939. Merged with the University of Arkansas and adopted present name 1971.

UNIVERSITY OF ARKANSAS AT PINE BLUFF. Pine Bluff, Ark. 71601. State institution. Established as Branch Normal College 1873. Became: Arkansas Agricultural, Mechanical and Normal College 1928. Merged with the University of Arkansas and adopted present name 1972.

UNIVERSITY OF BRIDGEPORT. Bridgeport, Conn. 06602. Non-public institution. Established as Junior College of Connecticut 1927. Adopted present name 1947.

University of Buffalo 1846. See State University of New York at Buffalo, Buffalo, N. Y.

University of California 1868. See University of California, Berkeley, Berkeley, Calif.

UNIVERSITY OF CALIFORNIA, BERKELEY. Berkeley, Calif. 94720. State institution. Established as College of California 1855 by private group. Became: University of California 1868, after transfer of control to state. Moved to present site 1873. Adopted present name 1952.

UNIVERSITY OF CALIFORNIA, DAVIS. Davis, Calif. 95616. State institution. Established as University Farm 1906. Became: College of Agricultural Branch at Davis 1922; College of Agriculture 1923. Adopted present name 1959.

UNIVERSITY OF CALIFORNIA, LOS ANGELES. Los Angeles, Calif. 90024. State institution. Established as State Normal School 1881. Became: Southern Branch, University of California 1919. Adopted present name 1927.

UNIVERSITY OF CALIFORNIA, RIVERSIDE. Riverside, Calif. 92502. State institution. Established as Citrus Experiment Station 1907. Became: University of California, Riverside Campus 1954. Adopted present name 1958.

University of California, Riverside Campus 1954. See University of California, Riverside, Riverside, Calif.

UNIVERSITY OF CALIFORNIA, SAN DIEGO. LaJolla, Calif. 92037. State institution. Established as Marine Biological Station of San Diego 1903. Became: Scripps Institution of Biological Research 1912, after joining University of California system; University of California Scripps Institution of Oceanography 1925. Adopted present name 1960 after becoming general campus of the University of California 1958.

UNIVERSITY OF CALIFORNIA, SAN FRANCISCO. San Francisco, Calif. 94122. State institution. Established as Toland Medical College 1864. Became a department of the University of California 1873; University of California, San Francisco Medical Center 1958. Adopted present name 1970.

University of California, San Francisco Medical Center 1958. See University of California, San Francisco, San Francisco, Calif.

UNIVERSITY OF CALIFORNIA, SANTA BARBARA. Santa Barbara, Calif. 93106. State institution. Established as Anna S. C. Blake

Manual Training School by private group 1891. Control transferred to City of Santa Barbara 1892. Became: Santa Barbara Normal School of Manual Arts and Home Economics 1909, after state assumed control, then became Santa Barbara Normal School 1919; Santa Barbara State Teachers College 1921; Santa Barbara State College 1935; Santa Barbara College 1944, after becoming part of the University of California. Adopted present name 1958.

University of California Scripps Institution of Oceanography 1925. See University of California, San Diego, La Jolla, Calif.

UNIVERSITY OF CENTRAL ARKANSAS. Conway, Ark. 72032. State institution. Established as Arkansas State Normal School 1907. Became: Arkansas State Teachers College 1925; State College of Arkansas 1967. Adopted present name 1975.

University of Chattanooga 1907. See The University of Tennessee at Chattanooga, Chattanooga, Tenn.

UNIVERSITY OF CINCINNATI. Cincinnati, Oh. 45221. State institution. Established as Cincinnati College and Medical College of Ohio 1819. Other predecessor, The McKicken University, established in 1859, became the University of Cincinnati 1870, a municipal institution. Merged with Medical College of Ohio 1896, Cincinnati College 1897. Other mergers: Cincinnati Astronomical Society 1872; School of Household Economics of the Cincinnati General Hospital 1916; Cincinnati College of Pharmacy 1954; College Conservatory of Music 1962; Ohio Mechanics Institute 1969; Ohio College of Applied Science 1969. Adopted present name 1870. State assumed control July 1977.

UNIVERSITY OF CONNECTICUT. Storrs, Conn. 06268. State institution. Established as Storrs Agricultural School 1881. Became: Storrs Agricultural College 1893; Connecticut Agricultural College 1899; Connecticut State College 1933. Adopted present name 1939.

University of Corpus Christi 1947. See Texas Agricultural and Industrial University at Corpus Christi, Corpus Christi, Tex.

University of Dakota 1862. See The University of South Dakota, Vermillion, S.D.

UNIVERSITY OF DAYTON. Dayton, Oh. 45409. Non-public institution. Affiliated with the Society of Mary, Roman Catholic Church. Established as St. Mary's Institute 1850. Became: St. Mary's College 1914. Adopted present name 1920.

UNIVERSITY OF DELAWARE. Newark, Del. 19711. State institution. Established as New London Academy 1743 by the Presbyterian Synod of Philadelphia in New London, Penn. Moved to Newark, Del. 1765. Became: Newark Academy 1769; Newark College 1833; Delaware College 1843. Transferred to state control 1843. Adopted present name 1921.

UNIVERSITY OF DENVER. Denver, Colo. 80210. Non-public institution. Affiliated with The United Methodist Church. Established
as Colorado Seminary 1864. Adopted present name 1880.

University of Deseret 1850. See University of Utah, Salt Lake City,
Ut.

UNIVERSITY OF DETROIT. Detroit, Mich. 48221. Non-public institution. Conducted by the Society of Jesus, Roman Catholic Church.
Established as Detroit College 1877. Adopted present name 1911.

UNIVERSITY OF DUBUQUE. Dubuque, Ia. 52001. Non-public institution. Affiliated with The United Presbyterian Church in the U.S.
Established as German Theological School of the Northwest 1852.
Became: German Presbyterian Theological School of the Northwest
1891; Dubuque German College and Seminary 1911. Adopted present
name 1920.

UNIVERSITY OF EVANSVILLE. Evansville, Ind. 47701. Non-public
institution. Affiliated with The United Methodist Church. Incorporated as Moores Hill Male and Female Collegiate Institute 1845. Became: Moores Hill College 1887; Evansville College 1919. Adopted
present name 1967.

UNIVERSITY OF FLORIDA. Gainesville, Fla. 32601. State institution. Established as East Florida Seminary 1853. Adopted present name 1909.

UNIVERSITY OF GUAM. Agana, Guam 96910. State institution.
Established as Territorial College of Guam 1952. Became: College
of Guam 1960. Adopted present name 1968.

UNIVERSITY OF HAWAII. Honolulu, Haw. 96822. State institution.
Established as College of Hawaii 1907. Adopted present name 1920.

UNIVERSITY OF HAWAII AT HILO. Hilo, Haw. 96720. State institution. Established as Extension Division of the University of Hawaii
1947. Became: University of Hawaii Hilo College 1970. Adopted
present name 1970.

University of Hawaii Hilo College 1970. See University of Hawaii
at Hilo, Hilo, Haw.

THE UNIVERSITY OF HEALTH SCIENCES/THE CHICAGO MEDICAL
SCHOOL. Chicago, Ill. 60612. Non-public institution. Established
as The Chicago Hospital College of Medicine 1912. Became: The
Chicago Medical School 1919; The Chicago Medical School/University
of Health Sciences 1967. Adopted present name 1971.

UNIVERSITY OF HOUSTON. Houston, Tex. 77004. State institution.
Established as Houston Junior College 1927. Adopted present name
1934.

UNIVERSITY OF ILLINOIS AT CHICAGO CIRCLE.   Chicago, Ill.
60680.   State institution.   Established as Chicago Undergraduate
Division of the University of Illinois 1946.   Adopted present name
1965.

THE UNIVERSITY OF IOWA.   Iowa City, Ia. 52240.   State institution.   Established under present official name, State University of
Iowa 1855.

University of Kansas City, 1929.   See University of Missouri-Kansas City, Kansas City, Mo.

UNIVERSITY OF KENTUCKY.   Lexington, Ky. 40506.   State institution.   Established as Agricultural and Mechanical College of Kentucky University 1865.   Became: Agricultural and Mechanical College of Kentucky 1878; State University of Kentucky 1908.   Adopted
present name 1916.

UNIVERSITY OF LOUISVILLE.   Louisville, Ky. 40208.   State institution.   Established as Jefferson Seminary 1798.   Became: Collegiate Institute of Louisville 1937; President and Trustees of the University of Louisville 1846.   Adopted present name 1926.   Merged
with Kentucky Southern College 1969, became part of state system
1970.

UNIVERSITY OF LOWELL.   Lowell, Mass. 01854.   State institution.
Established as Lowell Textile School 1895.   Became: Lowell Tex-
tile Institute 1928; Lowell Technological Institute 1953.   Lowell State
College annexed 1975.   Adopted present name 1975.

UNIVERSITY OF MAINE AT FARMINGTON.   Farmington, Me. 04938.
State institution.   Established as Western Maine Normal School 1863.
Became: Farmington State Normal School 1868; Farmington State
Teachers College 1945; Farmington State College of the University
of Maine 1968.   Adopted present name 1970.

UNIVERSITY OF MAINE AT FORT KENT.   Fort Kent, Me. 04743.
State institution.   Established as Madawaska Training School 1878.
Became: Fort Kent State Normal School 1955; Fort Kent State Teachers College 1961; Fort Kent State College 1965; Fort Kent State College of the University of Maine 1968.   Adopted present name 1970.

UNIVERSITY OF MAINE AT MACHIAS.   Machias, Me. 14654.   State
institution.   Established as Washington State Normal School 1909.
Became: Washington State Teachers College 1952; Washington State
College of the University of Maine 1968.   Adopted present name 1970.

UNIVERSITY OF MAINE AT ORONO.   Orono, Me. 04473.   State institution.   Established as State College of Agriculture and Mechanic
Arts 1862.   Adopted present name 1897.

UNIVERSITY OF MAINE AT PORTLAND-GORHAM.   Gorham, Me.
04038.   State institution.   Established as Gorham State College 1878.

Adopted present name 1970 after merger with Portland Campus of the University of Maine at Orono 1970.

UNIVERSITY OF MAINE AT PRESQUE ISLE. Presque Isle, Me. 04769. State institution. Established as Aroostook State Normal School 1903. Became: Aroostook State Teachers College 1952; Aroostook State College 1965; Aroostook State College of the University of Maine 1968. Adopted present name 1970.

UNIVERSITY OF MARYLAND. College Park, Md. 20742. State institution. Established as College of Medicine of Maryland 1807. Adopted present name 1812. Merged with Maryland State College of Agriculture 1920.

UNIVERSITY OF MARYLAND, EASTERN SHORE. Princess Anne, Md. 21853. State institution. Established as Delaware Conference Academy 1886 by the Methodist Church. Became: Princess Anne Academy 1886; Eastern Branch of the Maryland Agricultural College 1919; Industrial Branch of Morgan State College 1935. State assumed control 1936. Became: Princess Anne College 1936; Maryland State College 1948. Adopted present name 1970.

UNIVERSITY OF MASSACHUSETTS-AMHERST. Amherst, Mass. 01002. State institution. Established as Massachusetts Agricultural College 1863. Became: Massachusetts State College 1931. Adopted present name 1947.

UNIVERSITY OF MICHIGAN. Ann Arbor, Mich. 48104. State institution. Established as Catholepistemiad or University of Michigania 1817. Adopted present name 1821. Became state-supported institution, moved to present location 1837.

UNIVERSITY OF MICHIGAN-FLINT. Flint, Mich. 48503. State institution. Established as Flint College of University of Michigan 1956. Adopted present name 1971.

UNIVERSITY OF MINNESOTA, DULUTH. Duluth, Minn. 55812. State institution. Established as State Normal School 1895. Became: Duluth State Normal School 1905; Duluth State Teachers College 1921. Adopted present name on becoming part of the University of Minnesota 1947.

UNIVERSITY OF MISSOURI-KANSAS CITY. Kansas City, Mo. 64110. State institution. Established as University of Kansas City, 1929. Became part of the University of Missouri system and adopted present name 1963.

UNIVERSITY OF MISSOURI-ROLLA. Rolla, Mo. 65401. State institution. Established as University of Missouri School of Mines and Metallurgy 1870. Became campus of the University of Missouri and adopted present name 1964.

UNIVERSITY OF MISSOURI-ST. LOUIS. St. Louis, Mo. 63121.

State institution.   Established as Normandy Residence Center of the
University of Missouri 1960.   Adopted present name 1963.

University of Missouri School of Mines and Metallurgy 1870.   See
University of Missouri-Rolla, Rolla, Mo.

UNIVERSITY OF MONTANA.   Missoula, Mont. 59801.   State institution.   Established as University of Montana 1893.   Became: State
University of Montana 1913; Montana State University 1935.   Readopted present name 1965.

University of Montana 1893.   See   University of Montana, Missoula,
Mont.

UNIVERSITY OF MONTEVALLO.   Montevallo, Ala. 35115.   State
institution.   Established as Alabama College 1892.   Adopted present
name 1969.

University of Nashville 1826.   See   George Peabody College for
Teachers, Nashville, Tenn.

University of Nashville 1851.   See   The University of Tennessee
Medical Units, Memphis, Tenn.

University of Natural Healing Arts 1965.   See   National College of
Chiropractic, Lombard, Ill.

UNIVERSITY OF NEBRASKA AT OMAHA.   Omaha, Neb. 68101.
State institution.   Established as University of Omaha 1908.   Became: Municipal University of Omaha 1931.   Adopted present name
1968 after becoming part of the state university system.

University of Nevada 1887.   See   University of Nevada, Reno, Reno,
Nev.

UNIVERSITY OF NEVADA, LAS VEGAS.   Las Vegas, Nev. 89109.
State institution.   Established as Southern Regional Branch of the
University of Nevada 1951.   Became: Nevada Southern University
1965.   Adopted present name 1969.

UNIVERSITY OF NEVADA, RENO.   Reno, Nev. 89507.   State institution.   Established as Nevada State University 1874.   Became:
University of Nevada 1887.   Adopted present name 1969.

UNIVERSITY OF NEW HAMPSHIRE.   Durham, N.H. 03824.   State
institution.   Established as New Hampshire College of Agriculture
and the Mechanic Arts, a division of Dartmouth College, in Hanover,
N.H. 1866.   Moved to present location 1893.   Adopted present name
1923.

UNIVERSITY OF NEW HAVEN.   New Haven, Conn. 06516.   Non-
public institution.   Established as New Haven College 1920.   Became: New Haven YMCA Junior College 1926; New Haven College
1958.   Adopted present name 1970.

UNIVERSITY OF NORTH ALABAMA. Florence, Ala. 35630. State institution. Established as LaGrange College, LaGrange, Ga. 1830. Became: Wesleyan University 1855, Florence, Ala. with control assumed by Methodist Church; Florence Normal School 1872, with control assumed by state; Florence State Teachers College 1929; Florence State College 1957; Florence State University 1968. Adopted present name 1974.

UNIVERSITY OF NORTH CAROLINA AT ASHEVILLE. Asheville, N.C. 28804. State institution. Established as Biltmore Junior College 1927. Became: Biltmore College 1934; Asheville-Biltmore College 1936. Adopted present name 1969, after becoming part of the University of North Carolina system.

UNIVERSITY OF NORTH CAROLINA AT BOONE. Boone, N.C. 28607. State institution. Established as Appalachian Training School 1903. Became: Appalachian State Normal School 1925; Appalachian State Teachers College 1929; Appalachian State University 1967. Adopted present name 1972.

UNIVERSITY OF NORTH CAROLINA AT CHARLOTTE. Charlotte, N.C. 28213. State institution. Established as Charlotte Center of the University of N.C. 1946. Became: Charlotte College 1949. Control assumed by state 1958. Adopted present name 1965, after becoming part of the University of North Carolina system.

UNIVERSITY OF NORTH CAROLINA AT GREENSBORO. Greensboro, N.C. 27412. State institution. Established as State Normal and Industrial School 1891. Became: State Normal and Industrial College 1897; North Carolina College for Women 1919; Women's College of the University of North Carolina 1932. Adopted present name 1963.

UNIVERSITY OF NORTH CAROLINA AT WILMINGTON. Wilmington, N.C. 28401. State institution. Established as College Center 1946. Became: Wilmington College 1947. Adopted present name 1969 after becoming part of the University of North Carolina system.

UNIVERSITY OF NORTH CAROLINA AT WINSTON-SALEM. Winston-Salem, N.C. 27102. State institution. Established as Slater Industrial Academy 1892. Became: Winston-Salem Teachers College 1925; Winston-Salem State College 1963; Winston-Salem State University 1969. Adopted present name 1972.

UNIVERSITY OF NORTHERN COLORADO. Greeley, Colo. 80631. State institution. Established as State Normal School 1889. Became: Colorado State Teachers College 1911; Colorado State College of Education 1935; Colorado State College 1957. Adopted present name 1970.

UNIVERSITY OF NORTHERN IOWA. Cedar Falls, Ia. 50613. State institution. Established as Iowa State Normal School 1876. Became: Iowa State Teachers College 1909; State College of Iowa 1961. Adopted present name 1967.

UNIVERSITY OF NOTRE DAME. Notre Dame, Ind. 46556. Non-public institution. Affiliated with the Roman Catholic Church. Established under present official name University of Notre Dame du Lac 1842.

University of Notre Dame du Lac 1842. See University of Notre Dame, Notre Dame, Ind.

University of Omaha 1908. See University of Nebraska at Omaha, Omaha, Neb.

UNIVERSITY OF PENNSYLVANIA. Philadelphia, Pa. 19104. Non-public institution, receiving state aid. Established as Academy of Philadelphia 1753. Became: College and Academy of Philadelphia 1755; University of the State of Pennsylvania 1779. Adopted present name 1791.

UNIVERSITY OF PITTSBURGH. Pittsburgh, Pa. 15313. Non-public institution, state-related. Established as Pittsburgh Academy 1878. Became: Western University of Pennsylvania 1819; University of Pittsburgh 1908, after becoming state-aided institution. Adopted present official name University of Pittsburgh of the Commonwealth System of Higher Education 1966, after becoming state-related.

University of Pittsburgh 1908. See University of Pittsburgh, Pittsburgh, Pa.

University of Pittsburgh of the Commonwealth System of Higher Education 1966. See University of Pittsburgh, Pittsburgh, Pa.

University of Plano, Plano, Tex. Closed July 1976.

UNIVERSITY OF PORTLAND. Portland, Ore. 97203. Non-public institution. Established as Columbia University 1901. Adopted present name 1935.

UNIVERSITY OF PUERTO RICO. Rio Piedras, P. R. 00931. State institution. Established as Normal School 1900 in Fajardo, P. R. Moved to present location 1901. Adopted present name 1903.

UNIVERSITY OF PUGET SOUND. Tacoma, Wash. 98416. Non-public institution. Affiliated with The United Methodist Church. Established as University of Puget Sound 1888. Became: College of Puget Sound 1914. Readopted present name 1960.

UNIVERSITY OF RHODE ISLAND. Kingston, R. I. 02881. State institution. Established as State Agricultural School 1888. Became: Rhode Island College of Agriculture and Mechanic Arts 1892; Rhode Island State College 1909. Adopted present name 1951.

UNIVERSITY OF RICHMOND. Richmond, Va. 23173. Non-public institution. Affiliated with the Southern Baptist Convention. Established as Dunlora Academy 1830. Became: Virginia Baptist Sem-

inary 1832; Richmond College 1840. Merged with Westhampton College 1914. Adopted present name 1920.

UNIVERSITY OF SAN DIEGO. San Diego, Calif. 92110. Non-public
institution. Conducted by the Society of the Sacred Heart and the
Roman Catholic Diocese of San Diego. Established with the merger
of San Diego College for Women 1967 and University of San Diego
College for Men 1967. Adopted present name 1967. University of
San Diego School of Law became part of merger 1973.

University of San Diego College for Men 1967. See University of
San Diego, San Diego, Calif.

University of San Diego School of Law 1973. See University of
San Diego, San Diego, Calif.

UNIVERSITY OF SAN FRANCISCO. San Francisco, Calif. 94117.
Non-public institution. Affiliated with the Society of Jesus, Roman
Catholic Church. Established as St. Ignatius College 1855. Adopted
present name 1930.

UNIVERSITY OF SANTA CLARA. Santa Clara, Calif. 95053. Non-
public institution. Affiliated with the Society of Jesus, Roman Catholic Church. Established as Santa Clara College 1851. Adopted
present name 1912.

UNIVERSITY OF SCIENCES AND ARTS OF OKLAHOMA. Chickasha,
Okla. 73018. State institution. Established as Industrial Institute
and College 1908. Became: Oklahoma College for Women 1916;
Oklahoma College of Liberal Arts 1965. Adopted present name 1974.

UNIVERSITY OF SCRANTON. Scranton, Pa. 18510. Non-public institution. Established as Saint Thomas College 1888. Adopted present name 1938.

UNIVERSITY OF SOUTH CAROLINA. Columbia, S.C. 29208. State
institution. Established as South Carolina College 1801. Became:
University of South Carolina 1865; College of Agriculture and Mechanical Arts 1880; South Carolina College 1882; University of South
Carolina 1887; South Carolina College 1890. Readopted present name
1906.

University of South Carolina 1865. See University of South Carolina,
Columbia, S.C.

THE UNIVERSITY OF SOUTH DAKOTA. Vermillion, S.D. 57069.
State institution. Established as University of Dakota 1862. Be-
came: University of South Dakota 1891; State University of South
Dakota 1959. Adopted present name 1963.

UNIVERSITY OF SOUTH DAKOTA AT SPRINGFIELD. Springfield,
S.D. 57062. State institution. Established as Southern State Nor-
mal School 1881. Became: Southern State Teachers College 1947;
Southern State College 1964. Adopted present name 1971.

UNIVERSITY OF SOUTH FLORIDA. Tampa, Fla. 33620. State institution. Established in 1956 under present name. New College, Sarasota, Fla. became part of University of South Florida, 1975.

UNIVERSITY OF SOUTHERN COLORADO. Pueblo, Colo. 81001. State institution. Established as San Isabel Junior College 1933. Became: Southern Colorado Junior College 1934; Pueblo Junior College 1937; Southern Colorado State College 1963. Adopted present name 1975.

UNIVERSITY OF SOUTHERN MISSISSIPPI. Hattiesburg, Miss. 39401. State institution. Established as Mississippi Normal College 1910. Became: State Teachers College 1924; Mississippi Southern College 1940. Adopted present name 1962.

THE UNIVERSITY OF SOUTHWESTERN LOUISIANA. Lafayette, La. 70501. State institution. Established as Southwestern Louisiana Industrial Institute. 1898. Became: Southwestern Louisiana Institute of Liberal and Technical Learning 1921. Adopted present name 1960.

UNIVERSITY OF TAMPA. Tampa, Fla. 33606. Non-public institution. Established as Tampa Junior College 1930. Adopted present name 1933.

University of Tennessee 1969. See The University of Tennessee at Chattanooga, Chattanooga, Tenn.

THE UNIVERSITY OF TENNESSEE AT CHATTANOOGA. Chattanooga, Tenn. 37401. State institution. Established as Chattanooga University 1886 by Methodist Episcopal Church. Became: Grant University 1889; University of Chattanooga 1907, independent of church 1909. Merged with University of Tennessee 1969 and Chattanooga City College 1969. Adopted present name 1969.

THE UNIVERSITY OF TENNESSEE AT MARTIN. Martin, Tenn. 38237. State institution. Established as Hall-Moody Institute 1900, under private control. Became: Hall-Moody Normal School 1905; Hall-Moody Junior College 1917; University of Tennessee Junior College 1927, after state assumed control; University of Tennessee Martin Branch 1951. Adopted present name 1967.

THE UNIVERSITY OF TENNESSEE AT NASHVILLE. Nashville, Tenn. 37203. State institution. Established as University of Tennessee Nashville Center 1947. Adopted present name 1971.

University of Tennessee Junior College 1927. See The University of Tennessee at Martin, Martin, Tenn.

THE UNIVERSITY OF TENNESSEE, KNOXVILLE. Knoxville, Tenn. 37916. State institution. Established as Blount College 1794. Became: East Tennessee College 1807; East Tennessee University 1840. Adopted present name 1879.

University of Tennessee Martin Branch 1951. See The University of Tennessee at Martin, Martin, Tenn.

THE UNIVERSITY OF TENNESSEE MEDICAL UNITS. Memphis, Tenn. 38103. State institution. Established as University of Nashville 1851 in Nashville, Tenn. Adopted present name 1911, consolidating all units after moving to present location.

University of Tennessee Nashville Center 1947. See The University of Tennessee at Nashville, Nashville, Tenn.

UNIVERSITY OF TEXAS AT ARLINGTON. Arlington, Tex. 76010. State institution. Established as Arlington College 1895. Became: Carlisle Military Institute 1901; Arlington Training School 1913; Grubbs Vocational College 1917; North Texas Junior Agricultural, Mechanical and Industrial College 1923; Arlington State College 1949. Adopted present name 1967.

UNIVERSITY OF TEXAS AT AUSTIN. Austin, Tex. 78712. State institution. Established as University of Texas, Main University 1881. Became: University of Texas at Austin Main Campus 1967. Adopted present name 1974.

University of Texas at Austin Main Campus 1967. See University of Texas at Austin, Austin, Tex.

UNIVERSITY OF TEXAS AT EL PASO. El Paso, Tex. 79968. State institution. Established as Texas State School of Mines and Metallurgy 1913. Became: University of Texas, Department of Mines and Metallurgy 1919; Texas College of Mines and Metallurgy 1920; Texas Western College 1949. Adopted present name 1967.

University of Texas, Department of Mines and Metallurgy 1919. See University of Texas at El Paso, El Paso, Tex.

University of Texas, Main University, 1881. See University of Texas at Austin, Austin, Tex.

University of the City of New York 1831. See New York University, New York, N.Y.

University of the City of Toledo 1921. See University of Toledo, Toledo, Oh.

UNIVERSITY OF THE DISTRICT OF COLUMBIA. Washington, D.C. 20005. Municipal institution. Established under present name 1977 through merger of Federal City College, D.C. Teachers College and Washington Technical Institute.

University of the Holy Ghost 1911. See Duquesne University of the Holy Ghost, Pittsburgh, Pa.

University of the Northwest 1889. See Morningside College, Sioux City, Ia.

UNIVERSITY OF THE PACIFIC. Stockton, Calif. 95204. Non-public institution. Affiliated with The United Methodist Church. Established as California Wesleyan University 1951. Became: University of the Pacific 1852; College of the Pacific 1911. Readopted present name 1961.

University of the Pacific 1852. See University of the Pacific, Stockton, Calif.

University of the State of Pennsylvania 1779. See University of Pennsylvania, Philadelphia, Pa.

UNIVERSITY OF TOLEDO. Toledo, Oh. 43606. State institution. Established as Toledo University of Arts and Trades 1872. Became: Toledo University 1884; University of the City of Toledo 1921. Adopted present name 1940.

THE UNIVERSITY OF TULSA. Tulsa, Okla. 74104. Non-public institution. Affiliated with The United Presbyterian Church in the U.S. Established as Henry Kendall College 1894, in Muskogee, Indian Territory. Moved to Tulsa 1907. Adopted present name 1920.

UNIVERSITY OF UTAH. Salt Lake City, Ut. 84112. State institution. Established as University of Deseret 1950. Adopted present name 1892.

UNIVERSITY OF VERMONT. Burlington, Vt. 05401. State institution. Established under name University of Vermont 1791. Merged with Vermont Agricultural College 1865. Adopted present official name University of Vermont and State Agricultural College 1865.

University of Vermont and State Agricultural College 1865. See University of Vermont, Burlington, Vt.

UNIVERSITY OF WASHINGTON. Seattle, Wash. 98195. State institution. Established as Territorial University of Washington 1861. Adopted present name 1889.

University of Wichita 1956. See Wichita State University, Wichita, Kan.

University of Wisconsin 1848. See University of Wisconsin-Madison, Madison, Wisc.

UNIVERSITY OF WISCONSIN-EAU CLAIRE. Eau Claire, Wisc. 54701. State institution. Established as Eau Claire State Normal School 1916. Became: Eau Claire State Teachers College 1927; Wisconsin State College at Eau Claire 1951; Wisconsin State University-Eau Claire 1964. Adopted present name 1971.

University of Wisconsin Extension Division 1955. See University of Wisconsin-Milwaukee, Milwaukee, Wisc.

UNIVERSITY OF WISCONSIN-LA CROSSE. La Crosse, Wisc. 54601.
State institution. Established as State Normal School 1909. Became:
State Teachers College 1926; Wisconsin State College-La Crosse 1951;
Wisconsin State University-La Crosse 1964. Adopted present name
1971.

UNIVERSITY OF WISCONSIN-MADISON. Madison, Wisc. 53706. State
institution. Established as University of Wisconsin 1848. Adopted
present name 1968.

UNIVERSITY OF WISCONSIN-MILWAUKEE. Milwaukee, Wisc. 53201.
State institution. Established under present name after merger of
Wisconsin State College, Milwaukee 1955 and University of Wiscon-
sin Extension Division 1955.

UNIVERSITY OF WISCONSIN-OSHKOSH. Oshkosh, Wisc. 54901.
State institution. Established as Oshkosh Normal School 1871. Became: Oshkosh Teachers College 1925; Wisconsin State College-
Oshkosh 1949; Wisconsin State University-Oshkosh 1964. Adopted
present name 1971.

UNIVERSITY OF WISCONSIN-PLATTEVILLE. Platteville, Wisc.
53818. State institution. Established as Platteville Normal School
1866. Became: Platteville State Teachers College 1927; Wisconsin
State College-Platteville 1951; Wisconsin State College and Institute
for Technology, Platteville 1959, after merger with Wisconsin Institute for Technology 1959; Wisconsin State University-Platteville 1964.
Adopted present name 1971.

UNIVERSITY OF WISCONSIN-RIVER FALLS. River Falls, Wisc.
54022. State institution. Established as State Normal School 1874.
Became: River Falls State Teachers College 1926; Wisconsin State
College at River Falls 1951; Wisconsin State University-River Falls
1964. Adopted present name 1971.

UNIVERSITY OF WISCONSIN-STEVENS POINT. Stevens Point, Wisc.
54481. State institution. Established as Stevens Point State Normal
School 1894. Became: Central State Teachers College 1926; Wisconsin State College 1951; Wisconsin State University-Stevens Point
1963. Adopted present name 1971.

UNIVERSITY OF WISCONSIN-STOUT. Menomonie, Wisc. 54751.
State institution. Established as Stout Manual Training and Domestic
Science School 1891. Became: Stout Institute 1908; Stout State College 1955; Stout State University 1964. Adopted present name 1971
after becoming part of the state system.

UNIVERSITY OF WISCONSIN-SUPERIOR. Superior, Wisc. 54880.
State institution. Established as Superior Normal School 1893. Became: State Teachers College-Superior 1925; Wisconsin State College-Superior 1952; Wisconsin State University-Superior 1964. Adopted present name 1971.

UNIVERSITY OF WISCONSIN-WHITEWATER.   Whitewater, Wisc.
53190.   State institution.   Established as Whitewater Normal School
1868.   Became: Whitewater State Teachers College 1925; Wisconsin
State College-Whitewater 1951; Wisconsin State University-Whitewater
1964.   Adopted present name 1971.

University of Wooster 1866.   See   The College of Wooster, Wooster,
Oh.

University System Center 1932.   See   Georgia State University, Atlanta, Ga.

Upland College 1965.   See   Messiah College, Grantham, Pa.

UPPER IOWA COLLEGE.   Fayette, Ia. 52142.   Non-public institution.
Established as The Fayette Seminary of the Upper Iowa Conference
1850.   Adopted present official name Upper Iowa University 1857.

Upper Iowa University 1857.   See   Upper Iowa College, Fayette, Ia.

URBANA COLLEGE.   Urbana, Oh. 43087.   Non-public institution.
Affiliated with the General Convention The Swedenborgian Churches.
Established as Urbana University 1850.   Became: Urbana Junior
College 1920.   Adopted present name 1962.

Urbana Junior College 1920.   See   Urbana College, Urbana, Oh.

Urbana University 1850.   See   Urbana College, Urbana, Oh.

URSULINE COLLEGE.   Cleveland, Oh. 44124.   Non-public institution.   Affiliated with the Ursuline Nuns of Cleveland, Roman Catholic Church.   Established as Ursuline College for Women 1871.
Adopted present name 1968.

Ursuline College for Women 1871.   See   Ursuline College, Cleveland,
Oh.

Utah Agricultural College 1929.   See   Utah State University, Logan,
Ut.

UTAH STATE UNIVERSITY.   Logan, Ut. 84322.   State institution.
Established as Agricultural College of Utah 1888.   Became: Utah
Agricultural College 1929.   Adopted present official name Utah State
University of Agriculture and Applied Science 1957.

Utah State University of Agriculture and Applied Science 1957.   See
Utah State University, Logan, Ut.

- V -

VALDOSTA STATE COLLEGE.   Valdosta, Ga. 31601.   State insti-

tution. Established as South Georgia State Normal College 1906.
Became: Georgia State Womans College 1922. Adopted present
name 1950.

Valley City Normal School 1889. See Valley City State College,
Valley City, N.D.

VALLEY CITY STATE COLLEGE. Valley City, N.D. 58072. State
institution. Established as Valley City Normal School 1889. Became: Valley City State Teachers College 1912. Adopted present
name 1963.

Valley City State Teachers College 1912. See Valley City State
College, Valley City, N.D.

VALLEY FORGE CHRISTIAN COLLEGE. Green Lane, Pa. 18054.
Non-public institution. Affiliated with the Assemblies of God Church.
Established as Northeast Bible College 1938. Adopted present name
1977.

Valley Union Seminary 1842. See Hollins College, Hollins College,
Va.

Valparaiso College 1900. See Valparaiso University, Valparaiso,
Ind.

Valparaiso Male and Female College 1859. See Valparaiso University, Valparaiso, Ind.

VALPARAISO UNIVERSITY. Valparaiso, Ind. 46383. Non-public
institution. Affiliated with the Lutheran Church, Missouri Synod.
Established as Valparaiso Male and Female College 1859. Became:
Northern Indiana Normal School and Business Institute 1873. Valparaiso College 1900. Adopted present name 1907.

THE VANDERBILT UNIVERSITY. Nashville, Tenn. 37203. Non-
public institution. Established as The Central University of Methodist Episcopal Church, South 1872. Adopted present name 1873.
Became nonsectarian 1914.

VANDERCOOK COLLEGE OF MUSIC. Chicago, Ill. 60616. Non-
public institution. Established as Vandercook School of Music 1909
by Hale A. Vandercook. Adopted present name 1950.

Vandercook School of Music 1909. See Vandercook College of
Music, Chicago, Ill.

Vanport Extension Center 1946. See Portland State University,
Portland, Ore.

VASSAR COLLEGE. Poughkeepsie, N.Y. 12601. Non-public institution. Established as Vassar Female College 1861. Adopted present name 1867.

Vassar Female College 1861. See Vassar College, Poughkeepsie, N. Y.

Vermont Agricultural College 1865. See University of Vermont, Burlington, Vt.

Vermont Classical High School 1828. See Castleton State College, Castleton, Vt.

VERMONT COLLEGE. Montpelier, Vt. 05602. State institution. Established as Newbury Seminary 1834 by New Hampshire Methodist Conference. Became: Vermont Conference Seminary and Female College 1868; Vermont Methodist Seminary and Female College 1871; Vermont Methodist Seminary 1889; Montpelier Seminary 1895; Vermont Junior College 1937, when control was assumed by state. Adopted present name 1958. Became Division of Norwich University 1972.

Vermont College 1972. See Norwich University, Northfield, Vt.

Vermont Conference Seminary and Female College 1868. See Vermont College, Montpelier, Vt.

Vermont Institute of Special Studies 1951. See Windham College, Putney, Vt.

Vermont Junior College 1937. See Vermont College, Montpelier, Vt.

Vermont Methodist Seminary 1889. See Vermont College, Montpelier, Vt.

Vermont Methodist Seminary and Female College 1871. See Vermont College, Montpelier, Vt.

Verrazzano College, Saratoga Springs, N. Y. Closed June 1975.

Villa Madonna College 1921. See Thomas More College, Ft. Mitchell, Ky.

Villa Maria Academy for Girls 1914. See Immaculata College, Immaculata, Pa.

Villa Maria College 1920. See Immaculata College, Immaculata, Pa.

Villanova College 1842. See Villanova University, Villanova, Pa.

VILLANOVA UNIVERSITY. Villanova, Pa. 19085. Non-public institution. Owned by the Order of St. Augustine, Roman Catholic Church. Established as St. Augustine's Academy 1811. Became: Villanova College 1842. Adopted present name 1953.

Virginia Agricultural and Mechanical College 1872. See Virginia
Polytechnic Institute and State University, Blacksburg, Va.

Virginia Agricultural and Mechanical College and Polytechnic Institute 1885. See Virginia Polytechnic Institute and State University,
Blacksburg, Va.

Virginia Baptist Seminary 1832. See University of Richmond,
Richmond, Va.

Virginia Christian College 1903. See Lynchburg College, Lynchburg,
Va.

The Virginia Collegiate Institute 1845. See Roanoke College, Salem,
Va.

VIRGINIA COMMONWEALTH UNIVERSITY. Richmond, Va. 23220.
State institution. Established by merger of the Medical College of
Virginia 1968 and Richmond Professional Institute 1968. Adopted
present name 1968.

The Virginia Institute 1842. See Roanoke College, Salem, Va.

Virginia Institute 1891. See Virginia Intermont College, Bristol, Va.

VIRGINIA INTERMONT COLLEGE. Bristol, Va. 20201. Non-public
institution. Affiliated with the Southern Baptist Association. Established as Southwest Virginia Institute 1888, by J. R. Harrison. Became: Virginia Institute 1891. Adopted present name 1922.

Virginia Normal and Collegiate Institute 1882. See Virginia State
College, Petersburg, Va.

Virginia Normal and Industrial Institute 1902. See Virginia State
College, Petersburg, Va.

Virginia Normal School 1882. See Bridgewater College, Bridgewater, Va.

Virginia Polytechnic Institute 1944. See Virginia Polytechnic Institute and State University, Blacksburg, Va.

VIRGINIA POLYTECHNIC INSTITUTE AND STATE UNIVERSITY.
Blacksburg, Va. 24061. State institution. Established as Virginia
Agricultural and Mechanical College 1872. Became: Virginia Agricultural and Mechanical College and Polytechnic Institute 1885; Virginia Polytechnic Institute 1944. Adopted present name 1970.

VIRGINIA STATE COLLEGE. Petersburg, Va. 23803. State insti-
tution. Established as Virginia Normal and Collegiate Institute 1882.
Became: Virginia Normal and Industrial Institute 1902; Virginia
State College for Negroes 1922. Adopted present name 1946.

Virginia State College for Negroes 1922. <u>See</u> Virginia State College, Petersburg, Va.

VIRGINIA UNION UNIVERSITY. Richmond, Va. 23220. Non-public institution. Affiliated with the American Baptist Convention. Established by merger of Wayland Seminary, Washington, D.C. 1899 and Richmond Theological Seminary 1899. Adopted present name 1899.

VITERBO COLLEGE. La Crosse, Wisc. 54601. Non-public institution. Owned by the Franciscan Sisters of Perpetual Adoration of La Crosse, Roman Catholic Church. Established as St. Rose Junior College 1931. Adopted present name 1937.

VOORHEES COLLEGE. Denmark, S.C. 29042. Non-public institution. Affiliated with The Episcopal Church. Established as Denmark Industrial School 1897. Became: Voorhees School 1902; Voorhees School and Junior College 1947. Adopted present name 1962.

Voorhees School 1902. <u>See</u> Voorhees College, Denmark, S.C.

Voorhees School and Junior College 1947. <u>See</u> Voorhees College, Denmark, S.C.

- W -

WABASH COLLEGE. Crawfordsville, Ind. 47933. Non-public institution. Established as Wabash Manual Labor College and Teachers Seminary 1832. Adopted present name 1851.

Wabash Manual Labor College and Teachers Seminary 1832. <u>See</u> Wabash College, Crawfordsville, Ind.

WAGNER COLLEGE. Staten Island, N.Y. 10301. Non-public institution. Affiliated with the Metropolitan and Upper New York Synods of the Lutheran Church in America. Established as Lutheran Proseminary in Rochester 1885. Became: Wagner Memorial Lutheran College 1886; moved to Staten Island 1918; Wagner Lutheran College 1952. Adopted present name 1959.

Wagner Lutheran College 1952. <u>See</u> Wagner College, Staten Island, N.Y.

Wagner Memorial Lutheran College 1886. <u>See</u> Wagner College, Staten Island, N.Y.

Wake Forest College 1838. <u>See</u> Wake Forest University, Winston-Salem, N.C.

Wake Forest Manual Labor Institute 1833. <u>See</u> Wake Forest University, Winston-Salem, N.C.

235   Wake Forest

WAKE FOREST UNIVERSITY. Winston-Salem, N.C. 27109. Non-public institution. Affiliated with the Baptist State Convention of N.C. (Southern Baptist). Established as Wake Forest Manual Labor Institute 1833. Became: Wake Forest College 1838. Adopted present name 1967.

Walden Seminary 1877. See Philander Smith College, Little Rock, Ark.

Wallamet University 1853. See Willamette University, Salem, Ore.

Walnut Grove Academy 1848. See Eureka College, Eureka, Ill.

WALSH COLLEGE OF ACCOUNTANCY AND BUSINESS ADMINISTRA-TION. Troy, Mich. 48084. Non-public institution. Established as Walsh Institute of Accountancy 1922. Adopted present name 1968.

Walsh Institute of Accountancy 1922. See Walsh College of Accountancy and Business Administration, Troy, Mich.

Ward-Belmont, Inc. 1951. See Belmont College, Nashville, Tenn.

WARNER PACIFIC COLLEGE. Portland, Ore. 97215. Non-public institution. Owned by the Church of God, Anderson, Ind. Established as Pacific Bible College 1937. Adopted present name 1959.

WARREN WILSON COLLEGE. Swannanoa, N.C. 28778. Non-public institution. Affiliated with the United Presbyterian Church in the U.S. Established as Asheville Farm School 1894. Merged with Dorland-Bell School 1942. Adopted present name 1942.

WARTBURG COLLEGE. Waverly, Ia. 50677. Non-public institution. Owned by the American Lutheran Church. Established as Wartburg Normal School 1852. Became: Wartburg Normal College 1920. Adopted present name 1935, after merger with four other Lutheran colleges.

Wartburg Normal College 1920. See Wartburg College, Waverly, Ia.

Wartburg Normal School 1852. See Wartburg College, Waverly, Ia.

Washburn College 1868. See Washburn University of Topeka, Topeka, Kan.

WASHBURN UNIVERSITY OF TOPEKA. Topeka, Kan. 66621. Municipal institution. Established as Lincoln College 1865 by the Congregational Church. Became: Washburn College 1868. Control transferred to city and became Washburne Municipal University of Topeka 1941. Adopted present name 1952.

Washburne Municipal University of Topeka 1941. See Washburn University of Topeka, Topeka, Kan.

Washington Academy 1787.   See   Washington and Jefferson College,
Washington, Pa.

Washington Academy 1798.   See   Washington and Lee University,
Lexington, Va.

WASHINGTON AND JEFFERSON COLLEGE.   Washington, Pa. 15301.
Non-public institution.   Established as Washington Academy 1787.
Adopted present name 1865, after merging with Jefferson College
1865.

WASHINGTON AND LEE UNIVERSITY.   Lexington, Va. 24450.   Non-
public institution.   Established as Augusta Academy 1749.   Became:
Liberty Hall 1776; Liberty Hall Academy 1782; Washington Academy
1798; Washington College 1813.   Adopted present name 1871.

WASHINGTON COLLEGE.   Chestertown, Md. 21620.   Non-public
institution.   Established as Kent County School 1718.   Adopted present name 1782.

Washington College 1813.   See   Washington and Lee University, Lexington, Va.

Washington College 1823.   See   Trinity College, Hartford, Conn.

Washington Foreign Mission Seminary 1907.   See   Columbia Union
College, Takoma Park, Md.

Washington Missionary College 1913.   See   Columbia Union College,
Takoma Park, Md.

Washington State Agricultural College and School of Science 1890.
See   Washington State University, Pullman, Wash.

Washington State College of the University of Maine 1968.   See   University of Maine at Machias, Machias, Me.

Washington State Normal School 1890.   See   Central Washington State
College, Ellensburg, Wash.

Washington State Normal School 1893.   See   Western Washington
State College, Bellingham, Wash.

Washington State Normal School 1909.   See   University of Maine at
Machias, Machias, Me.

Washington State Teachers College 1952.   See   University of Maine
at Machias, Machias, Me.

WASHINGTON STATE UNIVERSITY.   Pullman, Wash. 99163.   State
institution.   Established as Washington State Agricultural College
and School of Science 1890.   Became: Agricultural College, Experiment Station and School of Science of the State of Washington 1891;
State College of Washington 1905.   Adopted present name 1959.

Washington Technical Institute 1977. See University of the District of Columbia, Washington, D. C.

WASHINGTON THEOLOGICAL COALITION. Silver Spring, Md. 20910. Non-public institution. Owned by seven religious orders of the Roman Catholic Church. Established as Coalition of Religious Seminaries 1968. Adopted present name 1969.

Washington Training College 1904. See Columbia Union College, Takoma Park, Md.

WASHINGTON UNIVERSITY. St. Louis, Mo. 63130. Non-public institution. Established as Eliot Seminary 1853. Adopted present official name, The Washington University 1857.

WAYLAND BAPTIST COLLEGE. Plainview, Tex. 79072. Non-public institution. Affiliated with the Southern Baptist Convention. Established as Wayland Literary and Technical Institution 1908. Adopted present name 1910.

Wayland Literary and Technical Institution 1908. See Wayland Baptist College, Plainview, Tex.

Wayland Seminary, Washington, D. C. 1899. See Virginia Union University, Richmond, Va.

WAYNE STATE COLLEGE. Wayne, Neb. 68787. State institution. Established as Nebraska State Normal School 1910. Became: Nebraska State Normal School and Teachers College 1921; Nebraska State Teachers College 1949. Adopted present name 1963.

WAYNE STATE UNIVERSITY. Detroit, Mich. 48202. State institution. Established as Detroit College of Medicine 1868. Became: Colleges of the City of Detroit 1933; Wayne University 1934. Adopted present name 1956.

Wayne University 1934. See Wayne State University, Detroit, Mich.

WAYNESBURG COLLEGE. Waynesburg, Pa. 15370. Non-public institution. Affiliated with The United Presbyterian Church in the U. S. A. Established by merger of Greence Academy 1849 and Madison College 1849.

WEBB INSTITUTE OF NAVAL ARCHITECTURE. Glen Cove, N. Y. 11542. Non-public institution. Established as Webb's Academy and Home for Shipbuilders 1889. Adopted present name 1920.

Webb's Academy and Home for Shipbuilders 1889. See Webb Institute of Naval Architecture, Glen Cove, N. Y.

Weber Academy 1908. See Weber State College, Ogden, Ut.

Weber College 1923. See Weber State College, Ogden, Ut.

Weber Normal College 1918. See Weber State College, Ogden, Ut.

Weber State Academy 1889. See Weber State College, Ogden, Ut.

WEBER STATE COLLEGE. Ogden, Ut. 84403. State institution.
Established as Weber State Academy 1889 by The Church of Jesus
Christ of Latter-day Saints. Became: Weber Academy 1908; Weber
Normal College 1918; Weber College 1923. State assumed control
1933. Adopted present name 1963.

WEBSTER COLLEGE. St. Louis, Mo. 63119. Non-public institution. Established as Loretto College by Sisters of Loretta, Roman
Catholic Church 1915. Adopted present name 1925. Became legally
secular 1967.

WELLESLEY COLLEGE. Wellesley, Mass. 02181. Non-public institution. Established as Wellesley Female Seminary 1870. Adopted
present name 1872.

Wellesley Female Seminary 1870. See Wellesley College, Wellesley,
Mass.

WELLS COLLEGE. Aurora, N. Y. 13026. Non-public institution.
Established as Wells Seminary 1868. Adopted present name 1870.

Wells Seminary 1868. See Wells College, Aurora, N. Y.

Welsh Neck Academy 1896. See Coker College, Hartsville, S. C.

WESLEY COLLEGE. Florence, Miss. 39073. Non-public institution.
Affiliated with the Congregational Methodist Church. Established as
Westminister College 1972. Adopted present name 1976.

WESLEYAN COLLEGE. Macon, Ga. 31201. Non-public institution.
Affiliated with The United Methodist Church. Established as The
Georgia Female College 1836. Became: Wesleyan Female College
1843. Adopted present name 1919.

Wesleyan College 1873. See Southwestern University, Georgetown,
Tex.

Wesleyan College, Frankfort, Ind. 1972. See United Wesleyan College, Allentown, Pa.

Wesleyan College, Kernersville, N. C. 1972. See United Wesleyan
College, Allentown, Pa.

Wesleyan Female College 1843. See Wesleyan College, Macon, Ga.

Wesleyan Methodist Bible Institute 1906. See Central Wesleyan
College, Central, S. C.

Wesleyan Methodist College 1909. See Central Wesleyan College,
Central, S. C.

Wesleyan Seminary and Female College at Albion 1857. See Albion College, Albion, Mich.

Wesleyan Seminary at Albion 1839. See Albion College, Albion, Mich.

Wesleyan University 1855. See University of North Alabama, Florence, Ala.

Wesleyan University of West Virginia 1904. See West Virginia Wesleyan College, Buckhannon, W. Va.

West Chester Academy 1812. See West Chester State College, West Chester, Pa.

WEST CHESTER STATE COLLEGE. West Chester, Pa. 19380. State institution. Established as West Chester Academy 1812. Became: West Chester State Normal School 1871; West Chester State Teacher's College 1927. Adopted present name 1960.

West Chester State Normal School 1871. See West Chester State College, West Chester, Pa.

West Chester State Teacher's College 1927. See West Chester State College, West Chester, Pa.

WEST COAST UNIVERSITY. Los Angeles, Calif. 90020. Non-public institution. Established as American College of Neuro-ophthalmology and Ocular Myology 1909. Adopted present name 1936.

West Liberty Academy 1837. See West Liberty State College, West Liberty, W. Va.

WEST LIBERTY STATE COLLEGE. West Liberty, W. Va. 26074. State institution. Established as West Liberty Academy 1837. Became: West Liberty State Normal School 1870; West Liberty State Teachers College 1931. Adopted present name 1943.

West Liberty State Normal School 1870. See West Liberty State College, West Liberty, W. Va.

West Liberty State Teachers College 1931. See West Liberty State College, West Liberty, W. Va.

West Tennessee Christian College 1885. See Freed-Hardeman College, Henderson, Tenn.

West Tennessee College 1844. See Union University, Jackson, Tenn.

West Tennessee State Normal School 1909. See Memphis State University, Memphis, Tenn.

West Tennessee State Teachers College 1929. See Memphis State University, Memphis, Tenn.

West Texas State College 1949. See West Texas State University, Canyon, Tex.

West Texas State Normal College 1910. See West Texas State University, Canyon, Tex.

West Texas State Teachers College 1923. See West Texas State University, Canyon, Tex.

WEST TEXAS STATE UNIVERSITY. Canyon, Tex. 79015. State institution. Established as West Texas State Normal College 1910. Became: West Texas State Teachers College 1923; West Texas State College 1949. Adopted present name 1963.

West Virginia Collegiate Institute 1915. See West Virginia State College, Institute, W. Va.

West Virginia Colored Institute 1891. See West Virginia State College, Institute, W. Va.

West Virginia Conference Seminary 1890. See West Virginia Wesleyan College, Buckhannon, W. Va.

WEST VIRGINIA INSTITUTE OF TECHNOLOGY. Montgomery, W. Va. 25136. State institution. Established as Montgomery Preparatory Branch of West Virginia University 1895. Became: West Virginia Trades School 1917; New River State School 1921; New River State College 1931. Adopted present name 1941.

WEST VIRGINIA SCHOOL OF OSTEOPATHIC MEDICINE. Lewisburg, W. Va. 24901. Non-public institution. Established as Greenbrier College of Osteopathic Medicine 1974 by Dr. Roland P. Sharp and others. Adopted present name 1976.

WEST VIRGINIA STATE COLLEGE. Institute, W. Va. 25112. State institution. Established as West Virginia Colored Institute 1891. Became: West Virginia Collegiate Institute 1915. Adopted present name 1929.

West Virginia State Normal School 1867. See Marshall University, Huntington, W. Va.

West Virginia Trades School 1917. See West Virginia Institute of Technology, Montgomery, W. Va.

WEST VIRGINIA UNIVERSITY. Morgantown, W. Va. 26506. State institution. Established as Monogalia Academy 1814. Became: Agricultural College of West Virginia 1867. Adopted present name 1868.

WEST VIRGINIA WESLEYAN COLLEGE. Buckhannon, W. Va. 26201. Non-public institution. Owned by The United Methodist Church. Established as West Virginia Conference Seminary 1890. Became:

Wesleyan University of West Virginia 1904. Adopted present name 1906.

WESTBROOK COLLEGE. Portland, Me. 04103. Non-public institution. Established as Westbrook Seminary 1831 by the Kennebec Association of Universalists. Became: Westbrook Seminary and Junior College 1929, after becoming independent institution 1917. Adopted present name 1970.

Westbrook Seminary 1831. See Westbrook College, Portland, Me.

Westbrook Seminary and Junior College 1929. See Westbrook College, Portland, Me.

The Western, A College and Seminary for Women 1894. See The Western College, Oxford, Oh.

WESTERN BAPTIST BIBLE COLLEGE. Salem, Ore. 97302. Non-public institution. Affiliated with the General Association of Regular Baptist Churches. Established as Western Baptist Bible College and Theological Seminary 1946. Adopted present name 1969.

Western Baptist Bible College and Theological Seminary 1946. See Western Baptist Bible College, Salem, Ore.

Western Baptist Theological Seminary 1927. See Western Conservative Baptist Seminary, Portland, Ore.

Western Bible College 1939. See Westmont College, Santa Barbara, Calif.

Western Branch of Kansas Normal School of Emporia 1901. See Fort Hayes Kansas State College, Hayes, Kan.

Western Carolina College 1953. See Western Carolina University, Cullowhee, N.C.

Western Carolina Teachers College 1929. See Western Carolina University, Cullowhee, N.C.

WESTERN CAROLINA UNIVERSITY. Cullowhee, N.C. 28723. State institution. Established as Cullowhee High School 1889. Became: Cullowhee Normal and Industrial School 1905; Cullowhee State Normal School 1925; Western Carolina Teachers College 1929; Western Carolina College 1953. Adopted present name 1967. Became part of the University of North Carolina system 1972.

THE WESTERN COLLEGE. Oxford, Oh. 45056. Non-public institution. Established as The Western Female Seminary 1853. Became: The Western, A College and Seminary for Women 1894; The Western College for Women 1904. Adopted present name 1971. Became affiliated with Miami University, Oxford, Oh. , 1974.

The Western College for Women 1904. See The Western College, Oxford, Oh.

WESTERN CONNECTICUT STATE COLLEGE. Danbury, Conn. 06810. State institution. Established as Danbury State Normal School 1903. Became: Danbury State Teachers College 1937; Danbury State College 1959. Adopted present name 1967.

WESTERN CONSERVATIVE BAPTIST SEMINARY. Portland, Ore. 97215. Non-public institution. Affiliated with the Conservative Baptist Association of America. Established as Western Baptist Theological Seminary 1927. Became: Western Conservative Baptist Theological Seminary 1951. Adopted present name 1968.

Western Conservative Baptist Theological Seminary 1951. See Western Conservative Baptist Seminary, Portland, Ore.

The Western Female Seminary 1853. See The Western College, Oxford, Oh.

Western Illinois State College 1947. See Western Illinois University, Macomb, Ill.

Western Illinois State Normal School 1899. See Western Illinois University, Macomb, Ill.

Western Illinois State Teachers College 1921. See Western Illinois University, Macomb, Ill.

WESTERN ILLINOIS UNIVERSITY. Macomb, Ill. 61455. State institution. Established as Western Illinois State Normal School 1899. Became: Western Illinois State Teachers College 1921; Western Illinois State College 1947. Adopted present name 1957.

Western Kentucky State College 1948. See Western Kentucky University, Bowling Green, Ky.

Western Kentucky State Normal School 1906. See Western Kentucky University, Bowling Green, Ky.

Western Kentucky State Normal School and Teachers College 1922. See Western Kentucky University, Bowling Green, Ky.

Western Kentucky State Teachers College 1930. See Western Kentucky University, Bowling Green, Ky.

WESTERN KENTUCKY UNIVERSITY. Bowling Green, Ky. 42101. State institution. Established as Western Kentucky State Normal School 1906. Became: Western Kentucky State Normal School and Teachers College 1922; Western Kentucky State Teachers College 1930; Western Kentucky State College 1948. Adopted present name 1966.

Western Maine Normal School 1863. See University of Maine at
Farmington, Farmington, Me.

Western Michigan College 1955. See Western Michigan University,
Kalamazoo, Mich.

Western Michigan College of Education 1941. See Western Michigan University, Kalamazoo, Mich.

WESTERN MICHIGAN UNIVERSITY. Kalamazoo, Mich. 49001. State
institution. Established as Western State Normal School 1903. Became: Western State Teachers College 1927; Western Michigan College of Education 1941; Western Michigan College 1955. Adopted
present name 1957.

WESTERN MONTANA COLLEGE. Dillon, Mont. 59725. State insti-
tution. Established as State Normal School 1893. Became: State
Normal College 1903; Western Montana College of Education 1949.
Adopted present name 1965.

Western Montana College of Education 1949. See Western Montana
College, Dillon, Mont.

WESTERN NEW ENGLAND COLLEGE. Springfield, Mass. 01119.
Non-public institution. Established as Springfield Division, Northeastern University 1915. Adopted present name 1951.

WESTERN NEW MEXICO UNIVERSITY. Silver City, N. M. 88061.
State institution. Established as Territorial Normal School 1893.
Became: New Mexico Normal School 1912; New Mexico State Teachers College 1923; New Mexico Western College 1949. Adopted present name 1963.

Western Reserve Eclectic Institute 1850. See Hiram College,
Hiram, Oh.

Western Reserve University 1967. See Case Western Reserve University, Cleveland, Oh.

WESTERN STATE COLLEGE OF COLORADO. Gunnison, Colo. 81230.
State institution. Established as Colorado State Normal School 1901.
Adopted present name 1923.

Western State Normal School 1903. See Western Michigan University, Kalamazoo, Mich.

Western State Teachers College 1927. See Western Michigan University, Kalamazoo, Mich.

Western Theological Seminary 1958. See Pittsburgh Theological
Seminary, Pittsburgh, Pa.

Western Union College 1955. See Westmar College, LeMars, Ia.

Western University of Pennsylvania 1819. See University of Pittsburgh, Pittsburgh, Pa.

Western Washington College of Education 1937. See Western Washington State College, Bellingham, Wash.

WESTERN WASHINGTON STATE COLLEGE. Bellingham, Wash.
98225. State institution. Established as Washington State Normal
School 1893. Became: Western Washington College of Education
1937. Adopted present name 1961.

Westfield Normal School 1844. See Westfield State College, Westfield, Mass.

WESTFIELD STATE COLLEGE. Westfield, Mass. 01085. Non-
public institution. Established as Barre Normal School 1838. Became: Westfield Normal School 1844; State Teachers College at
Westfield 1932; State College at Westfield 1960. Adopted present
name 1968.

Westhampton College 1914. See University of Richmond, Richmond,
Va.

WESTMAR COLLEGE. LeMars, Ia. 51031. Non-public institution.
Affiliated with The United Methodist Church. Established in 1955
through merger of York College and Western Union College. Adopted present name 1955.

WESTMINSTER CHOIR COLLEGE. Princeton, N.J. 08540. Non-
public institution. Established as Dayton Westminister Choir School,
Ohio 1926. Moved to Ithaca, N.Y., became affiliated with Ithaca
College 1929. Moved to Princeton, N.J. 1932. Adopted present
name 1940.

WESTMINSTER COLLEGE. New Wilmington, Pa. 16142. Non-public institution. Affiliated with The United Presbyterian Church in
the U.S.A. Established as Westminister Collegiate Institute 1852.
Adopted present name 1897.

WESTMINSTER COLLEGE. Salt Lake City, Ut. 84105. Non-public
institution. Affiliated with The United Presbyterian Church in the
U.S.A. Established as Salt Lake Collegiate Institute 1875. Merged
with Sheldon Jackson College 1902. Adopted present name 1902.

Westminister College 1972. See Wesley College, Florence, Miss.

Westminister College and Bible Institute 1953. See Wesley College,
Florence, Miss.

Westminster Collegiate Institute 1852. See Westminster College,
New Wilmington, Pa.

WESTMONT COLLEGE. Santa Barbara, Calif. 93103. Non-public

institution. Established as Bible Missionary Institute 1937. Became: Western Bible College 1939. Adopted present name 1940.

WHEATON COLLEGE. Norton, Mass. 02766. Non-public institution. Established as Wheaton Female Seminary 1834. Adopted present name 1912.

WHEATON COLLEGE. Wheaton, Ill. 60187. Non-public institution. Established as Illinois Institute 1853. Adopted present name 1860.

Wheaton Female Seminary 1834. See Wheaton College, Norton, Mass.

WHEELOCK COLLEGE. Boston, Mass. 02215. Non-public institution. Established as Wheelock School 1889. Adopted present name 1941.

Wheelock School 1889. See Wheelock College, Boston, Mass.

Whitewater Normal School 1868. See University of Wisconsin-Whitewater, Whitewater, Wisc.

Whitewater State Teachers College 1925. See University of Wisconsin-Whitewater, Whitewater, Wisc.

WHITMAN COLLEGE. Walla Walla, Wash. 99362. Established as Whitman Seminary 1859. Adopted present name 1882.

Whitman Seminary 1859. See Whitman College, Walla Walla, Wash.

Wichita Falls Junior College 1922. See Midwestern State University, Wichita Falls, Tex.

WICHITA STATE UNIVERSITY. Wichita, Kan. 67208. State institution. Established as Fairmount College 1887. Re-established as Fairmount Institute 1892 by Congregational Church. Became: Fairmount College 1895; Municipal University of Wichita 1926, after transfer to the City of Wichita; University of Wichita 1956. Adopted present name 1964 after becoming part of the state system.

WIDENER COLLEGE. Chester, Pa. 19013. Non-public institution. Established as Bullock School 1821. Became: Hyatt School 1853; Delaware Military Academy 1859; Pennsylvania Military Academy 1862; Pennsylvania Military College 1892; PMC Colleges (Pennsylvania Military College and Penn Morton College) 1966. Adopted present name 1972.

WILEY COLLEGE. Marshall, Tex. 75670. Non-public institution. Affiliated with The United Methodist Church. Established as Wiley University 1873. Adopted present name 1929.

Wiley University 1873. See Wiley College, Marshall, Tex.

WILKES COLLEGE. Wilkes-Barre, Pa. 18703. Non-public institution. Established as Bucknell University Junior College 1933. Adopted present name 1947.

WILLAMETTE UNIVERSITY. Salem, Ore. 97301. Non-public institution. Affiliated with The United Methodist Church. Established as Oregon Institute 1842. Became: Wallamet University 1853. Adopted present name 1865.

WILLIAM CAREY COLLEGE. Hattiesburg, Miss. 39401. Non-public institution. Owned by the Mississippi Baptist Convention (Southern Baptist). Established as Mississippi Women's College 1911. Adopted present name 1954.

William Jennings Bryan College 1930. See Bryan College, Dayton, Tenn.

William Marsh Rice University 1960. See Rice University, Houston, Tex.

WILLIAM MITCHELL COLLEGE OF LAW. St. Paul, Minn. 55105. Non-public institution. Established as St. Paul College of Law 1900. Merged with Minneapolis-Minnesota College of Law 1956. Adopted present name 1956.

William N. Rice Institute 1891. See Rice University, Houston, Tex.

THE WILLIAM PATERSON COLLEGE OF NEW JERSEY. Wayne, N.J. 07470. State institution. Established as Paterson Normal School 1855. Became: Paterson State Normal School 1923; New Jersey State Teachers College 1939; Paterson State College 1958. Adopted present name 1971.

WILLIAM PENN COLLEGE. Oskaloosa, Ia. 52577. Non-public institution. Affiliated with the Iowa Yearly Meeting of Friends. Established as Penn College 1873. Adopted present name 1933.

William Warren School 1915. See Menlo College School of Business Administration, Menlo Park, Calif.

WILLIAM WOODS COLLEGE. Fulton, Mo. 65251. Non-public institution. Established as Female Orphans School of the Christian Church of Missouri 1870, in northwestern Missouri. Moved to Fulton 1890. Became: Daughters College of the Christian Church of Missouri 1890. Adopted present name 1901.

Williamsburg Institute 1889. See Cumberland College, Williamsburg, Ky.

Williamsport Academy 1812. See Lycoming College, Williamsport, Pa.

Williamsport Dickinson Seminary 1848. See Lycoming College, Williamsport, Pa.

Williamsport Dickinson Seminary and Junior College 1929. See Lycoming College, Williamsport, Pa.

Williamston Female College 1872. See Lander College, Greenwood, S. C.

Willimantic Normal School 1889. See Eastern Connecticut State College, Willimantic, Conn.

Willimantic State Teachers College 1937. See Eastern Connecticut State College, Willimantic, Conn.

WILMINGTON COLLEGE. Wilmington, Oh. 45177. Non-public institution. Affiliated with the Wilmington Yearly Meeting of the Religious Society of Friends. Established as Franklin College 1863. Adopted present name 1870.

Wilmington College 1947. See University of North Carolina at Wilmington, Wilmington, N. C.

WINDHAM COLLEGE. Putney, Vt. 05346. Non-public institution. Established as Vermont Institute of Special Studies 1951. Adopted present name 1952.

Winfield College of Music 1926. See Southwestern College, Winfield, Kan.

Winona Seminary 1907. See College of Saint Teresa, Winona, Minn.

Winona State College 1957. See Winona State University, Winona, Minn.

Winona State Normal School 1905. See Winona State University, Winona, Minn.

Winona State Teachers College 1921. See Winona State University, Winona, Minn.

WINONA STATE UNIVERSITY. Winona, Minn. 55987. State institution. Established as First State Normal School at Winona 1858. Became: Winona State Normal School 1905; Winona State Teachers College 1921; Winona State College 1957. Adopted present name 1975.

Winston Churchill College, Pontiac, Ill. Closed June 1971.

Winston-Salem State College 1963. See University of North Carolina at Winston-Salem, Winston-Salem, N. C.

Winston-Salem State University 1969. See University of North Carolina at Winston-Salem, Winston-Salem, N. C.

Winston-Salem Teachers College 1925. See University of North Carolina at Winston-Salem, Winston-Salem, N. C.

WINTHROP COLLEGE. Rock Hill, S.C. 29730. State institution. Established as Winthrop Training School for Teachers 1886. Became: South Carolina Industrial and Winthrop Normal College 1891, after state assumed control; Winthrop Normal and Industrial College of South Carolina 1893. Adopted present name 1920.

Winthrop Normal and Industrial College of South Carolina 1893. See Winthrop College, Rock Hill, S.C.

Winthrop Training School for Teachers 1886. See Winthrop College, Rock Hill, S.C.

Wisconsin College of Physicians and Surgeons 1913. See The Medical College Wisconsin, Milwaukee, Wisc.

Wisconsin Institute for Technology 1959. See University of Wisconsin-Platteville, Platteville, Wisc.

Wisconsin State College 1951. See University of Wisconsin-Stevens Point, Stevens Point, Wisc.

Wisconsin State College and Institute for Technology, Platteville 1959. See University of Wisconsin-Platteville, Platteville, Wisc.

Wisconsin State College at Eau Claire 1951. See University of Wisconsin-Eau Claire, Eau Claire, Wisc.

Wisconsin State College at River Falls 1951. See University of Wisconsin-River Falls, River Falls, Wisc.

Wisconsin State College-La Crosse 1951. See University of Wisconsin-La Crosse, La Crosse, Wisc.

Wisconsin State College, Milwaukee 1955. See University of Wisconsin-Milwaukee, Milwaukee, Wisc.

Wisconsin State College-Oshkosh 1949. See University of Wisconsin-Oshkosh, Oshkosh, Wisc.

Wisconsin State College-Platteville 1951. See University of Wisconsin-Platteville, Platteville, Wisc.

Wisconsin State College-Superior 1952. See University of Wisconsin-Superior, Superior, Wisc.

Wisconsin State College-Whitewater 1951. See University of Wisconsin-Whitewater, Whitewater, Wisc.

Wisconsin State University-Eau Claire 1964. See University of Wisconsin-Eau Claire, Eau Claire, Wisc.

Wisconsin State University-La Crosse 1964. See University of Wisconsin-La Crosse, La Crosse, Wisc.

Wisconsin State University-Oshkosh 1964. See University of Wisconsin-Oshkosh, Oshkosh, Wisc.

Wisconsin State University-Platteville 1964. See University of Wisconsin-Platteville, Platteville, Wisc.

Wisconsin State University-River Falls 1964. See University of Wisconsin-River Falls, River Falls, Wisc.

Wisconsin State University-Stevens Point 1963. See University of Wisconsin-Stevens Point, Stevens Point, Wisc.

Wisconsin State University-Superior 1964. See University of Wisconsin-Superior, Superior, Wisc.

Wisconsin State University-Whitewater 1964. See University of Wisconsin-Whitewater, Whitewater, Wisc.

Woman's College of Alabama 1909. See Huntingdon College, Montgomery, Ala.

Woman's College of Baltimore 1890. See Goucher College, Towson, Md.

Woman's College of Baltimore City 1885. See Goucher College, Towson, Md.

Woman's College of Frederick, Md. 1893. See Hood College of Frederick, Md.

The Woman's College of Georgia 1961. See Georgia College, Milledgeville, Ga.

Woman's Medical College of Pennsylvania 1867. See The Medical College of Pennsylvania, Philadelphia, Pa.

Women's College of the University of North Carolina 1932. See University of North Carolina at Greensboro, Greensboro, N. C.

Women's Division Baylor University 1845. See Mary Hardin-Baylor College, Belton, Tex.

Women's Division, Virginia Polytechnic Institute 1944. See Radford College, Radford, Va.

Woodstock College, New York, N. Y. Closed June 1975.

Worcester County Free Institute of Industrial Science 1865. See Worcester Polytechnic Institute, Worcester, Mass.

Worcester Normal School 1874. See Worcester State College, Worcester, Mass.

WORCESTER POLYTECHNIC INSTITUTE. Worcester, Mass. 01609.
Non-public institution. Established as Worcester County Free Institute of Industrial Science 1865. Adopted present name 1887.

WORCESTER STATE COLLEGE. Worcester, Mass. 01602. State
institution. Established as Worcester Normal School 1874. Became:
State Teachers College at Worcester 1932; State College at Worcester 1960. Adopted present name 1968.

- X, Y, Z -

Xaverian College. Silver Spring, Md. Closed June 1970.

XAVIER UNIVERSITY. Cincinnati, Oh. 45207. Non-public institution. Owned by the Society of Jesus, Roman Catholic Church. Established as The Athenaeum 1831. Became: St. Xavier College
1840. Adopted present name 1930.

Xavier University 1915. See Xavier University of Louisiana, New
Orleans, La.

XAVIER UNIVERSITY OF LOUISIANA. New Orleans, La. 70125.
Non-public institution. Owned by the Sisters of the Blessed Sacra-
ment, Roman Catholic Church. Established as Xavier University,
a secondary school, 1915, then as a college 1925. Adopted present
name 1966.

Xenia Theological Seminary 1858. See Pittsburgh Theological Seminary, Pittsburgh, Pa.

YMCA Educational Branch 1881. See The Cleveland State University, Cleveland, Oh.

YMCA Institute 1942. See Roger Williams College Main Campus,
Bristol, R.I.

Yale College 1718. See Yale University, New Haven, Conn.

YALE UNIVERSITY. New Haven, Conn. 06520. Non-public institution. Established as The Collegiate School 1701. Became: Yale
College 1718. Adopted present name 1887.

Yeshiva College 1928. See Yeshiva University, New York, N.Y.

YESHIVA UNIVERSITY. New York, N.Y. 10033. Non-public institution. Established as Yeshiva College 1928. Adopted present name
1945.

YORK COLLEGE. Jamaica, N.Y. 11432. Municipal institution.
Established under present official name York College of The City
University of New York 1966.

York College 1955. See Westmar College, LeMars, Ia.

YORK COLLEGE OF PENNSYLVANIA. York, Pa. 17405. Non-public institution. Established as York Junior College 1929 through merger of The York County Academy 1929 and the York Collegiate Institute 1929. Adopted present name 1968.

York College of The City University of New York 1966. See York College, Jamaica, N. Y.

York Collegiate Institute 1929. See York College of Pennsylvania, York, Pa.

The York County Academy 1929. See York College of Pennsylvania, York, Pa.

York Junior College 1929. See York College of Pennsylvania, York, Pa.

Young Ladies Seminary, Benecia, Calif. 1852. See Mills College, Oakland, Calif.

Young Men's Christian Association College 1913. See George Williams College, Downers Grove, Ill.

Young Men's Christian Association Training School 1884. See George Williams College, Downers Grove, Ill.

Youngstown College 1928. See Youngstown State University, Youngstown, Oh.

Youngstown Institute of Technology 1921. See Youngstown State University, Youngstown, Oh.

YOUNGSTOWN STATE UNIVERSITY. Youngstown, Oh. 44503. State institution. Established as School of Law of the Youngstown Association School 1908. Became: Youngstown Institute of Technology 1921; Youngstown College 1928; Youngstown University 1955. Adopted present name 1967.

Youngstown University 1955. See Youngstown State University, Youngstown, Oh.

Zion Wesley College 1885. See Livingstone College, Salisbury, N. C.

Zion Wesley Institute 1879. See Livingstone College, Salisbury, N. C.

APPENDIX

LOCATION OF ACADEMIC RECORDS FOR
INSTITUTIONS LISTED AS CLOSED

State	Name of Institution	Location of Records
Alaska	Alaska Methodist University	Information not available. Contact source listed below.

Source: Board of Regents, University of Alaska Statewide System, Fairbanks 99701. Tel.: (907) 479-7311

Arizona	Arizona Bible College of Biola College	Biola College, La Mirada, Calif. 90639
	College Del Rey	Same as above
	Prescott College	Yavapai Community College, Prescott, Ariz. 86301

Source: Arizona Board of Regents, 1535 West Jefferson, Phoenix, 85007. Tel.: (602) 271-4082.

California	California Concordia College Highland College Pasadena Playhouse College of the Theater Arts Russell College San Luis Rey College Santa Barbara Art Institute Tahoe College	Information not available. Contact source listed below.

Source: California Postsecondary Education Commission, 1020 12th St. Sacramento, 95814. Tel.: (916) 445-7933.

Connecticut	College of Notre Dame of Wilton	Conn. Commission for Higher Education 340 Capitol Ave. Hartford, Conn. 06115

Appendix   254

State	Name of Institution	Location of Records
Connecticut (cont'd.)	Diocesan Sisters College, Bloomfield Branch	St. Joseph College 1678 Asylum Ave. West Hartford, Conn. 06117
	Holy Family Seminary	Department of Education State Office Bldg. Hartford, Conn. 06115
	Longview College	Connecticut Commission for Higher Education
	Silvermine College of Art	Connecticut Commission for Higher Education

Source: Connecticut Commission for Higher Education, 340 Capitol Ave., Hartford 06115. Tel.: (203) 566-3913.

District of Columbia	College of the Potomac Dunbarton College of the Holy Cross Holy Cross College St. Joseph's Seminary College St. Paul's College	Information not available. Contact source listed below.

Source: District of Columbia Commission on Postsecondary Education, 1329 E Street, N.W. Washington 20004. Tel.: (202) 347-5905.

Florida	College of Orlando Hollywood College St. Joseph College of Florida	Information not available. Contact source listed below.

Source: Florida Board of Regents, Collins Building, 107 West Gaines Street, Tallahassee 32304. Tel.: (904) 488-4234.

Illinois	Aquinas Institute of Theology	Aquinas Institute Dubuque, Ia. 52001
	Chicago School of Nursing	Mr. D. O. Bolander 1500 Cardinal Drive Little Falls, N.J.

Illinois (cont'd.)	Divine Word Seminary	Illinois Office of Education 100 North First St. Springfield, Ill. 62777
	Immaculata College	Bartlett Developmental Learning Center 801 W. Bartlett Road Bartlett, Ill. 60103
	Lincoln Open University	Illinois Office of Education. Address Cited above.
	Maryknoll College	Director of Education The Maryknoll Fathers, Maryknoll, N.Y. 10545
	Monticello College	Registrar Lewis and Clark College 5605 Godfrey Road, Godfrey, Ill. 62035
	Pestalozzi Froebel Teachers College	National College of Education 180 N. Wabash Street Chicago, Ill. 60601
	St. Dominic College	Siena Heights College Adrian, Mich. 49221
	Tolentine College	Tolentine Center 20300 Governors Highway, Olympia Fields, Ill. 60461
	Winston Churchill College	Mr. William Lower Pontiac High School Pontiac, Ill. 61764

Source: Illinois Board of Higher Education, 500 Reisch Bldg., 119 South Fifth St., Springfield 62701. Tel. (217) 782-2251.

Indiana	St. Benedict College	Sister Mary Clare Convent of the Immaculate Conception Ferdinand, Ind. 47532

Source: Indiana Commission for Higher Education, 143 West Market St., Indianapolis 46204.   Tel.:   (317) 633-6474.

State	Name of Institution	Location of Records
Iowa	Midwestern College	University of Iowa Iowa City, Ia. 52242
	Parsons College	Same as above

Source: Iowa State Board of Regents, Grimes State Office Bldg., Des Moines 50319. Tel.: (515) 281-3924.

Kansas	College of Emporia	Emporia Kansas State College, Emporia, Kan. 66801

Source: Board of Regents, State of Kansas, Merchants National Bank Tower, Topeka 66612. Tel.: (913) 296-3421.

Kentucky	Kentucky Southern College	Office of the Registrar, University of Louisville, Louisville, Ky. 40208
	St. Mary's College	Archdiocese Office of Education, Roman Catholic Church Louisville, Ky. 40201

Source: Council on Public Higher Education, Capital Plaza Tower, Frankfort, 40601. Tel.: (502) 564-3553.

Maine	Bliss College	State Department of Educational and Cultural Services State Education Bldg. Augusta, Me. 04333
	Northern Conservatory of Music	Same as above.
	Oblate College and Seminary	Same as above.

Source: Maine Postsecondary Education Commission, Dept. of Education and Cultural Services, Education Bldg., Augusta 04333. Tel.: (207) 289-2541.

Maryland	Baltimore College of Commerce	University of Baltimore, Baltimore, Md. 21201

Maryland (cont'd.)	St. Joseph College	Maryland State Department of Education Baltimore, Md. 21240
	St. Peters College	Same as above.
	Trinitarian College	Same as above.
	Xaverian College	Same as above.

Source: Maryland State Board for Higher Education, 93 Main St., Annapolis 21401. Tel.: (301) 267-5961.

Massachusetts	Calvin Coolidge College	Registrar's Office New England School of Law Boston, Mass. 02116
	Cardinal Cushing College	Archivist St. Mary's College Notre Dame, Ind. 46556
	Mount Alvernia College	Sr. Mary Angelica McMahon, 790 Centre Street, Newton, Mass. 02158
	Newton College	Registrar's Office Boston College Chestnut Hill, Mass. 02167
	Oblate College and Seminary	Oblate Order Oblate Provincial House, 216 Nesmith St., Lowell, Mass. 01852

Source: Board of Higher Education, 182 Tremont St., Boston 02111. Tel.: (617) 727-5360.

Michigan	Mackinac College	Lake Superior College Sault Ste. Marie, Mich. 49783
	Maryglade College	P.I.M.E. Missionaries, 9800 Oakland Ave., Detroit, Mich. 48211

Source: Michigan Dept. of Education, Lansing 48902. Tel.: (517) 373-3354.

State	Name of Institution	Location of Records
Minnesota	Lea College	Upper Iowa College Fayette, Iowa 52142

Source: Minnesota Higher Education Coordinating Board, Capitol Square Bldg., 550 Cedar Street, St. Paul 55101.

Mississippi	Okolona College Our Lady of Snows Scholasticate	Information not available. Contact source listed below.

Source: Board of Trustees of State Institution of Higher Learning, P. O. Box 2336, Jackson 39205. Tel.: (601) 982-6611.

Missouri	Marillac College	Daughters of Charity of St. Vincent de Paul 7800 Natural Bridge Road, St. Louis, Mo. 63121
	National College	Scarritt College 1008 19th Ave. South Nashville, Tenn. 37203
	Notre Dame College	Notre Dame College Office, 320 E. Ripa Ave., St. Louis, Mo. 63125

Source: Coordinating Board for Higher Education, 600 Clark Ave., Jefferson City 65101. Tel.: (314) 751-2361.

Nebraska	Duchesne College of the Sacred Heart	Barat College Lake Forest, Ill. 60045
	Hiram Scott College	Univ. of Nebraska, Lincoln, Neb. 68508
	John F. Kennedy College	Same as above.
	John J. Pershing College	University of Nebraska, Lincoln, Neb. 68508
	St. John Vianney Seminary	Mount Michael High School, Elkhorn, Neb. 68022

Nebraska
(cont'd.)

Source: Nebraska Coordinating Commission for Postsecondary Education, 1315 State Capitol, Lincoln 68509.

New Hampshire	Belknap College	Office of Postsecondary Education Commission, 66 South Street, Concord, N.H. 03301
	Canaan College	Same as above.
	Pierce College for Women	Same as above.
	Queen of Peace College	Washington Theological Coalition 9001 New Hampshire Ave., Silver Spring, Md. 20910

Source: New Hampshire Postsecondary Education Commission, 66 South St., Concord 03301. Tel.: (606) 271-2555.

| New Jersey | Shelton College | Shelton College 8810 Astronaut Blvd. Cape Canaveral, Florida 32820 |

Source: Board of Higher Education, 225 West State Street, Trenton 08625. Tel.: (609) 292-4310.

| New Mexico | College of Artesia | Eastern New Mexico University Portales, New Mexico 88130 |

Source: Board of Educational Finance, Legislative Executive Bldg., Santa Fe. 87503. Tel.: (505) 827-2115.

| New York | Brentwood College | St. Joseph's Convent Brentwood, New York 11717 |
| | Briarcliff College | Pace University, White Plains, N.Y. 10603 |

State	Name of Institution	Location of Records
New York (cont'd.)	Capuchin Theological Seminary	Capuchin Theological Seminary, Box 192 Glenclyffe, Garrison, New York 10524
	Catherine McAuley College	Administrative Secretary Office Sisters of Mercy Motherhouse, 1437 Blossom Road Rochester, New York 14610
	College of Pharmaceutical Sciences	Columbia University New York, New York 10027
	Finch College	Marymount Manhattan College, 221 East 71st Street, New York, New York 10021
	Mater Christi Seminary	Chancery Office Roman Catholic Diocese of Albany Box 6297, Albany, New York 12206
	Mills College of Education	Bank Street College 610 West 112th St. New York, N.Y. 10025
	New York College of Music	New York University School of Education 100 Washington Sq. E. New York, N.Y. 10003
	Our Lady of Hope Mission Seminary	Registrar Oblate College, 391 Michigan Ave. N.W. Washington, D.C. 20017
	Packer Collegiate Institute	Packer Institute 170 Jaralimon Street Brooklyn Heights, N.Y. 11201

New York (cont'd.)	Passionist Monastic Semi- nary	Office of Passionist Monastery of the Immaculate Conception, Inc., 86-45 178th Street, Jamaica, N.Y. 11400
	Rogers College	Order of Maryknoll Sisters, Maryknoll, N.Y. 10545
	St. Clare College	St. Mary of the Angels Convent 400 Mill Street Williamsville, N.Y. 14221
	St. John Vianney Seminary	Christ the King Seminary, East Aurora, N.Y. 14052
	St. Joseph Seraphic Seminary	Order of the Friars Minor of the Province of the Most Holy Name of New York Callicoon, New York 12723
	Verrazzano College	New York State Education Department Bureau of College Evaluation 99 Washington Avenue Albany, New York 12230
	Woodstock College	Fordham University Kohlmann Hall 501 East Fordham Rd. Bronx, N.Y. 10458

Source: Office of Postsecondary Research, Information Systems and Institutional Aid, The University of the State of New York, The State Department of Education, 99 Washington Ave., Albany 12230. Tel.: (518) 474-5093.

North Dakota	Assumption College	Assumption Abbey Richardton, N.D. 58652

Source: North Dakota State Board of Higher Education, State Capitol Building, Bismarck 58505. Tel.: (701) 224-2960.

State	Name of Institution	Location of Records
Ohio	College of the Dayton Art Institute	Dayton Art Institute Dayton, Oh. 45405
	Mary Manse College	University of Toledo Toledo, Oh. 43606
	St. John College of Cleveland	Ursuline College Cleveland, Oh. 44124

Source: Ohio Board of Regents, 30 East Broad Street, Columbus 43215.   Tel.: (614) 466-6000.

Oregon	Cascade College	Seattle Pacific College, Seattle, Wash. 98119
	Mt. Angel College	Mt. Angel Seminary St. Benedict, Ore. 97373

Source: Educational Coordinating Commission, 4263 Commercial St., S.E., Salem 97310.   Tel.: (505) 378-3921.

Rhode Island	Seminary of Our Lady of Providence	Providence College Providence, R.I. 02918
	Mt. St. Joseph College	Salve Regina College Newport, R.I. 02840

Source: Board of Regents for Education, 199 Promenade St., Providence 02908.   Tel.: (401) 277-2088.

Tennessee	Siena College	St. Catherine's College, St. Catherine's, Ky. 40061

Source: Tennessee Higher Education Commission, 501 Union Bldg., Nashville 37219.   Tel.: (615) 741-3605.

Texas	Christopher College	Chancery Office, Diocese of Corpus Christi, 620 Lipan St., Corpus Christi, Tex. 78401

Texas (cont'd.)	Dominican College	Sacred Heart Convent, 6501 Almeda Road, Houston, Tex. 77021
	University of Plano	Contact former President: Dr. Robert Morris, 523 Verde Vail, No. 1227 Dallas, Tex. 75240

Source: Coordinating Board, Texas College and University System, P. O. Box 12788, Capitol Station, Austin 78711. Tel.: (512) 475-3413.

Utah	Stephens Henager College	Los Business College 411 E. South Temple St., Salt Lake City, Ut. 84111

Source: State Board of Regents, 136 East Temple Street, Salt Lake City 84111. Tel.: (801) 533-5617

Virginia	Father Judge Mission Seminary	Holy Trinity Seminary, Silver Spring, Md. 20903
	Stratford College	Averett College Danville, Va. 24541

Source: State Council of Higher Education for Virginia, 700 Fidelity Bldg., Ninth and Main Streets, Richmond 23219. Tel.: (804) 786-2143.

West Virginia	Greenbrier College	Greenbrier Center for Mental Health Lewisburg, W. Va. 24901

Source: West Virginia Board of Regents, 950 Kanawha Boulevard East, Charleston, 25301. Tel.: (304) 348-2101.

Wisconsin	College of Racine	Sisters of St. Dominic Racine, Wisc. 53402
	Green County Teachers College	Office of County Clerk Monroe, Wisc. 53566

State	Name of Institution	Location of Records
Wisconsin (cont'd.)	Layton School of Art and Design	Layton School Records, 4650 North Port Milwaukee, Wisc. 53212
	Lincoln County Teachers College	Office of County Clerk Merrill, Wisc. 54452
	Mt. St. Paul College	See College of Racine
	Richland County Teachers College	Office of County Clerk Richland Center, Wisc. 53581

Source: Board of Regents of the University of Wisconsin System, 1860 Van Hise Hall, 1220 Linden Drive, Madison 53706. Tel.: (608) 262-2324.